Collectanea Hispanica:
Folklore and
Brief Narrative Studies

Collectanea Hispanica:
Folklore and
Brief Narrative Studies

by

JOHN ESTEN KELLER

University of Kentucky

Edited by

DENNIS P. SENIFF

Michigan State University

With the Assistance of

MARÍA ISABEL MONTOYA RAMÍREZ

University of Granada

Juan de la Cuesta
Newark, Delaware

MANUFACTURED IN THE UNITED STATES OF AMERICA

The pH of the paper this book is printed on is 7.00.

ISBN: 0-936388-37-4

TABLE OF CONTENTS

Preface

THE YEAR 1987 marks John Keller's seventieth birthday, and it is our distinct pleasure to be able to offer this selection of essays by him— this *collectanea hispanica*—as a modest tribute to one of the great Hispanists of the twentieth century. A true Southern gentleman in every way, John's contributions to medieval Spanish literature, folklore, and medieval culture—in the form of critical studies, editions, textbooks, and dozens of articles—are legion; the interested scholar will want to consult the "Publications" list that accompanies the introductory essay by Joseph R. Jones to the 1980 *homenaje: Medieval, Renaissance, and Folklore Studies in Honor of John Esten Keller*, published by this same Juan de la Cuesta, pp. xvii-xxii. We would be clearly remiss, however, not to mention several other publications not found in this list: a study on the skink's habits that appeared in the *Audubon Society Bulletin*; a novel about Queen Isabel and Christopher Columbus (that will hopefully be in print by 1992, the fifth centenary of the *Descubrimiento*); and, much to the surprise of many colleagues in the 1950s (but always to the credit of John's discretion and love of scholarship), a series of translations of medieval texts for *Playboy's* "Ribald Classics"(!). On the other hand, he published a children's story in *Walt Disney's Magazine* called "The Emperor's Elephant," which concerns the pet sent to Charlemagne by Hārūn ar-Rashíd.

As a university professor for more than forty years, John has masterfully communicated with audiences of all types, both academic and popular—witness the scores of slide lectures he has given on the *Cantigas de Santa Maria* alone during recent years in this country, Canada, Great Britain, Spain, and Portugal. His dedication to students, teaching, and scholarship over the years has yielded the following awards and distinctions: Corresponding Member of the Hispanic Society of America, New York City (1972); Corresponding Member of the "Instituto Miguel de Cervantes" of the Consejo Superior de

Investigaciones Científicas—Madrid (1972); the Award for Contribu-
tions to Graduate Education of the University of Kentucky (1972); a
Distinguished Professorship (University of Kentucky, 1979); the *home-
naje* volume (1980); the Cruz de Oficial of the Orden de Isabel la
Católica (1984); the Doctor Honoris Causa from the Universidad de
Granada (1986); and the Doctor of Humane Letters by Plymouth
State College of the Univerity of New Hampshire. Some forty-odd
Ph.D. students have looked to John to direct their dissertations over
the years while at Chapel Hill and at Lexington.

John Keller's first book, *Motif Index of Mediaeval Spanish* exempla, was
published in 1949 (Knoxville: University of Tennessee Press). His first
article, on the Spanish American author Horacio Quiroga, appeared in
the Costa Rican journal *Repertorio americano*, vol.. 46, núm. 10, in 1948
(what would have been the future of Latin American studies in the
United States had John continued in this vein of scholarship?). Since
then he has been active in the publication of books and articles; in the
reading of papers and organizing sections at conferences; as editor of
Kentucky Romance Quarterly (now *Romance Quarterly*) and *Studies in Romance
Languages*; and as editorial board member of *Crítica hispánica*, Studia
Humanitatis (now Scripta Humanistica), *Spanish Literature Studies*, *His-
pania*, Juan de la Cuesta—Hispanic Monographs, and most recently,
Discurso literario.

He considers his critical editions to be his most lasting work.
When he wrote his dissertation, "The *exemplum* in Spain" (University
of North Carolina, 1946), he realized that most of the editions of
medieval texts filled with *exempla* (OSp. *exienplos*) were long outdated. It
became clear to him that one of his life-long tasks would be to edit or
re-edit many of these books. Thus began a steady stream of publication of medieval Castilian prose works: *Libro de los engaños* (Chapel Hill:
University of North Carolina Press, 1953), *Libro de los gatos* (Madrid:
CSIC, 1958), *Libro de los exienplos por a.b.c.* (Madrid: CSIC, 1961), *Calila e
Digna* (Madrid: CSIC, 1969), and *Barlaam e Josafat* (Madrid: CSIC, 1980).
New editions of some of these are now being prepared. He is
currently collaborating with Dennis P. Seniff in the preparation of an
edition of Sancho IV's *Castigos e documentos para bien vivir*.

John Keller has opened new fields of scholarship. One of these is
medieval Spanish iconography, inasmuch as there is a close relation-

ship between the textual narrative of some manuscripts and their accompanying artwork. A key study here is *Iconography in Medieval Spanish Literature* (Lexington: University Press of Kentucky, 1984), which he co-authored with Richard P. Kinkade. The two scholars are currently working on visual narration in tapestries, stained glass, carvings in wood and stone, and other media.

For John, editing medieval books containing *exempla* was the beginning of many years of study in the realm of brief narrative in prose and verse. In particular, it is his belief that too many scholars have overlooked the matter of poetic brief narrative, which means that they have not been able to see the possibilities of such studies for works such as Berceo's *Milagros de Nuestra Señora* or Alfonso X's *Cantigas de Santa Maria*. It is very possible that he has written more studies on the latter book (which he calls the Learned King's "favorite work") than has any other scholar. It is a fitting tribute to John's devotion to the *Cantigas* that the very important volume of *actas* of the 1981 Symposium devoted to this poetic collection, of which he was one of the organizers and co-editors, has only just appeared: this *Studies on the Cantigas de Santa Maria: Art, Music, and Poetry* (Madison: Hispanic Seminary, 1987) is without a doubt the most significant collection of essays on the famous Alfonsine text that has ever been produced. The Keller *Pious Brief Narrative* (Lexington: University Press of Kentucky, 1978), which studies the verse of Berceo, Alfonso X, and other authors, has become a standard work on the topic; a Spanish version is now published (*Las narraciones breves piadosas versificadas en el castellano y gallego del Medioevo*, trans. Antonio Fernádez-Vázquez, Madrid: Alcalá, 1987). Complementing this book is the one he did with Albert Gier of the University of Heidelberg, *Les Formes narratives breves* (Heidelberg: Carl Winter, 1985). His most recent contribution to scholarship is the Society of the Cantigueiros de Santa Maria, which he founded in 1986, and whose *Bulletin*, to be published twice yearly, will begin publication in the fall of 1987.

John Keller's scholarship has always tended toward fundamental analyses of a given work. Witness his concern with such basic issues as visualization and verbalization in the medieval codex: these aspects put in relief the very essence of the book itself, but are a dichotomy that has generally been overlooked or ignored by scholars. "Why?" we want to ask somewhat sheepishly. No matter: Keller took the time to provide us with the necessary studies. Despite what some critics might have said, he was the one to "get the ball rolling." As a result, we are in his debt. Regarding current critical approaches to literature based on structuralism, narratology, grammatology, semiotics, deconstruction, post-deconstruction, etc., John is open-minded but uncertain as to how long they might stay in vogue. As he comments, "todo se pasa," while acknowledging the fact that they represent contributions to our general corpus of literary knowledge. Never one to try to second-guess the author of a work—Juan Ruiz, Juan Manuel, or anyone else—regarding his (or her) intent, or to seek its alleged *secretas razones*, John has always studied the text at face value. Not a bad policy.

The following twenty-two articles, in our opinion, are representative of some of John Keller's best writings. *Grosso modo*, they may be divided into the following seven categories: nos. 1-2, General Folklore; nos. 3-6, Diverse *exempla* Texts; nos. 7-8, Pilgrimage Rivalries; nos. 9-10, Gonzalo de Berceo and His Works; nos. 11-14, Juan Manuel and His Works; nos. 15-17, *Cantigas de Santa Maria* (General); and nos. 18-22, *Cantigas de Santa Maria* (Specific Monographic Studies). We hope that you will read (or reread, as the case may be) this worthy sampling of John's scholarly interests with the same profit and pleasure that we did in selecting them.

On a number of occasions, articles have been updated, or additional comments added, by authorial or editorial comments in brackets. These will be found both in the text and in the notes.

Acknowledgements for reprinting purposes appear as the first footnote of each article. Still, it is appropriate here to express our gratitude to the following organizations: the University of Miami Press (Coral Gables); the University of North Carolina Press (Chapel Hill); Editorial Gredos (Madrid); the American Association of Teachers of Spanish and Portuguese and *Hispania*; East Tennessee State University (Johnson City, Tennessee) and *Crítica hispánica*; the University Press of Kentucky (Lexington); Syracuse University and *Symposium* (Syracuse); the Medieval Spanish Division of the MLA and *La Corónica*; Ediciones Hispam (Barcelona); the Mediaeval Academy of America (Cambridge); Fordham University (New York); the University of Pennsylvania (Philadelphia); the Hispanic Seminary of Medieval Spanish Studies, Ltd. (Madison); Editorial Puvill (Barcelona); the University of Florida (Gainesville) and the *Southern Folklore Quarterly*.

Further thanks are due to Tom Lathrop, publisher of Juan de la Cuesta series, for his enthusiasm and support of this project, and to Diane M. Wright of Michigan State University for her assistance in proofreading galleys.

Mª. I. M. R.

D. P. S.

October 8, 1987

El cuento folklórico
en España y en
Hispanoamérica*

ARA ESTUDIAR EL CUENTO folklórico hispánico se
debe tener en cuenta las grandes obras de Stith
Thompson acerca del cuento folklórico mundial.[1]
Siendo Thompson una de las autoridades, o qui-
zás la autoridad principal, del mundo en estudios
narrativos de esta clase, es necesario llevar en
cuenta su obra como base de cualquier investigación especializada y regionalista del cuento folklórico. Por eso, será provechoso y conveniente aceptar su mismo
término que puede adaptarse por completo al cuento en lengua castellana. Ofrecemos sus palabras traducidas:

"En su acepción más amplia el término indica toda aquella narración heredada del pasado, ya sea en forma escrita u oral. En este
sentido las fábulas de Esopo y los cuentos de *Las mil y una noches* son
cuentos folklóricos. En el otro sentido, que es el adoptado en su
mayor parte en este ensayo, incluye toda clase de cuentos orientales
tradicionales de todo el mundo. Mientras *Las mil y una noches* sería
excluido como esencialmente un producto de la tradición escrita,
todo cuento, mito, y leyenda, ya sea serio, sagrado, o sencillamente
gracioso, se incluría. El tercer sentido iguala el término 'cuento folklórico' al alemán *Mabrchen*, de modo que se incluye dentro de este
concepto sólo cuentos de la clase hallada en la colección de los herma-
nos Grimm, o lo que se llama confusamente en inglés *fairy tales* . . . .
Para el estudio práctico del folklore hace falta un buen término,
válido en su aplicación exacta en todo el mundo, que abarque todas

1

las formas de la narración transmitidas principalmente por la tradición oral. Tal es el significado aquí atribuido al término 'cuento folklórico.'"[2]

En el estudio del cuento folklórico en España y en la América Hispánica es preciso estudiar las dos subdivisiones principales, los cuentos de España y los de Hispanoamérica. Es posible estudiar la primera como unidad separada con subdivisiones regionales. El estudio de la segunda es más complejo ya que debe dividirse en dos partes distintas. En el estudio de la segunda es menester incluir en primer lugar todos los cuentos folklóricos de las regiones en las cuales no se halla cultura indígena (india), y en segundo lugar incluir los cuentos que existen entre las personas de habla española en lugares de cultura y antecedentes aboriginales, es decir en los que existe una tradición nativa. El docto don Aurelio Espinosa, a quien agradecemos su profundo estudio de estas dos subdivisiones del cuento folklórico español, no ha querido incluir en ellas los cuentos de otros grupos que residen en el mundo hispánico, por ejemplo, los de los judíos sefardíes o los de los habitantes de las Islas Filipinas. Sin embargo, podemos tener la seguridad de que las condiciones que rigen estos grupos son iguales a las de Sudamérica o Méjico, y que pueden dividirse los cuentos en dos clasificaciones. Una vez decidido el método nos es posible emprender una investigación más o menos metódica del cuento folklórico del cuento español. Debemos examinar primero los cuentos de España y después los de Hispanoamérica bajo las siguientes subdivisiones: (1) origen; (2) relación entre el cuento folklórico y el literario; (3) variedad; (4) asunto; (5) estructura y presentación; (6) funciones en la sociedad tradicional.

1. Origen del cuento folklórico

España posee una herencia riquísima y antiquísima del cuento tradicional. Tres fueron las copiosas fuentes que contribuyeron a formar esta herencia: (1) en tiempos primitivos un caudal de cuentos europeos corrió hacia el sur de Europa y principalmente de Francia. Este caudal era la herencia del mundo clásico y de las tradiciones alemanas y célticas con un añadido más tarde del caudal medieval de las narraciones de la Iglesia y de Italia y Francia renacentistas; (2) un verdadero río de cuentos indostánicos, persas, árabes, judaicos, africanos con una cantidad ignorada de cuentos esporádicos de origen berberisco, egipciaco, etc.; (3) cuentos que aparecieron en España propia y en sus regiones vecinas de Portugal y Cataluña, y que podemos llamar nativos ya que se originaron en tiempos prehistóricos, romanos, mozárabes, etc., y que fueron el resultado de una mezcla de razas, religiones, culturas y tradiciones. A esta última categoría debemos añadir el caudal más reciente de cuentos del mundo hispano o sea de las Américas con su fondo de narraciones indias y negras, cuentos que ciertamente han penetrado en la tradición folklórica de España.

Una ojeada de cualquier historia de literatura española demostrará la predilección que sentían los escritores españoles por este género de cuentos a través de los siglos. Es lamentable que existan tan pocas colecciones de cuentos folklóricos antiguas, pero sabemos que en España como en otros países, los literatos han mantenido que lo tradicional aunque de mucho valor deba sacarse de su elemento natural y ponerse adornado en obras que pertenecen a la literatura. No ha sido esto tan lamentable en España como en la Grecia Antigua, por ejemplo, en la cual no se hizo ningún esfuerzo para conservar ni un solo cuento folklórico auténtico. Sin embargo, hasta el siglo pasado fue bastante limitada la cantidad de esos cuentos españoles legítimos. El cuento folklórico es la novela del pueblo y siendo así, no puede ocupar lugar literario debido a los requisitos de la literatura. Afortunadamente los españoles del siglo diez y nueve se dieron cuenta del valor del cuento tradicional en su forma original, y desde entonces muchas colecciones de estos cuentos se han conservado en esa forma.

Como no existieron cuentos folklóricos escritos para el uso de sus estudiantes ni para el entretenimiento del público en general hasta el siglo diez y nueve, tenemos que dirigirnos a la literatura para estudiar la historia de estos cuentos en la lengua castellana.

2. Enlace entre los cuentos folklóricos y los literarios.

La historia de la prosa narrativa española revela que los escritores de España se interesan por el cuento desde hace mucho tiempo. Las colecciones de cuentos se llamaban en la Edad Media libros de "enxienplos," palabra derivada del *exemplum* latino. Sabemos que estos depósitos de enxienplos o *exempla*, si se habla de colecciones en latín, eran muy populares en toda Europa durante la Edad Media. En España se les tuvo más cariño y estima que en ningún otro país y por eso en España estaban escritas muy a menudo en romance en vez de latín. Esta afición a las narraciones probablemente ha sido el resultado de la invasión árabe, la cual ejerció una influencia tan grande sobre la vida y cultura de las diferentes clases sociales de España.[3] Sea lo que fuere, el hecho es que había muchas clases de cuentos orientales, muchos de ellos tomados del folklore del Oriente y de su literatura, que entraron en España.

La primera colección de fábulas o cuentos que apareció en España en lengua occidental no estaba escrita en español, sino en el latín de la Edad Media. Este fue la *Disciplina Clericalis*[4] del judío converso Moisés Sefardí de Huesca bautizado Petrus Alfonsí, ahijado de don Alfonso el Batallador de Aragón. Es difícil darse cuenta de la importancia y casi maravillosa diseminación de este grupo de unos treinta cuentos. Sin embargo, fueron pocas las colecciones de cuentos o enxienplos en toda la Europa medieval que no están adecuadamente representadas en estas narraciones. Estas colecciones forman base de los cuentos que aparecen en tales obras famosas de la Edad Media como la *Gesta Romanorum* y el *Decamerone* de Boccaccio. El autor de la *Disciplina Clericalis* indicó que lo habia trasladado de una lengua oriental,—que suponemos era el árabe—, y es de creer que de la literatura pasó parcialmente al folklore.

Un siglo más tarde más o menos, en 1251, otra colección de cuentos del Oriente fue traducida a la lengua popular por primera vez, siendo esta lengua el español. El título de esta colección es el *Libro de Calila e Dimna*[5] y fue traducido por mandado del príncipe Alfonso, coronado Alfonso X de Castilla en 1252 y llamado el Sabio. Hemos dicho que este libro es de origen árabe, pero en parte es una versión de una obra indostánica llamada *Pantchatantra* (Cinco Libros) que según los eruditos tuvo su origen en los cuentos mitológicos de los antiguos indo-europeos.[6]

La traducción del famoso *Libro de Sindibad* bajo el titulo del *Libro de los engaños e asayamientos de las mugeres* es de 1253.[7] Vieron la luz durante el siglo catorce el *Libro de Patronio* o el *Conde Lucanor* de don Juan Manuel,[8] los *Castigos y documentos para buen vivir* del rey don Sancho,[9] hijo de Alfonso el Sabio, y el inimitable *Libro de Buen Amor* en verso del Arcipreste de Hita Juan Ruiz.[10]

Creemos que don Juan Manuel y su primo don Sancho, llamado el Bravo, obtuvieron algunos de sus cuentos del folklore de aquel tiempo en España. Ni el uno ni el otro hizo una mera traducción, sino que produjeron dos obras originales hasta cierto punto y obtenidos en fuentes diversos, parte eruditas y parte populares. Cierto es que hay elementos populares en la obra maestra de Juan Ruiz y también en el *Libro de los enxienplos por a. b. c.* de Clemente Sánchez,[11] excelente ejemplar éste del género del cuento moral cristiano el cual llegó a la cumbre de popularidad durante los siglos trece, catorce y quince. Nadie niega que el enxienplo número 45 de Sánchez [12] tenga fondo popular. Leemos en él que un íncubo persiguió a una pobre mujer que no pudo rechazar sus avances indecentes hasta que, por consejo de un santo, ella durmió con el báculo de él, remedio seguro de conjurar a los espíritus malos. ¿Quién duda que Sánchez y otros clérigos que recopilaron cuentos obtuvieron muchos del pueblo de sus parroquias?

Debemos mencionar que la narración de un pacto con el demonio que el Arcipreste de Hita usa en el *Libro de Buen Amor* fue uno de los temas más comunes del pueblo medieval y muy probablemente un cuento folklórico. El docto Fray Cejador y Frauca asegura que ese cuento lo había oído en su niñez de los labios de "una vieja muy devota." Y podríamos citar un gran número de ejemplos de este tipo de cuento literario-popular en las *Cantigas* de don Alfonso el Sabio,[13] que no es más que una colección de cuentos en verso de la gente española principalmente, aunque escrita en la lengua gallego-portuguesa.

Todas estas obras son literarias y escritas por autores más o menos eruditos y conocidos, de modo que se puede decir que son productos literarios que no merecen lugar entre los verdaderos cuentos populares. Esto nos conduce al problema perenne que aún no se ha resuelto: el decidir categóricamente si cierto cuento tiene su origen en el folklore o en la tradición literaria. En muchos casos no es posible resolver el problema porque de vez en cuando en la literatura aparece un cuento que es aceptado y narrado por la gente como producto popular, por ejemplo, el cuento del "Anillo de Policrates," objeto que perdido y tragado por un pez fue recobrado más tarde y devuelto a su dueño. Herodoto incluyó este cuento en sus famosas *Historias* y de aquella obra de la erudición griega llegó a ser un cuento tradicional europeo. En cambio hay cuentos verdaderamente populares, o así considerados por las mejores autoridades, que forman parte integral de la literatura erudita. Hemos mencionado el *Pantchatantra*, obra de una literatura sofisticada, producto de una civilización muy avanzada, que tuvo sus remotos orígenes en el folklore y que ha sido utilizado para originar otros cuentos folklóricos. Basta citar un ejemplo más antes de pasar a unos ejemplos más modernos de esta relación que existe entre los cuentos populares y los literarios y éste es el de *Martín Fierro*, epopeya argentina, producto de la mente de José Hernández (1834-86). Este poema tendrá su origen en las canciones populares del payador argentino, porque Hernández vivía entre los gauchos de la pampa quienes conocía muy bien, y hoy mismo este personaje, creado por un autor conocido, ha sido recibido por los gauchos como parte de su literatura popular. Así pues, resulta un ciclo completo: el folklore produce literatura erudita que en su tiempo produce más folklore.

Para evitar ser prolijo sólo mencionaremos brevemente otro parentesco entre el cuento erudito y el folklórico. Mencionaremos a autores tales como Lope de Vega, Calderón de la Barca, Ruiz de Alarcón, Quevedo, Cervantes y los autores conocidos y anónimos de la novela picaresca. Todos ellos a veces bebieron profundamente en las ricas fuentes del cuento popular español. Pedro de Urdemalas, un verdadero personaje popular, hace un papel interesante no sólo en España sino también en Hispanoamérica. Este personaje fue muy bien delineado, por ejemplo, por Timoneda en su *Sobremesa y alivio de caminantes* (1563) y en su *Patrañuelo* (1565), ambos ricos depósitos de temas folklóricos.[14]

No existen en España coleccionistas de cuentos populares hasta la mitad del siglo pasado cuando los romanticistas, novelistas regionales y costumbristas descubrieron el valor de la tradición popular en su país. Entre otros son de importancia los *Cuentos y fábulas* de Hartzenbusch, los *Cuentos populares* y las *Narraciones populares* de Trueba,[15] y desde luego las obras de Fernán Caballero.

La contribución de España al cuento popular es generosa. Esta forma de narración abunda en su literatura ya sea medieval, renacentista o moderna. Y entre el pueblo hay una tradición muy activa de cuentos populares, como se puede confirmar por la abundante cantidad de cuentos recopilados por los folkloristas del presente siglo.

3. *Las variedades de cuentos folklóricos en España.*

En España el gusto es variado en lo que se refiere al cuento folklórico. Ralph S. Boggs en su *Index of Spanish Folktales*[16] clasificó, según el sistema de Anti Aarne,[17] todos los cuentos populares publicados en España hasta 1930, citando más de ochenta y seis. Hace unos veinte y cuatro años que no se publica otra clasificación igual, aunque se han publicado varios índices de temas de cuentos españoles[18] y debemos decir que hoy día animados por la obra de Thompson[19] en este campo de investigación temática, los índices de temas son más numerosos que las clasificaciones de tipos de cuentos hechas según el sistema de Aarne.

Boggs mantiene, basándose en las conclusiones de su ya mencionado estudio definitivo de tipos comparado con estudios de otras nueve tradiciones nacionales, que los cuentos de España tienen una proporción mayor de cuentos de animales y menor de magia, los cuales son bastante numerosos, y aun menor es la de cuentos chistosos y enigmáticos. Boggs[20] nota también que los cuentos de tono religioso y didáctico son casi dos veces más estimados en España, debido esto, según creemos, no sólo a la influencia eclesiástica sino también en gran parte a la ya aludida herencia musulmana de moralizar en casi todos los cuentos. Sus descubrimientos concuerdan con los de Aurelio Espinosa[21] quien tuvo acceso a muchos cuentos españoles que Boggs no pudo estudiar porque no se habían publicado cuando hizo sus investigaciones. Revela Espinosa que los cuentos de origen esópico e indostánico son numerosos, excediendo la abundante cantidad de cuentos de asunto sobrenatural, v. g. cuentos de los milagros de Nuestra Señora, de los Santos, de agentes sobrenaturales tales como hadas, xanas, enanos, espíritos, ninfas, etc., y gran número de entes malévolos tales como el Nubero, Juan Cabrito, el cuélebre volante, las sirenas, el trasgu y la Estantigua o Güestia.[22]

Cuando contamos los temas compilados por mí y por Childers vemos que resulta algo más o menos parecido: predominan los cuentos de origen oriental, sean estos de origen esópico en el *Libro de los gatos*, sean indostánicos en *Calila e Dimna*, sea de la tradición oriental de las mujeres engañosas, representados por el *Libro de los engaños*. Siguen los numerosos cuentos de milagros de santos y de la Santa Virgen y del demonio y sus cohortes; y al fin encontramos los cuentos de tono chistoso, bromas y enigmas. Parece, en vista de los tres estudios mencionados, que en el dominio del cuento popular español existe lo que se puede llamar una norma fija y determinada.

4. *Los asuntos del cuento popular en España.*

Stith Thompson nos dice que en la gran área folklórica que se extiende desde Irlanda hasta la India el cuento popular está muy bien representado en la Península Ibérica.

En el castellano y desde luego en el portugués, catalán y en los varios dialectos de éstos existen muchísimos de los más importantes de estos cuentos, tales, por ejemplo, como *Cenicienta, Blancanieves,* o *el pescador y su esposa.*

5. *Estructura y manera de relatar los cuentos en España.*

Cuando se trata de este tipo de cuentos llamado en alemán *Märchen* y en inglés *fairy tale*, se ve que en España se emplean las mismas fórmulas[23] y desarrollo. Podemos decir lo mismo que Thompson manifiesta en su ensayo "El cuento folklórico" en *Folklore Américas* XII, No. 2, en lo que se refiere al cuento español de este tipo. Existe la misma vaga fraseología en la fórmula. En la introducción de casi todos los cuentos hallamos algo más o menos semejante: "Había una vez..." (*El lobo bobo y la zorra astuta*); "Erase vez y vez..." (*El pájaro de la verdad*); "Era un padre..." (*El muerto agradecido*); "Esta era una vez..." (*Las tres naranjas*) o "Este era un príncipe..." (*El castillo de irás-y-no-volverás*).[24]

Los ejemplos de conclusiones de cuentos en España también están de acuerdo con las siguientes fórmulas: "...y ellos se casaron luego y fueron muy felices por toda su vida." (*Las tres naranjas*); "...luego tuvieron nueve hijos y vivieron felices por muchos años." (*La piedra de mármol*).

Respecto al desarrollo, todo sucede en estos cuentos de una manera directa hasta la culminación y desde allí hasta la conclusión. Hablando del cuento de este tipo en general, Thompson dice que "...el lector u oyente amaestrado por lo general puede predecir no sólo el desenlace del cuento sino también casi todo el curso de la acción una vez que haya escuchado unos minutos o leído unas páginas."[25] Vemos que en casi todos estos cuentos el tema es el triunfo de los pobres o de los débiles, v.g. *El gato con botas, Cenicienta, y Blancanieves* y cien más; que todo sucede tres veces y que es siempre el tercer protagonista o suceso que sale con éxito, v.g. *Los tres hijos de oro, La novia negra y la novia blanca, y El pescador y su esposa*; y que el premio de éxito es ordinariamente un casamiento feliz, aunque nos dice Thompson, que "...a medida que uno deja el cuento (*Märchen*) más típico, encontraría que la riqueza o el esplendor material se considera de mayor importancia,"[26] v.g. *Mata siete, Blancanieves*, etc.

Thompson hubiera dicho todo en lo que se refiere al cuento español, porque todos los ejemplos que hemos citado más arriba aparecen no sólo en otros países sino también en España como parte integral del folklore hispánico.

6. La función del cuento popular en España

Casi todas las autoridades sobre el cuento popular están de acuerdo en lo que se refiere a las funciones de este género. Se dice, que estos cuentos son la novela de la gente y no está mal dicho porque no se encuentra mucho de la literatura formal o erudito entre al pueblo. De modo que el cuento folklórico sirve de diversión popular y de pasatiempo predilecto, y ésta es su función principal. No se puede negar que hay muchos cuentos cuya naturaleza es didáctica, y éstos abundan en España, debido como hemos dicho antes a las dos fuertes influencias—eclesiástica y oriental—, pero aun cuando se trate de cualquier cuento didáctico es de notar que muy a menudo el mismo cuento existe sin moraleja alguna, segura evidencia de que el papel didáctico es secundario y que la principal función de la mayoría de los cuentos es recreativa. Durante la Edad Media especialmente era la costumbre de los escritos de cuentos didácticos de valerse de temas diversos para llegar a una moraleja cristiana, y realmente queda uno escandalizado al leer algunos de ellos.[27] Y hoy día casi no es necesario recordarle a nadie que predicadores--católicos, protestantes y judíos—suelen adornar sus sermones con una variedad muy amplia de cuentos que no son todos piadosos ni completamente didácticos. Lo mismo sucede cuando uno hace algún cuento para moralizar o dar enseñanza a niños u otras personas. Por eso no es fácil ni prudente decir que todos los cuentos didácticos pertenecen a la tradición didáctica.

A pesar de todo lo que hemos dicho acerca de la popularidad del cuento de diversión, es necesario llevar en cuenta que siempre la función secundaria es didáctica. Nadie puede negar al cuento didáctico un lugar importante aunque sea secundario. En España como en gran parte del mundo siempre existirán cuentos de esta clase. Y es fácil explicarlo. España y Portugal constituyen unidades muy distintas entre las razas europeas en lo que se refiere a la tradición y folklore. La dominación musulmana y la consecuente introducción de una riqueza tan grande de elementos islámicos y orientales en la cultura ibérica dejaron una huella bien definida. La gente española es además ortodoxa en su catolicismo y hace siglos que se interesa en cuentos en los cuales se exalta la piedad. Una vez entendida la popularidad de los cuentos didácticos en España, podemos clasificarlos en tres grupos: primero, todos los cuentos didácticos narrados por gente devota para asustar y amonestar a los pecadores—cuentos de ánimas en pena, de cadáveres sepultados en llamas, del diablo y sus espíritus malos; en segundo lugar los cuentos en que se manifiesta el poder bondadoso de la Santa Familia y de los santos y en los que se dan pruebas de la gloria del Omnipotente y de la eficacia de la oración y de las buenas obras,—y aquí tenemos que decir que no hay tierra más aficionada al cuento piadoso que España; el tercer grupo de cuentos didácticos incluye los basados en fábulas esópicas que tratan de enseñar por medio de sabiduría práctica o eficaz para ganarse la vida astutamente o para escapar cualquier peligro, o engañar o burlarse de los crédulos.

La tercera función,—y ésta a veces es difícil de identificar— es la de perpetuar algún rito o costumbre. Muchos de estos cuentos pertenecen al género de la leyenda sobre la cual Thompson ha escrito explícitamente en su ensayo titulado "La leyenda" en *Folklore Américas* XII, No. 1.

En lo que se refiere al cuento folklórico, mucho de lo que es dicho en España puede aplicarse a Hispanoamérica. Tocante a los orígenes de los cuentos creemos que casi todas las versiones halladas en España existen en las Américas, tanto que no es preciso que nos ocupemos mucho de este particular. Notaremos más tarde que en casi todos los cuentos folklóricos españoles existe cierta norma que puede ser reconocida y que persiste aun en los cuentos populares hispanoamericanos. Desde luego el cuento popular hispanoamericano como ya se ha dicho, debe mucho al elemento indígena y por esta razón muchos de los asuntos de ellos se diferencian de los europeos. Pero en lo que se refiere a los otros aspectos del cuento en España, v.g. enlace entre cuentos populares y literarios, variedades de cuentos, forma y modo de narración y función es posible aceptar lo que se ha dicho acerca del cuento en España.

Sería de valor e interés hacer un estudio de la proporción de cuentos folklóricos españoles que también existen en Hispanoamérica. Las investigaciones del profesor Espinosa presentan datos estadísticos muy interesantes en lo que se refiere a la cantidad de cuentos de normas españolas que perduran en Hispanoamérica. Dice Espinosa[28] que en una colección de cuentos folklóricos hispanoamericanos de cualquiera de las regiones de cultura española se hallarán de 80 a 90 por ciento de cuentos típicos españoles. Existen variaciones, por supuesto, en el orden de los cuentos, pero generalmente se nota una gran semejanza entre ellos. El docto Espinosa basa sus datos sobre un estudio de 1800 cuentos españoles, pero sólo ha examinado ocho colecciones de cuentos hispanoamericanos. Sin embargo su computación ha sido cuidadosa y sus conclusiones indican una tendencia persistente que los cuentos españoles tienden de perpetuarse en las Américas.

Basando sus cálculos en dos colecciones de cuentos reunidos en regiones donde predomina la cultura india él encuentra que la razón a favor de los cuentos de origen español es de 55 a 50 por ciento sobre los de origen indio.

Existe hoy una cantidad impresionante de cuentos folklóricos españoles e hispanoamericanos. De España tenemos 1800 cuentos, más unos 1200 de Portugal y Cataluña; de Hispanoamérica 2200.

Los estudiantes del cuento popular español e hispanoamerica no tenemos los mismos problemas que menciona Stith Thompson en lo que se refiere al cuento popular mundial: nos hacen falta muchas colecciones de cuentos de regiones aun no examinadas; tenemos que emprender estudios mucho más exactos de cuentos individuales; tenemos que estudiar cuidadosamente todas las materias íntimamente relacionadas con el folklore—la etnología, la lengua, la dialectología, el ritual y las relaciones que existen entre los pueblos antiguos y modernos y la raza española y la hispanoamericana; tenemos también que estudiar las literaturas de España y de Hispanoamérica y sus relaciones con otras literaturas.

Quedan por hacerse todavía muchos estudios y será preciso llevarlos a cabo antes de que podamos comprender completamente el cuento folklórico del munco hispánico.

Notas

* Reprinted *Folklore Américas*, 14 (1954), 1-14.

1 Stith Thompson, *The Folktale*. Nueva York, 1951.

2 Stith Thompson, "El cuento folklórico," *Folklore Américas*, 12 (1952), 13.

3 Américo Castro, *España en su historia: Cristianos, Moros y Judíos*, Buenos Aires, 1948.

4 Pedro Alfonso *Disciplina Clericalis*, ed. Ángel González Palencia, Madrid, 1948.

5 *La antigua versión del Calila y Dimna cotejada con el original árabe de la misma*, ed. J. Alemany Bolúfer, Madrid, 1915; también la edición de Pascual de Gayangos en *Biblioteca de autores españoles*, LI, segunda edición, Madrid, 1952, p. 11-78. [AUTH. Robert White Linker and I published a new critical edition of this work, *El Libro de Calila e Digna*, Madrid: CSIC, 1967.]

6 Véase Stith Thompson, *The Folktale*, p. 367-90.

7 *El libro de los engaños e los asayamientos de las mugeres*, ed. A. Bonilla y San Martín, Barcelona-Madrid, 1914; también mi edición, Chapel Hill, 1953, asimismo contiene este texto la obra de A. González Palencia titulada *Versiones castellanas del «Sendebar»*, Madrid-Granada, 1946.

8 Juan Manuel, *El Libro de los enxiemplos del Conde Lucanor et de Patronio*, ed. Hermann Knust y Adolf Birch-Hirschfeld, Leipzig, 1900; también la edición de Pascual de Gayangos en *Biblioteca de autores españoles*, LI, p. 367-426. [AUTH. A more modern edition is that of José Manuel Blecua, *El Conde Lucanor o Libro de Patronio*, Madrid: Castalia, 1971.]

9 *Castigos e documentos para bien vivir ordenados por el rey don Sancho*, ed. Agapito Rey, Bloomington, Indiana, 1953 (Indiana University Publications Humanities series, No. 24), también la edición de Pascual de Gayangos en *Biblioteca de autores españoles* LI, 87-228. [AUTH. Dennis P. Seniff and I are preparing a new edition of this.]

10 Juan Ruiz, *Libro de Buen Amor*, ed. J. Cejador y Frauca, 5ª ed., Madrid, 1951.

11 *El libro de los enenplos por a. b. c.*, ed. A. Morel-Fatio en *Romania* VII, (1878), 481-526; también la edición de Pascual de Gayangos en *Biblioteca de autores españoles*, LI, p. 447-542. [AUTH. I published a new critical edition of this work, *Libro de los exemplos por a. b. c.*, Madrid: CSIC, 1961.]

12 *El libro de los enxenplos*, ed. Gayangos, p. 458.

¹³ Alfonso el Sabio *Las Cantigas de Santa Maria*, ed. del Marqués de Valmar, Madrid, 1889. [AUTH. Walter Mettman now has the definitive edition of this work, *Afonso X, O Sabio. Cantigas de Santa Maria*, 4 vols., Coimbra, 1959-72. Clásicos Castalia has begun to republish this work.]

¹⁴ Juan de Timoneda, *Sobremesa y alivio de caminantes*, ed. Aribau, *Biblioteca de autores españoles* III, Madrid, 1858. Su *Patrañuelo* se halla también en el mismo Vol. III.

¹⁵ J. E. Hartzenbusch, *Cuentos y fábulas*, Madrid, 1888; Antonio de Trueba, *Cuentos populares*, Madrid, 1864, y *Narraciones populares*, Leipzig, 1875.

¹⁶ Ralph S. Boggs, *Index of Spanish Folktales*, Helsinki, Finlandia, 1930 (Folklore Fellows Communications, No. 90).

¹⁷ A. Aarne y Stith Thompson, *Types of the Folktale: a Classification and Bibliography*, Helsinki, Finalandia, 1928 (Folklore fellows communications, No. 74).

¹⁸ Véase los siguientes: mi *Motif-Index of Mediaeval Spanish Exempla*, Knoxville, Tennessee, 1949; J. Wesley Childers, *Motif-Index of the* cuentos of Juan Timoneda, Bloomington, Indiana, 1948 (Indiana University Publications Folklore Series, No. 5).

¹⁹ Stith Thompson, *Motif-Index of Folk-Literature*, Bloomington, Indiana y Helsinki, Finlandia, 1932-1936, 6 vols. (Folklore fellows communications, nos. 106, 107, 108, 109, 116, 117; también Indiana University Studies, nos. 96, 97, 100, 101, 105, 108, 109, 110, 111, 112). [AUTH. A new edition was published by Indiana University Press, 4 vols., 1955-59.]

²⁰ R. S. Boggs y N. B. Adams, *Spanish Folktales*, Nueva York, 1932, p. xii.

²¹ Aurelio Espinosa, "Spanish and Spanish-American Folk Tales,' *Journal of American Folklore*, 64 (1951), 151-62.

²² Véase el artículo por A. Espinosa titulado "Spanish Folklore," en Funk and Wagnalls' *Standard Dictionary of Folklore, Mythology and Legend*, Nueva York, 1950, Vol. II, p. 1067-68.

²³ J. Bolte y G. Polivka. *Anmerkungen zu den Kinder-un Hausmärchen der Brüder Grimm*. Leipzig, 1913-31, IV, 41-46.

²⁴ Todos los títulos en paréntesis se sacan de R. S. Boggs y N. B. Adams, *Spanish Folktales*, Nueva York, 1932.

²⁵ Stith Thompson, "El cuento folklórico," *Folklore Américas*, 12 (1952), 16.

²⁶ *Ibid*, p. 16.

²⁷ J. A. Mosher, *The Exemplum in the Early Religious and Didactic Literature of England*, Nueva York, 1911, p. 17; J. T. Welter, *L'Exemplum dans la littérature religieuse et didactique du Moyen Âge*. Paris, 1927, p. 398 y sigs.

²⁸ A. Espinosa, *op. cit.*, p. 157.

Bibliografía

[AUTH. The bibliography has been updated per the notes.]
Aarne, Anti y Stith Thompson. *The Types of the Folk-Tale*. Helsinki, Finlandia, 1930 (Folklore Fellows Communications, No. 90), e Indiana University Press, 4 vols., 1955-59..

Alfonso, Pedro, *Disciplina clericalis*, ed. de A. González Palencia. Madrid, 1948.

Alfonso X, *Cantigas de Santa María*, ed. del Marqués de Valmar. Madrid, 1889.

Amador de los Ríos, José. *Historia crítica de la literatura española*. Madrid, 1861-65. 7 vols.

Andrade, Manuel J. *Folklore from the Dominican Republic*. Nueva York, 1930.

——. *Folklore de la República Dominicana*. Ciudad Trujillo, 1948. [Trad. del inglés.]

BAE. Biblioteca de autores españoles. Madrid, 1846-80. 71 vols.

Barker, W. H. y Cecilia Sinclair. *West African Folktales*. Londres, 1917.

Beckwith, Martha W. *Jamaica Anansi Stories*. Nueva York, 1924.

Bédier, J. *Les Fabliaux, Étude de littérature populaire et d'histoire littéraire du Moyen Âge*. París, 1895.

Benfey, T. *Pantschatantra: Fünf Bücher indischer Fabeln, Märchen und Erzählungen*. Leipzig, 1859.

Calila y Dimna, ed. de J. Alemany Bolufer. Madrid, 1915; ed. de *BAE* LI. [AUTH. See also my edition, below.]

Castigos y documentos, ed. de Agapito Rey. Bloomington, Indiana, 1953; ed. de *BAE* LI.

Chauvin, Victor. *Bibliographie des ouvrages arabes ou relatifs aux arabes, publiés dans l'Europe chrétienne de 1810 à 1885*. Lieja, 1892-1922. 12 vols.

Childers, J. Wesley. *Motif-Index of the cuentos of Juan Timoneda*. Bloomington, Indiana, 1948.

Eells, E. S. *Tales of Enchantment from Spain*. Nueva York, 1920.

Espinosa, Aurelio M. *Cuentos populares españoles*. Stanford University, 1923-26. 3 vols.

——. "Spanish and Spanish-American Folk-Tales," *Journal of American Folklore*, (64) 1951, 151-62.

Espinosa, José M. *Spanish Folktales from Nuevo Méjico*. Nueva York, 1937.

Fernán Caballero. *Cuentos y poesías populares andaluces*. Sevilla, 1859; Leipzig, 1866.

Fitzmaurice-Kelly, James. *Historia de la literatura española*. Madrid, 1921.

Gesta Romanorum, ed. de Hermann Oesterley. Berlín, 1872.

Haavio, Marrti. *Kettenmarchenstudien*. Helsinki, Finlandia 1931. (Folklore Fellows Communications, No. 45).

Gier, Albert and John E. Keller, *Les Formes narratives brèves en Espagne et au Portugal*. Heidelberg, Grundriss der Romanischen Literaturen der Mittelalters, 1985.

Jacobs, Joseph. *History of the Aesopic Fable*. Londres, 1889.

Jacobus de Voragine, *Leyenda áurea*, ed. de Th. Graesse. Breslau, 1890.

Krappe, Alexandre H. "Les Sources du *Libro de los exemplos*," *Bulletin Hispanique*, (39) 1937, 5-54.

Keller, John E. *Motif-Index of Mediaeval Spanish Exempla*. Knoxville, Tennessee, 1949.

——. "A Medieval Folklorist," *Folklore Studies in Honor of Arthur Palmer Hudson*. [The next essay in this collection.]

—— y Robert White Linker. *El Libro de Calila e Digna*, Madrid: CSIC, 1967.

Laval, Ramon A. *Cuentos populares en Chile*. Santiago, 1903.

Libro de los engaños, ed. John E. Keller. Chapel Hill, 1953; ed. de A. Bonilla y San Martin. Barcelona-Madrid, 1914; ed. de A. González Palencia en *Versiones castellanas del* Sendebar. Madrid-Granada, 1946.

Libro de los gatos, ed. de *BAE*, LI; ed. de G. T. Northrup en *Modern Philology*, 4 (1908).

Lyra, Carmen. *Los cuentos de mi tía Panchita.* Costa Rica, 1926.

Manuel, Don Juan. *Obras* en *BAE*, y José Manuel Blecua, *El Conde Lucanor o Libro de Patronio.* Madrid: Castalia, 1971

Maspons y Labros, F. *Lo rondallayre.* Barcelona, 1871-74. 3 vols.

Menéndez y Pelayo, M. *Orígenes de la novela.* Madrid, 1905; 2 ed. 1943.

Mettman, Walter. *Afonso X, O Sabio. Cantigas de Santa Maria,* 4 vols., Coimbra, 1959-72.

Montenegro, Ernesto. *Cuentos populares de Chile.* Santiago, 1938.

Müller, Max. "On the Emigration of Fables," *The Contemporary Review,* 14 (1870), 570-600.

Panchatantra, tr. del sánscrito por Arthur W. Ryder. Chicago, 1925.

Rael, Juan B. "Cuentos españoles de Colorado y de Nuevo Méjico," *Journal of American Folklore,* 52 (1939), 227-323 y 40 (1942), 1-93.

Ramírez de Arellano, R. *Folklore portorriqueño.* Madrid, 1926.

Reed, H. A. *Spanish Legends and Traditions.* Londres, 1914.

Romera-Navarro, M. *Historia de la literatura española.* Nueva York, 1928.

Sydow, Carl von. *Circulation des contes populaires.* Tours, 1938.

Thompson, Stith. *The Folktale.* Nueva York, 1951.

—————. *Tales of the North American Indians.* Cambridge, Massachusetts, 1929.

Valbuena Prat, A. *Historia de la literatura española.* Barcelona, 1937.

Welter, J. Th. *L'Exemplum dans la littérature religieuse et didactique du Moyen Âge.* París, 1927.

Wesselski, Albert. "Einstige Brucken zwischen Orient und Okzident," *Archiv Orientali,* 9 (1929), p. 1-18.

—————. *Versuch einer Theorie des Marchen.* Reichenberg, 1931.

Wheeler, Howard T. *Tales from Jalisco.* Nueva York, 1943.

A Medieval Folklorist*

OLKLORE AS A DEFINITE PART of Spanish letters was first given considerable prominence in the nineteenth century when *costumbrismo* filled the works of important writers. *Costumbrismo* is a variety of Spanish literature characterized by the intention to present popular customs, daily life, and, of course, many elements of true folklore. It was recognized as a definite literary movement, and its reputation was widely disseminated in the works of such masters as Fernán Caballero, Juan Valera, Pedro Antonio de Alarcón, and José María de Pereda. But *costumbrismo* was no new thing in Spanish letters, for Cervantes himself, in the opinion of some scholars, was the first to capitalize upon it in his *Rinconete y Cortadillo* (1613). And Cervantes was only following a Spanish custom old even in his day. Apparently Spaniards have always, from the very beginnings of their literature, felt the urge to depict the life that went on around them. There is even *costumbrismo* in the first monument of Spanish writing, the *Poem of the Cid*, written circa 1140, although the author's or the authors' interest in other things caused those other things to overshadow the depiction of customs and other folkloric elements. Perhaps the first to linger over customs, beliefs and folk motifs was Gonzalo de Berceo who wrote in the first half of the thirteenth century. His *Miracles of Our Lady* and his three saints' lives are filled with *costumbrismo* and true folklore;[1] but as his primary aim was to lead his readers to piety through the example of the Virgin and the saints, he used folkloric elements primarily because he thought they would give him greater rapport with the simple folk he hoped to teach. If he appeared to be one of the folk, perhaps he thought he could gain their trust. One might conceivably think of Berceo as the first Spanish folklorist had it

15

not been that another personage in the same century seems to have outshone him in the art of gathering and making known the folkloric elements of the times.

This personage, far more distinguished than Berceo, was no less than King Alfonso X, dubbed by his people as "El Sabio," that is, "the Wise."[2] This remarkable monarch, criticized for his zealous literary, scientific and artistic activities, apparently planned to give his people the benefits of the then known knowledge of the world. To accomplish this he employed the greatest specialists in law, history, the sciences, medicine, music and the pictorial arts, and perhaps, as we shall see below, in at least certain varieties of *costumbrismo* and folklore. His contributions are too numerous to list here, albeit it should be mentioned that he virtually produced the codex of Spanish law that was to become the foundation of all subsequent law in Spain and her possessions; the longest and most detailed medieval history of the world and the longest of his own country; and had rendered into Spanish books on astronomy, astrology, the lapidary science and the playing of chess, all of which influenced the learned until well into the Renaissance. And somehow, amid all this erudite activity, while he waged war upon the Moors, fought rebellious nobles, contended with his son, Sancho IV, who eventually deposed him, and even though he vied for the title of Emperor of the Holy Roman Empire, he managed to produce one of the great literary works of the Middle Ages, the *Canticles of Holy Mary*,[3] a book interesting to artists, musicians, students of sociology, history, daily life, comparativists and to folklorists. It is this book of Alfonso X's which gives him the honor of being considered as the first medieval folklorist.

The *Canticles* is a vast collection of the miracles ascribed to the Blessed Virgin. It follows the general pattern of the great Latin collections of miracles compiled in most of the important countries of Europe. It presents over 400 miracles in a wide variety of verse forms, and with each poetic rendition of a miracle there is the musical notation to which it was to be played or sung. And what is even more valuable and important is the fact that each miracle is accompanied by a full page (sometimes even by two pages) of miniatures in gorgeous colors and brilliant illumination. In these miniatures can be seen the whole panorama of medieval life, rural and urban, on land and on the sea, in Spain and abroad. When these pictures have been studied properly and with the care they merit, we will know a great deal more about the life and times of thirteenth-century man and about the elements of his folklore.[4]

It is well known that the king enlisted the assistance of great authorities in the preparation and production of the many books he caused to be written. This is especially true in the case of the histories, the scientific works, for the most part translated from Arabic, and for the musical and pictorial aspects of the *Canticles*. In a very few cases we know the names of specialists in the above-mentioned areas of activity. We know nothing of any expert help the King may have received in the compiling of the miracles included in the *Canticles*. But surely a monarch as busy as Alfonso X must have had to avail himself of some assistance. He simply would not have had time to assemble and research over four hundred miracles. Who could his helpers have been in this project? Most probably, at least for the purely literary or Scriptural miracles, he must have had the assistance of ecclesiastics, and most likely these were of the upper ranks of the hierarchy and not simple priests, friars or itinerant Dominican preachers. The first one hundred miracles, more or less, follow the Latin tradition of miracles and are little more than Latin miracles of the Virgin translated into the language of the *Canticles*. These miracles were the common property of the Church and represented some of the favorite themes of medieval Christendom. Any bishop could have offered a volume of such miracles in Latin, and the royal library itself in Toledo or in Burgos (Madrid, it will be recalled, was no more than the village it would remain until Philip II made it his capital in the sixteenth century) must have contained several such collections. So much for the first one hundred miracles. But the second one hundred contain a higher percentage of lesser known miracles, some of which were associated with remote or even inaccessible shrines far from the busy life of the court, and well out of range of the King and his perambulations through the kingdom. How did these make their way into Alfonso's ken and into the *Canticles of Holy Mary*? What bishop or important ecclesiastic would have known such miracles, many of which treat subject matter of the most homely variety, matters which one would expect to be of little interest for any one save peasants and farmers of a particular region. Actually, only the shrine of Our Lady of Villa Sirga in the Kingdom of León had anything like an international reputation, and even this shrine may have attracted attention because it lay on the route from France to the shrine of St. James at Compostela, a pilgrimage center so famous that even a bourgeois woman like the Wife of Bath had visited it.[5] But such shrines as that of Our Lady of Salas, at which the Virgin cured a man who had been attacked by a dragon, lay more or less in the hinterland. The poor and the lowly who lived as simple peasants and woodsmen along the Valley of the Guadiana and close to the Portuguese border did not visit such renowned centers of healing as Villa Sirga or Saragossa or Monserrat; they had recourse to Puerto de Santa María or Santa Maria de Terena. Out of the wilds of Huesca and from Borja and Daroca they came, and it is doubtful that the fame of their cures or the miracles wrought in these lesser shrines often reached the King or the higher ecclesiastics. Therefore, to repeat a question, how did King Alfonso learn of these insignificant miracles? In a very few cases we read that he actually made a trip to gain information about some miracle, thereby functioning as a true collector of folkloristic material, for such miracles attached to the lesser shrines were often no more than local legends or folktales. One very interesting miracle of this type (we read that the king went to the church associated with the miracle, and in the miniatures we see him depicted there examining the miraculous cloth) is number XVIII.[6] A woman in Segovia produced silk as a livelihood. When her silkworms became infected with some disease, she sought the aid of the Virgin of a small parish church, and she promised the Virgin, whose image wore a tattered garment, a new robe if the cure were effected. This woman forgot her pledge, even though all her silkworms recovered, but the worms themselves honored her obligation by weaving not one, but two pieces of cloth to replace the ragged garment. The king carried off one of the pieces of cloth for the Virgin to his own Chapel and stated in the final lines of the canticle that he had done so.

Since the king could not obviously turn folklorist to any great extent, he must have had assistance. And his assistants must have circulated through the provinces, even penetrating the Moorish Kingdom of Granada, and perhaps even journeying to foreign lands in search of miracles. This activity would have extended over a period of many years, for the king seems to have labored on the *Canticles of Holy Mary* from early in his reign (and possibly even before it began) until close to the time of his death.

Only such determined collecting could have turned up so many insignificant miracles, and only King Alfonso's interest in the beliefs and customs of his people could have persuaded him to edit and have miracles written down about insects, sick falcons, aging donkeys and peasant children. The *Canticles* is, then, a collection of folk miracles, as well as literary and ecclesiastical miracles, and represents what can logically and justifiably be termed folklore research in the thirteenth century.

The following miracles will illustrate the folkloric tone of this variety of popular miracle.[7] The tale of the Jewess Marisaltos of Segovia is a typical local legend of the type known well by all folklorists. The tale can still be heard in and around Segovia, and indeed has spread to other regions and even to the New World.[8] In it a Jewish girl decides to accept conversion and become a devotee of the Virgin Mary, but the Jewish community of the city decides otherwise. They judge her guilty of blasphemy and cast her down from a high crag, only to see her miraculously float to safety, saved by the Virgin's intervention.[9]

In Miracle CCCXV a woman in the fields near Madrid placed her child in the standing wheat as she helped with the harvest, and a head of wheat was swallowed by the infant. When the mother found the child, its belly swollen, and in great agony, she sped to the shrine of Our Lady of Atocha, and the head of wheat miraculously worked its way harmlessly through the infant's side.

Miracle CXCIX relates the story of a furrier who worked at his trade on one of the feast days of Our Lady. As a punishment, a needle he was using suddenly pierced his throat and would not be removed until he repented and begged aid of the Virgin. The man was healed in the shrine of Our Lady of Terena.

Many other examples could be given, but these will illustrate the subject matter treated in the more folkloristic of the *Canticles* and will, it is hoped, show how it is that King Alfonso X of Spain was interested in *costumbrismo* and in the folklore of his realm.

Notes

* Reprinted from *Folklore Studies in Honor of Arthur Palmer Hudson*, Chapel Hill, 1965, pp. 19-25.

1 The works of Berceo alluded to are the *Milagros de Nuestra Señora* and three saints' lives: *Vida de Santo Domingo de Silos, Vida de San Millán de la Cogolla* and *Vida de Santa Oria, Virgen.* The edition of A. G. Solalinde (Madrid: Clásicos Castellanos, 1958) has been the standard text of the *Milagros;* for the best text of the *Vida de Santo Domingo de Silos* see the edition of Fray Alfonso

Andrés, O. S. B. (Madrid, 1958); the *Vida de San Millán* and the *Vida de Santa Oria* may be read in the outdated edition of Florencio Janer, *Biblioteca de Autores Españoles*, Number 57. [AUTH. Since these editions, Brian Dutton has edited most of Berceo's works in what have come to be the standard editions. Dutton's *Milagros* was published in London by Tamesis in 1971.]

² Alfonso, son of King Ferdinand the Saint and of Princess Beatriz of Swabia, was born in 1221 and ruled from 1252 to 1284. A true forerunner of humanism, he was a better scholar than politician and his reign was marred by much civil discord. His repute as a patron of literature and learning, however, perpetuates his memory.

³ The best edition of the *Canticles* is that of Walter Mettmann, *Afonso X, O Sábio: Cantigas de Santa Maria* (Coimbra, 1959-72). All references to this work of Alfonso X refer to this edition. [AUTH. Editorial Castalia is publishing an updated edition, but so far only the first one hundred *Cantigas* have appeared in *Cantigas de Santa Maria (Cantigas 1 a 100)*, 1986. Some years may pass before all 400-odd *cantigas* are printed.]

⁴ See my brief article, "Daily Living as Presented in the *Canticles* of Alfonso the Learned," *Speculum*, 33 (1958), 484-89 [AUTH. This is reprinted in this collection as the sixteenth article.]

⁵ In the General Prologue to the *Canterbury Tales* we read of the Wife of Bath: "At Rome she hadde been, and at Boloyne, In Galice at Seint Jame, and at Coloyne."

⁶ A reproduction of the miniatures of the Miracle can be seen in the article cited in footnote 4. [AUTH. For reproduction of all the illustrations of the *Cantigas* see the facsimile volume. *Alfonso X, el Sabio, Cantigas de Santa Maria. Edición facsímil del Códice T.I.1 de la Biblioteca de San Lorenzo el Real de El Escorial, Siglo XIII*. Madrid: Editorial Internacional de Libros Antiguos, 2 vols. 1979.]

⁷ For a more complete study of the folkloric content of the *Canticles* see my "Folklore in the *Cantigas* of Alfonso El Sabio," *Southern Folklore Quarterly*, 23 (1959), 175-83 [AUTH. Reprinted here as the fifteenth article.].

⁸ A painting al fresco of this miracle can be seen in the cloister of the Cathedral of Segovia directly above the niche in which the converted Jewess lies entombed.

⁹ See also Fidel Fita, "La judería de Segovia," *BRAH*, 9 (1886), 349-89, in which on pp. 372-77 he treats this miracle and transcribes, from an unedited manuscript of the 13th century by Fray Rodrigo de Cerrato, that priest's account of the actual trial of the Jewess and of her life after the Blessed Virgin saved her. An account is found also in Ramón Menéndez Pidal, *Primera crónica general*, 2nd ed., Madrid: Gredos, 1955, II, Ch. 1006, 685.

Elements of White Magic
in Mediaeval Spanish *Exempla**

HE RELATIONSHIP OF WHITE MAGIC to Spanish me-
diaeval *exempla* has never been studied seriously
and comprehensively; nevertheless, a close rela-
tionship existed, and few were the collections of
this form of mediaeval narrative that did not
contain colorings and backgrounds in white
magic. The present approach to the subject will
take the form of a brief introductory study, the
aim of which will be that of focusing attention upon the prevalence
of white magic in Spanish mediaeval *exempla* repositories and of
showing clearly that most of the types or divisions of white magic
were represented in them.

A careful examination of the most representative *exempla* collections showed that white magic was present almost throughout the
entire period when the *exemplum* flourished, i. e., the 12th through the
15th centuries. Both lay and clerical works drew from the white
magic lore of the folk for motifs and subject matter; however, as
might be expected, collections of tales compiled by hagiographers
employed magic much more extensively than did those repositories
whose *exempla* concerned themselves with less exalted matters.

Miracles made up a large percentage of the examples of white
magic, but not all miracles can be classified as magic; most miracles,
indeed, are based upon faith and the power of prayer, and such
miracles did not emerge as a part of folk culture and cannot be
considered as true white magic. Sheer faith and its ability to move
mountains, heal the sick, raise the dead, and alter the course of
nature's laws was an element of the Christian credo of those times: it

21

was not of the folk; it was not white magic; it is not related to the subject of this article. For these reasons all miracles and marvelous happenings in the collections considered, if wrought by faith and faith alone, have been excluded from the study.

The folk—superstitious, credulous, and deeply rooted in an ancient lore of which magic, black and white, was an important part— would not willingly relinquish this age-old heritage. Ecclesiastics, therefore, found it necessary and profitable in their work to borrow deeds once attributed to the pagan gods and popular heroes, grafting these deeds, often with little in the way of modification, upon the new heroes, the saints. If the saints were to supersede the old gods, if the heroes of ancient cultures were to be supplanted, then the hagiographer had to conform to the tastes and beliefs of the people, had to supply, literally upon demand, the magic so deeply embedded in the fibre of the folk.

Magic we shall consider as a science or art by which the logical, normal forces of nature may be upset, nullified, or made to operate in a fashion not in accord with nature's laws. Unseen, often unknown, almost always incomprehensible forces come into play when magic is practiced, and these forces may be caused to operate for either good or for evil ends. Magic, then, is the art or science of producing preternatural effects through the aid of departed spirits, the occult powers of nature, or mysterious forces beyond the ken of man. Magic is always present to a greater or lesser degree. White magic, magic practiced for ends that are good, magic set in operation by the powers of good, by saints and other holy people, played an important role in Spain's *exempla*. An examination of the varieties of white magic is now in order.

A considerable body of *exempla* was the basis for this study. The collections comprehend chronologically the entire development of the form in Spain from its earliest beginnings, as represented by the *Disciplina Clericalis*, through the apogee of literary, popular, recreational, and didactic phases, exemplified by the master works of Don Juan Manuel, Juan Ruiz, and Clemente Sánchez. The works whose tales were carefully studied were the following: *El libro de buen amor; El libro de Calila y Dimna; Castigos y documentos del rey don Sancho; El libro del cauallero Zifar; Consolaciones de la vida humana; El Corbacho; Disciplina Clericalis; El libro de los engaños et los asayamientos de las mugeres; El libro de los estados;* and *El libro de enxienplos por a.b.c.; El libro de los gatos; El libro de los*

*enxienplos del Conde Lucanor et de Patronio; Milagros de Nuestra Sennora.***
In these works are found more than a thousand *exempla*. Not all contain examples of white magic. The *Disciplina Clericalis* might be cited as an example. Some, such as *El libro de los engaños*, contain only examples of black magic. Others are the repositories of numerous illustrations of black and of white magic. Of the last type the best example is *El libro de los enxemplos.*

No effort was made here to catalogue all the examples of white magic present in the collections mentioned above; but a sufficient number of illustrations has been included to strengthen the case for the frequent appearance of white magic in Spanish works of the *exenplum* genre.

The religious *exempla* collections, as has been noted, contain the greatest number of examples of white magic. Of these, the most numerous samples appear in *El libro de los enxemplos, Consolaciones de la vida humana, Castigos y documentos del rey don Sancho,* and *Milagros de Nuestra Sennora.*

The divisions employed here for convenience in the treatment of the types of white magic in mediaeval Spanish *exempla* collections are those used by Stith Thompson,[1] namely, A. Mythological Motifs, in which magic animals are included; D. Magic, under which are found magic transformation, magic control of the elements, magic invulnerability, destructive magic powers, magic automata, and miscellaneous magic manifestations; F. marvels, wherein are listed magic powers of perception, extraordinary plants that undergo miraculous growth, and magic multiplication; Q. Rewards and Punishments, the section that lists miraculous rewards and punishments; V. Religion, the section devoted to miraculous images, the saints, angels, the Virgin Mary, et cetera.

Magic animals
Motifs employing magic animals were quite common in the Spanish works studied: a dragon guarded the food of a holy hermit, frightened robbers so violently as to bring about their repentance;[2] bees left honey on the lips of a child destined to become a great man, and ants brought grains of wheat to another child whose future was bright;[3] a hyena guided a lost hermit out of the wilderness;[4] wild leopards accompanied the Holy Family through the desert on their flight into Egypt;[5] birds showed a monk where to dig for a hidden treasure.[6]

Magic transformation

Magic transformations were not uncommon. Sometimes the transformation was made from a human being to an animal, as when a holy hermit changed a girl into a mouse;[7] in a very graphic illustration of white magic transformation a saint caused maggots in a holy nun's sore to become precious gems;[8] water changed into wine in another *exemplum*.[9]

Magic control of the elements

In Spanish *exempla* saints and holy people control the elements with apparent ease: magic winds, raised at the command of saints, are present in at least three of the collections;[10] with a magic iron rod another saint made bodies of water open and close.[11]

Magic charms, talismans, and words

Among some of the most interesting and authentic examples of folk magic found in the *exempla* collections are those in which the saint employs a charm, talisman or magic word to bring about some miracle. Stories of this kind vividly illustrate the powerful underlying influence of the folk culture of Spain. A woman, beset nightly by the devil, is able to ward off his unwanted attentions by sleeping with the hose of a saint;[12] an evil spirit is adjured to depart by naming the Deity;[13] the sign of the cross is all that is required to banish the devil, in one case,[14] and wild beasts, in another;[15] holy water washes away marks left upon a man's face by the Fiend;[16] witchcraft involving the spirit of a dead child that attempts to lead its mother into peril is overcome by burning a lock of the dead infant's hair.[17]

In these examples the magic of the folk has been transplanted bodily into the soil of Christian white magic. One is led to believe that the clergyman[18] who used these instances of magic in a book designed to provide preachers with sermon topics was of the folk, and that he knew the folk remedies for averting supernatural perils so well that he allowed these old remedies to creep into his text with the more legitimate Christian miracles.

Magic powers of perception; magic senses

The magic of the saints gave them the power to foresee dangers, to be aware of events long before they happened, to see through solid matter, and to predict the future. All of these powers are well represented in the collections studied: a saint was able to warn a boy of a serpent that had hidden in a basket left by the child in a distant spot;[19] a blind holy man was aware that a man was poisoning his drink;[20] when pilgrims hid their clothing in a wood and begged a saint to clothe them, he was able to see the hidden garments and to send the false beggars away.[21]

Magic invulnerability

The magic invulnerability afforded certain saints was truly re-markable: fire consumed a house in which a saint was residing, burned the clothing from his back, but left the holy flesh unharmed;[22] another saint handled the most venemous serpents with no danger to his life;[23] more marvelous still was a saint who drank poison and suffered no ill effects.[24]

Saints were able to impart magic invulnerability to others whom they desired to protect; a saint sustained a man on the gallows for several days until his innocence had been established;[25] a young prince of holy inclinations was saved from murder at the hands of his uncle by a group of infant angels who slew his assailants.[26]

Celestial visitors; angels, the Virgin, et cetera

The appearance of celestial visitors in Spanish *exempla* collections merits study. Likewise, some study of the visitations of the Holy Virgin would seem to deserve a separate investigation. The Virgin appeared in so many of these Spanish *exempla* that no study, however brief, would be complete without at least some minor treatment of her place in the literature.

Berceo's *Milagros de Nuestra Sennora* is a collection of twenty-five miracles of the Virgin. *El libro de los enxemplos* in both its manuscripts devotes a great deal of space and a great many *exempla* to miracles and marvelous cures and protection afforded by the Mother of God. A few examples will have to suffice here to illustrate the folklore of the Virgin in the Spanish *exempla* repositories: the Virgin supported a man on the gallows because he was one of her devotees;[27] she resuscitated a drowned man;[28] she restored the hand to a saint after he had cut it off in an attempt to suppress lust;[29] she destroyed a great Moorish army at the gates of Constantinople;[30] she rescued a man from a watery grave after a shipwreck.[31]

Destructive magic power; magic punishment

Not always did the saints and holy hermits and pious nuns turn white magic into channels of kindness: at times it was necessary for them to destroy their enemies and the foes of their faith. A few examples will serve to explain the statement. A holy woman, a near-saint, was accused by her husband of infidelity. Innocent, she appealed for some sign to prove that she was guiltless. Her husband immediately became a leper.[32] A knight ravished a holy nun and then took flight on his horse. Miraculously, the nun appeared in front of him on the animal, grasped the reins and held them with such supernatural strength that those pursuing the knight were able to overtake and apprehend him.[33] One saint ruined a fine sword belonging to a man about to execute a good woman; the sword was hopelessly dulled.[34] A lewd girl, about to bear an illegitimate child, accused a holy bishop of fathering the unborn infant. She was kept in a state of miraculously and phenomenally prolonged labor until she confessed and absolved the bishop of all blame.[35]

Magic automata

Inanimate objects such as statues, images, the cross, and even things like trees and springs may be imbued with magic powers: a magic statue revealed a treasure;[36] an image of the Saviour descended from the cross to punish a nun about to desert the convent and flee with a lover;[37] His image bled when injured by a Jew;[38] a statue of the Virgin grasped the hem of an artist's garment when the devil pushed him from a lofty scaffolding.[39] The Virgin once wove a magic garment for an exceptionally pious priest. When an evil priest put the garment on, it strangled him to death.[40]

Miraculous growth and multiplication

Miraculous growth and multiplication was a favorite subject of the compilers of *exempla* and probably of the folk. Such miracles were doubtless suggested, in part at least, by Scripture; but it is possible, and even very likely, that marvels of this kind had formed a part of the lore of the people, for all peoples seem to produce such tales.

Vegetables and fruits matured in an unbelievably short time--indeed, they developed even as people watched them;[41] certain monks were so pious that their supply of flour was never low, even when they gave quantities away daily to the poor;[42] one amusing tale tells of a saint who cast dice with a man for the latter's soul, and caused the dice to split so as to make a higher score for himself.[43]

Closely related to this sort of magic multiplication is the miracles of the inexplicable replacement of objects removed by saints or of false relics made authentic for holy people. St. Nicholas, in order to feed the poor, was obliged to steal certain supplies of bread. Before the theft could be discovered, the bread was miraculously restored.[44] In another case, a man bought a finger which he believed to be a relic of a saint. The finger was not authentic; nevertheless, because of his piety, he soon received the true finger, which was missing thereafter from the corpse of the saint.[45]

White magic, then, was well represented in mediaeval Spanish *exempla* collections of both lay and clerical authorship. Indeed, during the course of this investigation, motifs founded upon magic, white and black, were found to be numerous enough to merit separate studies. It is seen that the principal divisions or types of white magic are represented in the Spanish collections, and there are indications pointing to the probable use of the various types or divisions of black magic.

The Spanish *exemplum* genre gathered and perpetuated numerous magic motifs which otherwise might well have been lost, since they do not appear in other literatures. Many of these motifs, it is true, were not original to Spanish writing; on the other hand, a large number of them may have appeared first in Spain. The difficulties involved in determining the origins of tales are well known. In many cases there is no certainty as to whether a motif was common lore, or not. Conclusions of this nature are so difficult to reach that it is often necessary to depend upon a feeling for motifs of Spanish background, and obviously such feelings are not reliable.

Notes

* Reprinted from *Romance Studies Presented to William Morton Dey*. Studies in the Romance Languages and Literatures, Chapel Hill: University of North Carolina Press, 1959, pp. 85-90.

** The titles of these collections are abbreviated as follows:

Barlaam, ed. Lauchert, Friedrich. "La estoria del rey Anemur e de Iosaphat e de Barlaam" *Romanische Forschungen*, 8 (1893), 33-402. [AUTH. The latest edition of *Barlaam e Josafat* is that of Robert W. Linker and myself, *Barlaam e Josafat, edición crítica*. Madrid: CSIC, 1979.];

Buen Amor, ed. Cejador y Frauca, Julio. *Juan Ruiz Arcipreste de Hita, Libro de buen amor* (Vol. 1) Madrid: Espasa-Calpe, 1937; Vol. II, 1941. [AUTH. More modern editions of Juan Ruiz's work include Jacques Joset, *Libro de buen amor*. Madrid: Espasa-Calpe, 1974. This one replaces Cejador y Frauca's edition.];

Calila, ed. Alemany, J. *La antigua versión del Calila y Dimna cotejada con el original árabe de la misma*, Madrid: Sucesores de Hernando, 1915 [AUTH. Two more recent editions of *Calila* are Robert W. Linker's and my *El libro de Calila e Digna.* Madrid: CSIC, 1967; and J. M. Cacho Blecua and María Jesús Lacarra. *Calila e Dimna.* Madrid: Castalia, 1984.];

Castigos, ed. Gayangos, Pascual de. *Castigos e documentos del rey don Sancho,* BAE, Vol. 51, Madrid: Rivadeneyra, 1912, 79-228. Agapito Rey, *Castigos e documentos para bien vivir ordenados por el rey don Sancho IV,* Bloomington: Indiana University Press, 1952;

Zifar, ed. Wagner, C. P. *El libro del cauallero Zifar* (Ann Arbor: University of Michigan, 1929). [AUTH. Two newer editions are Marilyn Olsen, *Libro del Cauallero Cifar.* Madison: Hispanic Seminary of Medieval Studies, 1984 and J. González Muela, *Libro del Caballero Zifar.* Madrid: Castalia, 1982.];

Corbacho, ed. Simpson, Lesley Byrd. *Alfonso Martínez de Toledo. El arcipreste de Talavera o sea El Corbacho* Berkeley: University of California Press, 1939 [AUTH. Newer editions include those of J. González Muela and Mario Penna, *Alfonso Martínez de Toledo. Arcipreste de Talavera.* Madrid: Clasicos Castalia, 1970, and Michael Gerli's, published by Cátedra (Madrid) in 1979.];

Disciplina, ed. Alfons Hilka and Werner Söderhjelm. *Die* Disciplina Clericalis *des Petrus Alfonsi* (Heidelberg: Carl Winter, 1911);

Engaños, ed. Comparetti, Domenico. *Researches Respecting the Book of Sindibad,* London: Elliot Stock, 1882 [AUTH. Newer editions include Ángel González Palencia, *Versiones castellanas del "Sendebar"* Madrid-Granada: CSIC, 1946; and my own *El libro de los engaños,* Chapel Hill: University of North Carolina Press, 1959.];

Estados, ed. Gayangos, Pascual de. *El libro de los estados,* BAE Vol. 51, Madrid: Rivadeneyra, 1912, 278-363;

Enxemplos (G), for *Libro de los enxemplos,* ed. Gayangos, Pascual de. *El libro de los enxempla,* BAE, Vol. 51, Madrid: Rivadeneyra, 1912 pp. 443-542;

Enxemplos (M), for *Libro de los enxienplos por a.b.c.* ed. Morel-Fatio, F. "*El libro de los enxienplos por a.b.c.* de Clemente Sanchez de Valderas," *Romania,* 7 (1878), 481-526 [AUTH. See also my newer edition, *Libro de los exenplos por a.b.c., edición crítica,* Madrid: CSIC, 1961];

Macpherson, Ian, and R. B. Tate, eds., *Libro de los estados,* Oxford: Clarendon Press 1974;

Gatos ed. Gayangos, Pascual de. *El libro de los gatos,* B.A.E. Vol 51, Madrid: Rivadeneyra, 1912, 543-60 [AUTH. See also my *Libro de los gatos, edición crítica,* Madrid, 1958];

Lucanor, ed. Knust, Hermann and Adolf Birch-Hirschfeld. *Juan Manuel El libro de los enxiemplos del Conde Lucanor et de Patronio* (Leipzig: Dr. Seele and Co., 1900) [AUTH. See also the newer edition by José Manuel Blecua, Don Juan Manuel. *El Conde Lucanor.* Madrid: Castalia, 1971.];

Milagros, ed. Janer, Florencio. *Milagros de Nuestra Sennora,* BAE Vol. 57, Madrid: Hernando, 1925, 103-31 [AUTH. See also Brian Dutton's *Milagros de Nuestra Señora,* London: Tamesis, 1971.].

1 Stith Thompson, *Motif-Index of Folk Literature,* New Enlarged and Revised Edition. Bloomington: Indiana University Press, 4 Vols., 1955-58.

2 *Enxemplos* (G), no. 377; *Enxemplos* (M), no. 3.

3 *Ibid.,* no. 109.

4 *Ibid.,* no. 50

5 *Castigos,* p. 145.

6 *Calila,* p. 453.

7 *Ibid.,* p. 289.

8 *Enxemplos* (G), no. 277.

9 *Consolaciones,* p. 369.

10 *Castigos,* p. 108; *Enxemplos* (M), no. 33; *Enxemplos* (G), no. 206.

11 *Castigos,* pp. 104, 122, 226.

12 *Enxemplos* (G), no. 45.

13 *Ibid.,* no. 86.

14 *Ibid.,* no. 21; *Buen amor,* I, 196.

15 *Barlaam,* p. 390.

16 *Enxemplos* (G), no. 125.

17 *Ibid.,* no. 378.

18 The clergyman was Clemente Sánchez, the Archdeacon of Valderas, who included several of these motifs in his *El libro de los enxemplos,* suggesting them as topics for sermons.

19 *Enxemplos* (G), no. 337.

20 *Ibid.,* no. 170.

21 *Ibid.,* no. 322.

22 *Ibid.,* no. 333; *Consolaciones,* p. 567; *Milagros,* no. 13.

23 *Estados,* p. 313.

24 *Loc. cit.*

25 *Enxemplos* (G), nos. 222, 223; *Enxemplos* (M), no. 33

26 *Zifar,* p. 271.

27 *Enxemplos* (G), no. 201; *Enxemplos* (m), no. 48; *Milagros,* no. 6.

28 *Enxemplos* (G), no. 198.

29 *Ibid.,* nos. 204, 335.

30 *Ibid.,* no. 206.

31 *Ibid.,* no. 213.

32 *Lucanor,* no. 44.

33 *Castigos,* p. 130.

34 *Enxemplos* (M), no. 14.

35 *Enxemplos* (G), nos. 18, 216.

36 *Ibid.,* no. 172.

37 *Castigos,* p. 130.

38 *Enxemplos* (G), nos. 19, 20.

39 *Ibid,* no. 194.

40 *Milagros,* no. 1.

41 *Zifar,* p. 226.

42 *Enxemplos* (G), nos. 75, 76.
43 *Ibid.*, no. 183.
44 *Castigos*, p. 99.
45 *Enxemplos* (G), no. 132.

Gatos Not Quentos*

VER SINCE *El libro de los gatos* became widely known in 1851,[1] it has been the subject of discussion and controversy. One question has been of particular interest to scholars: why was it named *The Book of the Cats?* The work, a collection of sixty-seven tales[2] accompanied by moralizations often much longer than the stories themselves, was written probably in the second quarter of the thirteenth century. It is almost an exact translation from the *Parabolae* or *Narrationes* of an English churchman named Odo of Cheriton.[3] Odo traveled in Spain and in France south of the Loire, preaching and gathering material for his fables some time between 1221 and 1225. The influence of his sermons and religious tracts was felt in Spain,[4] and versions of his fables appeared in French translation. There were Latin texts of the fables in France, Germany, Belgium, Italy, and Switzerland.[5] Odo is thus one of the earliest important literary contacts between England and the Continent.

Ticknor, the great American Hispanist, comments unfavorably on *El libro de los gatos* in the second English edition and in subsequent editions of his *History of Spanish Literature*.[6] He suggests no reason for the book's peculiar title. Gayangos, who translated Ticknor's first edition into Spanish, added a treatment of *El libro de los gatos* in which he stated that the title was entirely arbitrary and unusually meaningless for thirteenth- or fourteenth-century Spain.[7]

The first scholar to offer a possible explanation was Amador de los Ríos,[8] who considered the collection quite valuable and of considerable artistic merit. The tales, rich in satire against unscrupulous nobles and churchmen, suggested to this critic the *arañazos* 'scratches' of cats, verbal scratches, which might have given the book its name.

Hermann Knust[9] suggested that fables toward the beginning of

31

the work had been lost[10] and that these supposedly lost fables might have provided some cogent reason for including the word *gatos* in the title. Knust cited *El libro del oso* as proof that animal names might have been fashionable for the titles of books. But books were not often named after animals in Spain, and G. T. Northup has identified *El libro de oso* as an erroneous title for *El libro de Ose*.[11]

G. Baist ventured the suggestion that *El libro de los gatos* may have been embellished with cat illuminations;[12] but his idea, like that of Knust, seems unlikely, since other animals appear in the tales more frequently than cats.[13]

Menéndez y Pelayo wrote that "... acaso el autor entendía figuradamente por gatos a los que son blanco predilecto de su sátira."[14] Northup objected to this idea,[15] observing that since cats play a smaller role as sinners, lay and ecclesiastical, than certain other animals, they would hardly have lent their name to the whole group of tales.

Of all the theories about the use of the word *gatos*, Northup's is the most important because of its general acceptance by historians of Spanish literature.[16] "To my mind," wrote Northup, "the most natural explanation is that the word *gatos* is the result of a paleographic blunder ... *Quentos* and *gatos* could easily be confused. Throughout the text *g* and *q* are frequently interchanged."[17]

I am unable to understand how Professor Northup saw anything confusing in the scribe's *g* in the word *gatos*. In the unique manuscript (Biblioteca Nacional de Madrid, manuscript 1182) the title reads as follows: "Aqui comiença el libro de los gatos e cuenta luego un enxiemplo de lo acaesçio entre el galapago e el aguilla." the *g* in *gatos*, as will be seen on the accompanying facsimile page, is quite clear and is the same *g* employed by the scribe in many other words on the same page, and indeed in the same passage, for example, *galapago, rrogo, agora*, and *aguilla*. I have examined the entire manuscript with extreme care, in the preparation of a new edition of the text, and I have found no interchange of *g* and *q*. It is true that the scribe used in the abbreviation for *que*, whether this *que* was the shortened form of the word *que* or formed a part of such a word as *querer*, a *q* that resembled somewhat his *g*; but this abbreviation was common in much of Western Europe and could hardly have been confused with the letter *g*. All the other *q*'s in the manuscript are quite regular and bear only slight resemblance to *g*, for every *g* set down by this scribe

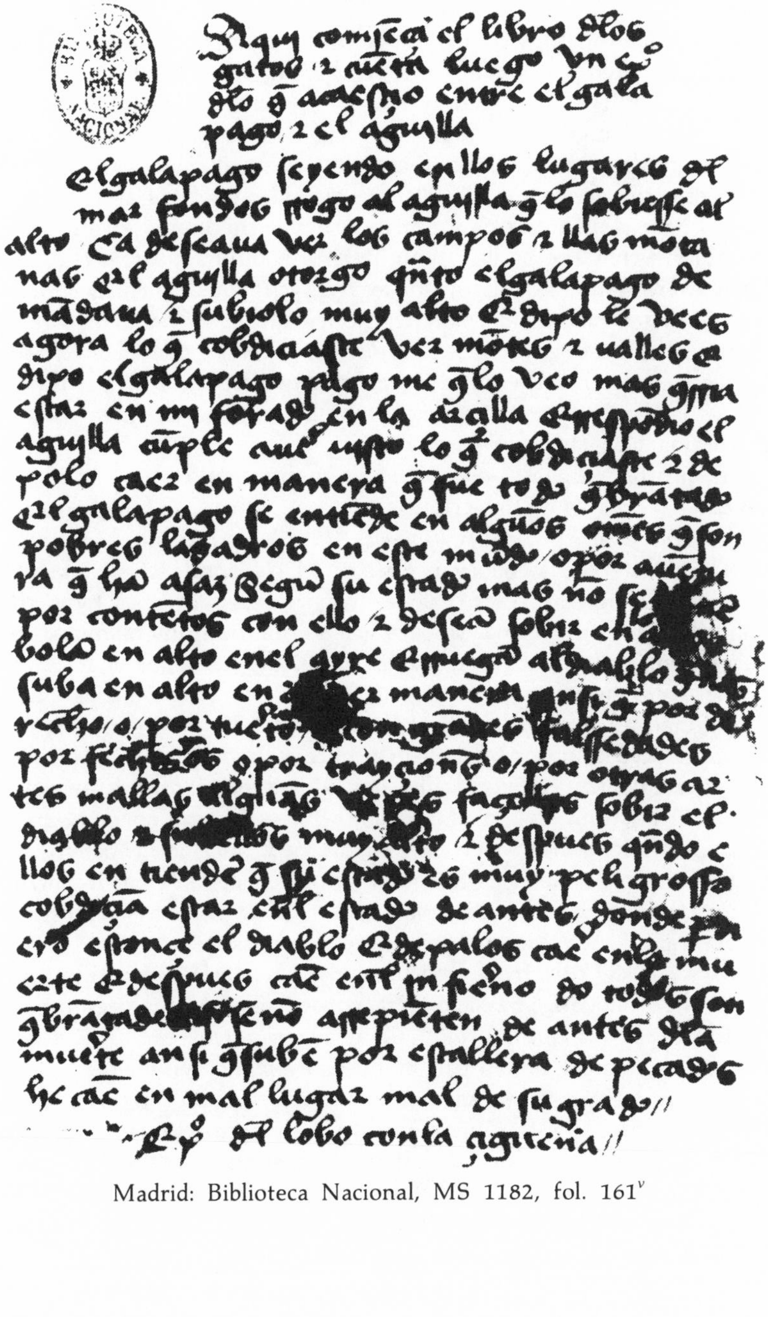

Madrid: Biblioteca Nacional, MS 1182, fol. 161v

has a horizontal topstroke that connects it to the following letter. Modern printed *g* still bears this stroke. No single example of *q*, not even the *q* in the abbreviation, has this stroke. Certainly, then, there is no interchange of *g* and *q* in *El libro de los gatos*.

Careful scrutiny of the facsimile page will show, immediately following the scribe's *g,* the letters *-atos*. These letters are unmistakable. There is no sign of a *u* nor an *e*; nor is there an *n* or a nasal bar to indicate that the scribe thought an *n* should appear in the word. Thus there can be no reason to say that *gatos* could be easily confused with *quentos*, which incidentally the scribe spelled with a *c* consistently. Note in the first sentence "... *el libro de los gatos e cuenta*...." It seems perfectly clear that the word is *gatos* and not *quentos*, and that the title is *The Book of the Cats*, unless *gatos* is the Spanish development of some word not hitherto considered.

Two other suggestions should be mentioned. L. G. Zelson[18] believed that *gatos* is a transcription of some word unintelligible to the scribe and cites the Hebrew *agadot* "fable" in rabbinical writing.

The most recent theory is that of María Rosa Lida de Malkiel.[19] She holds that *gatos* 'cats,' have always been known as hypocrites, that the cats in *El libro de los gatos* are personifications of hypocritical clergymen, and that hence it is a book of cats, that is to say, of hypocrites. She notes that twenty-six of the tales satirize wicked churchmen and points out that in the Middle Ages one of the most constant accusations made against heretics was that they practiced religious austerity hypocritically. Her idea is not fantastic, except for the fact that only seven of the sixty-two tales are concerned with cats, and that of the seven cats mentioned, only one is a hypocrite; moreover, only nine tales from the entire collection treat hypocrites, and of these nine, five might be construed to treat as well of some other frailty such as ambition, greed, or pride.[20]

Mrs. Malkiel cites from Don Juan Manuel's *Conde Lucanor* (Enxiemplo XLII) the following passage: "Et conséiovos yo que siempre vos guardades de los que vierdes que se fazen gatos religiosos, que los mas dellos siempre andan con mal e con engaño." She cites also two Spanish proverbs: "Gato segoviano, colmillos agudos fíngese santo," and "Palabras de santo y uñas de gato."[21] In connection with Spanish proverbs, it should be noted that the largest and most widely known collection of these sayings[22] lists fifty-five that deal with the cat, and that of these fifty-five, only two—the same cited by Mrs. Malkiel— mention the cat as anything approaching a hypocrite.

According to the theory of Mrs. Malkiel, a thirteenth-century copyist, or perhaps the scribe of the fourteenth century who later penned the only existing manuscript of *El libro de los gatos*, seeing that hypocrites are violently satirized [in possibly nine out of sixty-seven tales], decided to use *gatos* for a title. This seems to me to be a peculiar thing for him to have done in view of the facts that so few stories treat of hypocrisy and that one cat story in the collection (Enxiemplo XL) likens the cat to "los simples e los buenos que non saben usar sinon la verdad, e de servir a Dios e facer obras para sobir al cielo."[23]

If Mrs. Malkiel's theory could be accepted, it would serve to strengthen rather than weaken the contention that the word is *gatos* in the title and that the word meant *cats*.

There is a very different conception of the cat in the Middle Ages that may shed some light on the question. Was hypocrisy the cat's outstanding quality for mediaeval man? We know that cats from remote antiquity in Egypt held a place of high esteem and were even adored as gods. They are not mentioned in the Bible, but the Talmud cites them. Hellenic and Roman civilization read of them in Aesop. The Moslem world held them in reverence: they graced the courts of Persia; Egyptian Mohammedans sent cats as favored pilgrims to Mecca, according them as much honor as their ancestors had when cats were sacred to Bubastis;[24] and the Prophet himself, according to tradition, so respected his pet cat Muezza, that rather than disturb her meditations, he cut off the sleeve of his garment upon which she was lying and promised her a place beside him in Paradise.[25]

But what did men think of cats in mediaeval Europe? Certainly, hypocrisy was not their outstanding quality. Observant mediaeval man saw the cat as a respectable creature, clean, relatively law-abiding, intelligent, shrewd, at times crafty. To Spain and her literature from the Moslem world came collections of stories in which such wise cats figured. *Calila e Dimna* contains two tales of shrewd or resourceful cats.[26]

In France in the *Roman de Renart*, the cat, Tibert, is represented as a respectable character, sometimes led into trouble by Renart or tricked by him, sometimes shrewd enough to dupe even the wily fox.[27] The cycle of tales revolving around Renart must have been known fairly well in Spain, and although the episodes of Tibert and Renart are not numbered among the most famous motifs,[28] they could have been abroad in the Iberian Peninsula.

Current in Spain is a version of a world-famous tale in which a wise cat makes his master rich. Thompson lists this as type 545B.[29] It is the tale we know as "Puss in Boots," made famous by Perrault, but known from antiquity and alive, in altered form, in the Spanish version cited by Boggs.[30]

Studying the matter of the cat from a linguistic point of view suggests some interesting possibilities. Latin had an adjective, *catus, a um* "intelligent" in the meliorative sense, "crafty" in the pejorative. This adjective, which had no etymological association with the noun *cattus,* "cat," might have entered into the subsequent development of the problem.

Several of the Romance tongues had developments of Latin *captare* "to seize." Amado Alonso lists the following: "CAPTARE, prender una cosa, ital. cattare, adquirir; esp. y port. catar, ver, observar, investigar... M. Raynouard trae el prov. catar, 'voir,' esto es con la misma forma y significado que en español."[31]

The meanings of Old Spanish *catar* as found in representative texts are as follows: to look at, to stare at, to examine, to investigate, to look for, to consider, to look after [to care for], to pay attention to, to see.[32]

What might have been the connection between *catus,* "cat," *catus, a, um* "intelligent" or "shrewd," and the verb *catar?* Etymologically, of course, there is no connection, but vulgar association between the several words seems to have been active. Isidore of Seville (A.D. 570-636), writing his famous *Etymologies* (XII, 2, 38), reveals that he believed such a connection existed in the mind of the people. He wrote: "Musio appellatus, quod muribus infestus sit. Hunc vulgus *catum* a captura vocant. Alii dicunt, quod *catat,* id est videt. Nam tanto acute cernit, ut fulgore luminis noctis tenebras superet. Unde et a Graeco venit *catus,* id est ingeniosus."[33]

This comment by Isidore upon the popular concept of the word *cat* and its connection with the verb *catare* is most revealing. It shows us that the Spaniard of the sixth and seventh centuries, speaking the Hispanic Romance of the period, related the verb *catare,* which became Old Spanish *catar,* to the manner in which a cat looked at things, probably in reference to the cat's careful, intent scrutiny of strange objects; although it might also have meant the wise, understanding, shrewdly considering stare of the cat. Whether the Spaniard of those times thought of the cat as the personification of curiosity or of shrewdness, we may never know, for the meanings might well have overlapped; but in either case we have the word of a great authority on early Romance speech that the stare of a cat lent intensity and depth of meaning to a Romance world. Isidore's explanation in no way points to the hypocrisy of felines. Certainly Old Spanish *catar* had no connotation of looking at something hypocritically.

It would be rather futile to set up a probable etymology for *gato* stemming from the verb *catar*; but the word might have developed so. Be that as it may, the popular etymology given by Isidore lends a good deal of strength to the argument that *gatos* in the title of the work in question meant *cats* or those that see as cats see.

I should suggest at least one other possibility. Supposing the word *gatos* was, as Knust and Zelson thought, the Spanish copyist's transcription of some word that held no meaning for him or that had come into Spanish from some other form than *catus* and associated words, what might that word have been? There was a *Libro de los cuentos*, and more than one *Libro de los enxienplos* was known; might not *gatos* have developed from some word whose connotation was "tale"? At least three Arabic words come to mind: the first and perhaps the most likely is the noun *khatta*, one of the meanings of which might be "writing" and hence possibly "tale." This could have given the Spanish *gata* and then *gato*; the second, *gat'ah*, literally "piece," can carry the meaning of "piece of writing," and so "story"; and the verb *ghatta* "to cover" and "to hide" might have had some influence.[34] The *enxienplos* in *El libro de los gatos* are parabolic and therefore needed the moralizations that accompanied them.

It does seem likely, then, that *gato*,—for the word is *gato* in the manuscript—may have grown out of a blend of popular folk conception of the ethical, wise and curious qualities of members of the cat tribe and of a Romance word whose background was lost to the vulgar speaker's mind in early Spain, a word that came to mean "to see as a cat sees," which perhaps meant to see wisely or to regard with curiosity.

Notes

* Reprinted from *Studies in Philology*, 50, (1953), 437-45.

[1] Pascual de Gayangos, trans. *Historiá de la literatura española* by George Ticknor, Madrid, 1851, I, 502.

[2] The edition of Gayangos contains fifty-eight tales or chapters bearing numbers supplied by the editor. Northup's edition contains fifty-nine. Actually, there are sixty-seven separate tales, because some of the chapters contain more than one story. [AUTH. See my edition, *Libro de los gatos. edicion crítica.* Madrid: CSIC, 1958: the edition of Darbord, *Libro de los gatos*, Paris: Seminaire d'études médiévales hispaniques de l'Université de Paris-XIII, 1985, and of Annie-Noële Peïdro, *El Libro de los gatos*, mémoire de maîtrese dactylographié, sous la direction de J. Roudil, Paris-XIII, 1979.]

[3] M. H. Oesterley, who published an edition of Odo's fables, "Die Narrationes des Odo de Cirintonia (Odo de Shirton)" in *Jrb. f. rom. u. eng. Lit.*, 9 (1868), 121-54, was the first to recognize that these were the sources of *El libro de los gatos*.

[4] Albert C. Friend, "Master Odo of Cheriton," *Speculum*, 33 (1948), 654-55.

[5] Leopold Hervieux, *Les Fabulistes latins, IV: "Etudes de Cheriton et ses Dérivés,"* Paris, 1896, 85-106.

[6] George Ticknor, *History of Spanish Literature*, Boston, 1891, I, 81.

[7] Pascual de Gayangos, *BAE*, LI, 445.

[8] J. Amador de los Ríos, *Historia crítica de la literatura española*, Madrid, 1865, IV, 319.

[9] Hermann Knust, *Jhr. f. rom. u. eng. Lit.*, 4 (1865), 130.

[10] The first nine of the stories found in Odo's *Narrationes* do not occur in *El libro de los gatos*. None of these nine tales contains anything suggestive of the cat nor is there anything in Odo's prologue concerning this animal.

[11] G. T. Northup, *MLN*, 20 (1905), 30-31.

[12] G. Baist, in Gröber's *Grundiss der romanische Philologie* (2nd ed., Strassburg, 1904), II, 414, note.

[13] The wolf appears in nine tales (II, XIV, XV, XX, XXI, XXIII, XXVIII, XLVI, LVIII); the fox in eight (XIV, XV, XXIV, XXV, XXVII, XXV, XLIX, LIII); the cat figures in seven stories (IX, XI, XVI, XXXVII, XL, LV, XLIX, LIII); the cat figures in seven stories (IX, XI, XVI, XXXVII, XL, LV, LVI). These numbers come from the Gayangos edition.

[15] G. T. Northup, "*El libro de los gatos*, a Text with Introduction and Notes," *MPh*, 5 (1908), 491.

[16] The following are some who have accepted Northup's theory: P. Henríquez Ureña, *Tables cronológicas de la literatura española* (Boston, 1920), 17; A. Valbuena Prat, *Historia de la literatura española* (Barcelona, 1946), I, 184; Mérimée and Morley, *History of Spanish Literature* (New York, 1930), 73; F. Morel-Fatio and J. Carroll Marden in their reviews of Northup's edition in *Rom.*, 38 (1909), 143 and *MLN*, 24 (1909), 57.

[17] Northup, p. 492.

[18] L. G. Zelson, "The Title of *Libro de los gatos*," *RR*, XXI (1930), 237-38.

¹⁹ María Rosa Lida de Malkiel, "¿*Libro de los gatos* o de los *quentos?*," *RPh*, 4 (1951), 46-49. [AUTH. Since her article appeared a number have been published. To be noted are: George T. Artola, "El *libro de los gatos*: An Orientalist's View of its Title," *Romance Philology*, 9 (1955-56), 17-19; W. Mettmann, "Zum Title *El Libro de los gatos*," *Romanische Forschungen*, 73 (1961), 391-92; and M. Roy Harris, "*Bufo* 'owl' or 'toad' in the *Libro de los gatos?*", *Hispanic Review*, 33 (1965), 147-51.

²⁰ The hypocritical cat appears in tale IX. Four other rather unmistakable hypocrites are a hunter in IV, a fox in XXIV and XXV, and a count in XXVI; possible hypocrites are a wolf in XIX, asses in XXII, a spider in XXIX and LII, and a fox in LIII.

²¹ Malkiel, p. 48.

²² José María Sbarbi, *Diccionario de refranes...*, Madrid, 1922, 410-11.

²³ Tale XL in the edition of Gayangos and tale XXXVII in that of Northup.

²⁴ Agnes Repplier, *The Fireside Sphinx*, New York, 1901, 8.

²⁵ J. Collin Plancy, *Dictionnaire infernal...*, Brussels, 1845, 125.

²⁶ J. Alemany Bolúfer, *La antigua versión del Calila y Dimna...*, Madrid, 1915, 269 and 475.

²⁷ Ernest Martin, *Le Roman de Renart*, Paris, 1882, Branch I, lines 725-915, Branch II, lines 665-815.

²⁸ Urban T. Holmes, Jr., "The Beast Epic of Reynard the Fox," *University of North Carolina Extension Bulletin, Lectures in the Humanities*, 31 (1952), 55-56.

²⁹ Stith Thompson, *The Folktale...*, p. 58.

³⁰ Ralph S. Boggs, *FCC*, 32 (1930), 70.

³¹ Amado Alonso, "La subagrupación románica del Catalán," *RFE*, 13 (1926), 233.

³² *Tentative Dictionary of Medieval Spanish*, Chapel Hill, 1946, 104-5.

³³ Migne, *Patrologia Latina*, 58, 440.

³⁴ F. Steinglass, *English-Arabic Dictionary*, London, 1882.

Some Stylistic and Conceptual Differences in Texts A and B of *El libro de los engaños**

N THE YEAR 1291 of the Spanish era, which, of course, is the year 1253 of our own Christian era, Prince Fadrique, blood brother of Alfonso X, El Sabio, caused to be written a remarkable book, generally referred to as *El libro de los engaños e asayamientos de las mugeres*.[1] This work, as scholars well know, is the medieval Spanish version of the *Book of Sindibad* which appeared in numerous renditions and in many eastern and western languages.[2] Obviously, an Arabic version was the source of Prince Fadrique's translation, which is by no means surprising. The thirteenth century represented the apogee of such translations, and the Prince was but following the precedent set by his learned brother whose translation of *Calila e Digna* had a year earlier brought another eastern collection of tales into Castilian.[3]

But to return to the subject of the present article, i. e., to the stylistic and conceptual corrections in the *Libro de los engaños*' two texts, it should be made clear that only one actual manuscript of this work has survived the ages. This particular manuscript may not be the original penned in the thirteenth century, but is quite possible a fourteenth century copy of that original.[4]

This is an extremely interesting manuscript, whether it be the thirteenth-century original or a later copy of it. It can in actuality be regarded as two texts, as I have regarded it. It is this duality that makes it possible to present this study. The basic text, written in a firm and clear minuscule hand, can be quite easily read by the naked eye.[5] This basic text, then, I have considered as one of two distinct manuscripts. The other is produced by the insertion, marginally and interlinearly, of almost three hundred emendations into the original writing. These emendations are so pronounced as to provide a surprisingly divergent set of readings, often completely changing the meaning of the older and original version.

Amador de los Ríos lamented the inclusion of the emendations, since to him they did not contribute to the meaning, but on the contrary, deformed it. In a letter to Domenico Comparetti, who was at the time editing the *Libro*, he wrote, after commenting upon the fact that the scribe who copied the extant manuscript had himself doubtless not followed the original of the thirteenth-century text with any degree of faithfulness: "Pero, como si no bastara este para desfigurar el original del siglo XIII, el poseedor u otro que lo leyó en el XVI, ha enmendado sin discreción ni criterio palabras y frases, a fin de hacerlo más accesible a la ignorancia."[6]

How wrong Amador was! The emendations, since they were penned into the manuscript without in any way disfiguring the original physically (the emendations do not cover, erase or in any way damage the original hand), provide an interesting comparison of meanings, and one is able to see the extent to which such meanings were altered or lost across the centuries.

How erroneous, too, were those who, disregarding the basic hand, preferred to produce editions based upon the emendations, relegating the older original words and phrases to variant readings placed in profusion at the foot of the appropriate pages! [7]

These editions, in effect, produce a sixteenth-century rendition, since the emendations are in a sixteenth-century hand (according to Amador, although more probably the emender's hand is of the fifteenth or even the fourteenth) and since even the parts of the extant manuscript left unemended seem to have been acceptable to the scribe of the sixteenth century (or earlier) who emended only where he believed it necessary to emend. The one edition of the original hand, listed under note 7 which gives the emendations in variant readings produces a text far closer to the original of the thirteenth century.

So it is that the unemended text, together with the emended text, offer for study two divergent versions and enable one to view the

aforementioned stylistic and conceptual differences. The list of divergencies, substitutions and deletions is long. It is not feasible,
therefore, to include all these in a short article. The emendations
which follow are quite selective, but are calculated to illustrate the
variety of changes made by the emender.

With these facts in mind, we can proceed to a study of the
emendations. Why did the later scribe feel constrained to emend,
deleting words and phrases, substituting others, correcting orthography and otherwise altering the original? A careful study would
seem to indicate a plurality of reasons.

The set of classifications for emendation I present are arbitrary,
admittedly. Another investigator might well suggest a longer and
more diverse list. The opportunity for further investigation is by no
means, then, vitiated by what follows, but is rather enhanced, since
the examples presented represent only a few from the many in each
category.

I suggest that with four divisions, within which are four subdivi-
sions, one can classify the changes: 1) orthographical emendations
seen by the emender as corrections of archaic spellings; 2) substitution of archaic words for words the emender considered contemporary; 3) changes in phraseology made by the emender to clarify
meaning; 4) miscellaneous changes made for a variety of purposes—
incomprehension on the emender's part, reasons of taste, reasons of
ultracorrection, etc.

1. *Orthographical Emendations*

Orthographical emendations are numerous. Some, like *sano* (line
64) substituted by the emender with *saño* and *engeño* (line 179), deleted
in favor of *engeñyo*, seem to me needless, and, in the first case, even
erroneous. Most changes in orthography were made to correct what
the emender recognized as archaic spellings. The most prevalent is
the correction of apocopation of words whose final -*e* had been
omitted by the earlier scribe. The spelling *pud* (line 113) is corrected to
read *pude*; *fiz* (line 158) to *fize*; *quel* (line 175) to *que le*; *pesol* (line 225) to
pesole; *faza* (line 1472) is corrected to *fazya*; and *amas* (line 977) clearly a
second person plural, has been corrected by the emender to read
amays; and the older *seades* (line 71) becomes in the emended text *seays*.

2. *Substitution of Contemporary Words for Archaic*

The emender often changed words like the following, often to return them to a Latinized spelling, as in the case of original text's *fesigo* (line 412) which the emender corrected to *fysico*. Another is the original's *gabla* (line 347) for which the emender substituted contemporary *jaula*. The old adverb *y* 'there' (line 435) is changed to *ay*; the older *estudo* (line 73) is corrected to *estuvo*; the older *finco* (line 82) was deleted in favor of *quedo* in the sentence, *Quando oyo dezir esto, finco muy espantado*; the old adjective *sabidor* 'wise, learned' (lines 104 and 106) was changed to *sabio*, but the noun *sabio* (line 108) was not changed, leading to the likelihood that in the time· of the original scribe the adjectival form was *sabidor* and the noun form was *sabio*, while in the emender's period *sabio* served both as adjective and a noun; *tuelle* (line 131) was changed to *desiste* in the phrase, *La cosa que non le tuelle el estomago, despues come con sus manos...*; the older *saberes* (line 132 and in several other places) was corrected to *sçienças*. For *saber* he substitutes *sçienças* (lines 185 and 186 respectively: *aprendio todos los saberes que Çendubete, su maestro, avia escripto del saber de los omnes*).

He replaces *fallesçer* with *faltar* (line 205): *...e yo non le he de fallesçer fijo* (lines 378-9).

In line 160 an interesting change may also indicate the emender's failure to understand the meaning of a noun. The older text reads: *E quando esto ovo dicho, ovo miedo el rrey que se mataria con el tosigo que tenia en la mano*. Now *tosigo* is from *toxicum* ('poison'). The emender probably understood the word and replaced it with *cuchillo*, in the belief that his reader would not recognize *tosigo*.

Still another interesting substitution is that of *pisadas* for *pies* in the phrase: *...en pos dellos fasta que perdi los pies* (line 491). The emender did not like the idea of one's losing his 'feet', which must have meant 'trail' as well to the original scribe.

Interesting, too, is the substitituion of *mañana* for *cras* (line 1376), and *mensajero* for the more colloquial and antique *mandadero* (line 1221).

3. *Changes Made to Clarify Meaning*

Some phrases and sentences contain older words and expressions which could have been treated above, since their archaic quality is partially responsible for the emendations they suffered. Even so, they have been placed in the section now under consideration.

The sentence, *Non se si podre fazimiento con muger* (line 623) becomes in the emender's language, *Non se si podre holgar y yazer con muger*.

Occasionally the emender erred greatly in his interpretations of a passage, producing a non-sequitur or even an illogical concept. This is specially apparent in the prefatory remarks which attribute the *Libro's* patronage to Prince Fadrique. The old text reads: ... *que quien bien faze nunca se le muere el saber.* The emendation reads (lines 5-6): ... *que quien bien faze nunca se le muere la fama sabyendo que...* In another place the emender erred so greatly as to give the wrong subject to a verb. The preface makes it plain that Prince Fadrique caused the book to be written. It mentions his parents, as was customary in such prefaces, and names his mother Queen Beatriz. This confused the later scribe. Where the original reads: ... *pues tomo el* [Fadrique] *la entençion en fin de los saberes...* the emender substituted... *pues tomo ella en su entençion...* Obviously Queen Beatriz had no active part in the book's production.

The phrase, ... *e catole la falsedat que le fiziera el privado* (lines 84-5) is rendered in the emended text to read, ... *e dixole la falsedat,* etc.

The old expression *mas que mas* 'especially' (line 1144) is altered considerably by the emender. The original reads: ... *que la muger quando vido al niño tan fermoso e apuesto, ovo sabor del mas que mas quando se aparto con el.* ... The emendation is rendered: ... *ovo sabor del e mas quando se aparto con el.*

A very interesting emendation developed because the emender misunderstood the meaning of an unfamiliar word—*garpios.* He replaced the word with *grytos* (in line 253):[8] he considered it as a noun, and substituted by a noun. The phrase in which the word appears merits examination. it reads: *entendio ella que seria en peligro de muerte, e dio bozes e garpios, e començó de mesar sus cabellos...* To the emender, it can readily be seen, *bozes e garpios* meant 'cries' and 'complaints' (?). In actuality *garpios* was the original scribe's orthography for *garpiose,* from the verb *garpir,* an archaic form of *carpir,* attested in other works of the thirteenth century. The apocopation of the preterite ending in *e* was a common phenomenon in the thirteenth century. The emender added final *e* to all words in which such apocopation occurred, no matter what the part of speech: *dixol* becomes *dixole* (line 30); *pud* becomes *pude* (line 113); *pesol* becomes *pesole* (line 293); *fiz* becomes *fize* (line 394); and *rascos* becomes *rascose* (line 707).

The verb *aduxo* was preferred by the emender who substituted it for the original's *truxo* (*e aduxolo a la vieja...,* line 795).

Delicacy dictated the substitution of *mienbros* for *cojones* (*e echol mano de los cojones,* line 884).

Fuste in the older text is replaced by *palo (... que non ay en el mundo fuste mas frio que el sandalo...*, line 1133).

Tuelga gives way to *quyte* in the phrase: *E agora ruega a Dios que te las tuelga...*, line 982.

The older word *adobo* was deleted in favor of *aparejo (... que un ome que adobo su yantar...*, line 1162).

The emender favored *manjares* over *comeres (... quel omne non puede gostar tantos comeres,* line 1189).

4. Miscellaneous Changes

Plain erudite taste must have made the emender change *gota* to *destello (...e non dexes cosa ninguna nin destello,* line 1369).

An interesting preference, I believe, dictated also by delicacy and propriety, caused several other emendations. In the original we read (line 61) that the king, after speaking to his pious favorite wife, and after praying for a son, took her to bed *e yazio con ella el rrey, e empreñose luego.* The emender lined out *yazio,* replacing it with *holgo.* The reason I suggest is this: in many jocose or merry tales in medieval times, primarily those of oriental provenience, the verb *yazer* (to lie with) connoted adulterous or salacious intercourse and therefore, from its association with such activities in such stories it was considered indelicate and subject to deletion by the emender. The verb *folgar* or *holgar,* apparently, to the emender, meant a more legitimate and proper sexual union, hence its inclusion.

More to the point, as to delicacy is the emender's substitution of *paryo* (in line 64) for *encaesçio: E quando fueron conplidos los nueve meses, encaesçio de un fijo sano...* (and when the nine months were accomplished she dropped, that is, gave birth to, a healthy son). *Encaesçer* ('to let fall', 'drop', and by extension, 'to give birth to') might have seemed an improper expression to the emender. The birth of a prince to a queen in the emender's mind should not have been recorded in the terminology of the stable and farmyard where foals and calves and lambs were 'dropped', hence the more erudite and euphemistic *paryo.*

The learned emender sometimes deleted down-to-earth nouns as well as verbs. He replaced the word for 'musk' in the original, *musgaño* (the shrew mouse from which is derived a strong, musky odor, and by extension the musk itself), by a word more in keeping with literary concepts. The phrase reads: ... *tal es el saber con el coraçon como el musgaño e el agua.* The emender substituted the word *almyscle* (modern *almizcle* 'the musk from a Tibetan musk deer'). One surmises that as Fadrique's translators in the thirteenth century rendered the Arabic into Spanish, they in their time, had opined that the Arabic word *al misc* 'musk' would mean little to Spanish readers and had substituted a term for musk familiar to their readers, i. e. *musgaño*. The emender, frowning upon the folksy Spanish *musgaño*, changed it to *almyscle*, restoring inadvertently the original Arabic.

The prefatory passage, a species of introduction, is one of the most carelessly written of the entire book. It is no wonder that emendations were inserted in it. Nor is it strange that the emender, in his efforts to improve and make the text clear to himself and his readers, created further confusion. He simply did not understand what the original meaning was, and had to paraphrase and otherwise create a to-him-readable passage. One can read both texts in my edition and can, with difficulty, by using the emended text of Bonilla and his variants, view both texts, and therefore it will not be necessary to provide both here. Even so, one important correction should be mentioned, for it leads to interesting speculations as to the very title of the book. Line 28 in the original state clearly that the book was translated ... *de aravigo en castellano para aperçebir a los* engañados (italics mine) *e los asayamientos de las mugeres*. The word *engañados* is quite clearly discernable through the inked-in correction of the emender, who changed it to *engaños*. This means, I believe, that the title might actually have been *El libro de los engañados* ('The Book of the Deceived', rather than the 'Book of the Deceits').[9]

One last example, returning for it to the body of the *Libro* and leaving the prefatory section, appears in line 120 of my edition. We read that certain aspects of life, indeed, certain inidividuals, should be praised only so long as the praise is justified, brings into play a common word used in an unusual way. One should praise ... *el que va a lydiar, fasta que torne da la* hedat (italics mine). Here *hedat* from the context in which it appears, must mean the 'time a soldier is required to serve in the army.' It is the only occurrence I have encountered of *hedat's* being so used, but the usage makes sense. It is roughly analogous to our own current slang expression in English, i. e., 'a hitch in the army.' To the emender, however, it took on a different connotation, or perhaps it meant to him what I have suggested, but was not acceptable to him on the grounds that it was colloquial or archaic. At any rate he penned out *hedat* and wrote above it the word *guerra*.

A case in similar vein is to be found in line 155. The original mentions the dangers of dealing with physicians and reads: ... *el físico fuere loçano con su fiesta que non la emuestra a los enfermos*, the emender rephrases this passage so that it reads: ... *el físico fuere tan loçano que con su loçania y locura non curare de los enfermos*.

The multiplicity of emendations in the *Libro de los engaños* which stem from the two different scribes who treated it—the one who penned it originally and he who emended the text—lays the groundwork for a more lengthy study than can be set down in so brief an article as this. Perhaps the few samplings herein presented can at least indicate the shifting concepts of the Spanish language as it progressed across a century or more of its development toward its modern form. [More clearly stated, Keller's edition cited in note 7, presents all the variant readings, that is, the emender's readings. EDS.]

Notes

* Reprinted from *Estudios Hispánicos in Honorem Rafael Lapesa*, Vol. 3. Madrid: Gredos, 1972, 100-15.

1 The lines attributing the book to Prince Fadrique appear in the introductory passages as follows: *El ynfante don Fadrique... plogo e tovo por bien que aqueste libro [fuese trasladado] de aravigo en castellano... Este libro fue trasladado en noventa e un años.*

2 My introduction to *El libro de los engaños*, page XIV, lists the Eastern versions. Angel González Palencia lists the Eastern and the Western versions in his edition and study. See note 7 for complete bibliography listings of these and other studies and editions. Citations refer to my version.

3 Despite arguments to the contrary, we are of the belief that Alfonso el Sabio did, indeed, cause the Arabic *Kalilah wa Dimma* to be translated from the Arabic. At least one of the codices of *Calila* states this: *Aqui se acaba el libro de Calina* [sic] *e Digna, e fue sacado de aravigo en latyn, e rromançado por mandado del infante don Alfonso, fijo del noble rrey don Fernando en la era de mill e dozientos e noventa e nueve años.*

4 Menéndez y Pelayo, as well as Amador de los Ríos, considered the extant manuscript to have been penned as late as the fifteenth century and that the emendations, apparently in a quite different hand, were written in the sixteenth. Their reasons for this belief are not quite clear to me, for the handwriting seems to be no older than the fourteenth, although the emendations may indeed be as late as the sixteenth century.

5 The manuscript is written on paper 25.5 x 19.8 m. with chapter headings or divisions in red ink. The *Libro de los engaños* itself is only one of

four documents bound together and entitled *El Conde Lucanor, Ms. Antigua*. Folios 1^v-62^v is *El Conde Lucanor*; folios 63^r-79^v is the *Libro de los engaños*; folios 86^r-86^v is a letter from St. Bernard to one Ramón, señor del Castillo de Santo Ambrosio; and folios 88^v-163^r is *El lucidario*. The manuscript, formerly the property of the Count of Puñonrostro, is now in the archives of the Real Academia de la Lengua in Madrid. A facsimile of the manuscript's first page may be seen in my edition.

⁶ Domenico Comparetti, *Researches Respecting the Book of Sindibad, The Folklore Society* (London), 9 (1882), 68.

⁷ The three editions which follow the emendations and disregard the original parts are the following: Adolfo Bonilla y San Martin, *Libro de los engaños e los asayamientos de las mugeres*, Barcelona-Madrid, 1914; Domenico Comparetti, *Researches Respecting the Book of Sindibad*, The Folk-Lore Society, No. IX (London, 1882), and *Ricerche intorno al libro de Sindibad (Atti del Instituto Lombardo*, Florence, 1869, and its 2nd edition, Florence, 1896). Angel González Palencia, *Versiones Castellanas del Sendebar* (Consejo Superior de Investigaciones Científicas), Madrid-Granada, 1946. (This edition reproduces the text of Bonilla y San Martín). The edition which follows the text of the extant version exclusively, relegating the emendations to variants, is my *El Libro de los engaños*, University of North Carolina Studies in the Romance Languages and Literatures, No. 20. Chapel Hill, 1959. All line numbers cited refer to this edition.

⁸ See my article,"Old Spanish *garpios*," *Hispanic Review*, 23 (1954), 227-32.

⁹ See the facsimile page in my edition, left hand column, line 28.

The *Libro de los exenplos por a.b.c.*

HE *Libro de los exenplos por a.b.c.* IS THE largest collection of tales in the Spanish language; it is the only extant alphabet of *exempla* or moralized tales in this language; it draws from a wider body of source materials than any other such collection, indeed, than any other medieval Spanish work, with the exception of the Alfonsine histories; it preserves more themes and motifs than any other. In spite of all this less has been written about it than any comparably deserving work.

In the hundred and five years since Pascual de Gayangos and Enrique de Vedia made brief mention of the *Libro de los exenplos* in their translation of Ticknor's history of Spanish writing (*Historia de la literatura española*, Madrid, 1851, pp. 502-03) only a modicum of investigation has been accorded this important work. This is partly due, of course, to the fact that there has never been an adequate edition of the entire book. Then, too, the extreme length of this great collection of stories has prevented many from reading it. But even these factors can hardly explain satisfactorily why there has been so great a divergence of opinion as regards such basic matters as the quality of the author's prose, his use of original sources or his failure to use them, and even the actual number of *exempla* in his book.

A brief review of these differences in scholarly opinion will be of some value. When Gayangos and Vedia translated Ticknor's work, they gave only the briefest of notices about the *Libro de los exenplos*; but when Gayangos later edited the manuscript (*Biblioteca de Autores Españoles*, LI, 443-542) he mentioned it in his introduction to the text (p. 443-45) and made a few observations that have been handed down from generation to scholarly generation. Gayangos noted that the *exempla* were set off in sections without any numeration and that there were 395 of these sections or divisions. He remarked that the divisions each represented one *exemplum* and that they were arranged in alphabetical order according to the first word of the Latin maxim that preceded each section; that all the divisions under the letters *a* and *b*, and under *c* as far as the maxim that began "Confessio debet esse..." were lacking, due to some damage to the manuscript; he pointed out that after each of the Latin maxims a Spanish translation of it appeared and stated that all of these translations were written in Spanish verses, a fact mentioned in the translation of Ticknor, but not stressed there. It is to Pascual de Gayangos, most probably, that we owe the constant echoing of these two facts, namely, that the book contains 395 *exempla* and that each and every maxim in its Spanish form was couched in verse. Due to Gayangos, also, no doubt, is the belief that all the *exempla* of the *Disciplina Clericalis* appear in the *Libro de los exenplos*, although touching this matter he merely wrote that "... el autor anónimo de la presente colección insertó en ella casi todos los cuentos *que halló en la Disciplina clericalis*" (*BAE*, LI, 444) (italics mine).

Gayangos considered the style of the *Libro de los exenplos* good, although not as polished as that of Don Juan Manuel; he did not know the date of the writing, but hazarded the correct guess that the book had been written later than the works of Don Juan; Gayangos did not know the authorship of the great book he had edited; he barely touched upon its sources; he offered very little in the nature of criticism. Still, he had prepared the only edition, and even though it was not a critical edition and he had made great changes, especially as regards orthography, it was all scholars had. It served, therefore, together with his brief remarks, as a careful guide for most of the study that followed.

Spain's great, and perhaps her first truly critical historian of Spanish literature, Amador de los Ríos, next treated the *Libro de los exenplos* (*Historia crítica de la literatura española*, Madrid, 1863, IV, 305-18). He differed little with what Gayangos had written, but he added certain interesting observations and the first true criticism of the book. He believed that the author, whose name was still unknown, had drawn directly from the sources he cited, and that by reading the *Libro de los exenplos* one could form a good idea of the remarkable scope of a well-read man of the period. He revealed for the first time the great wealth of themes contained in the many *exempla* and stated that 25 of the tales from the *Disciplina Clericalis* appeared among them. He did not say that all from the *Disciplina Clericalis* were there, for he knew that this Latin work contained over 30 tales; but he opined that probably all had been included and that the lost first pages of the *Libro de los exenplos* had contained those not found in the manuscript edited by Gayangos.

It was almost certainly this statement on the part of Amador de los Ríos that led Menéndez y Pelayo to state (*Orígenes de la novela,* Madrid, 1950, p. 170) that the entire repertoire of the *Disciplina Clericalis* appeared in the *Libro de los exenplos,* an error perpetuated by subsequent writers.

Amador de los Ríos liked the style of the *Libro de los exenplos* and commented favorably upon the poetic translations of the Latin maxims, strengthening even more the erroneous idea that all of these translations were written in rhyme. The statements of this great critic about the *Libro de los exenplos* were accepted in Spain and to this day prevail.

Menéndez y Pelayo (*Orígenes,* I, 168-70) agreed with what his famous predecessor had written, adding little that was original except the name of the author, which had been discovered by Morel-Fatio in a second manuscript that contained the pages missing from the manuscript edited by Gayangos. As Morel-Fatio edited only the divisions missing from the first manuscript, and as these divisions were 71 in number, Menéndez y Pelayo wrote that the *Libro de los exenplos* contained, counting the 395 sections in the first manuscript, 467 *exempla.* Insofar as the writer of this article knows, all subsequent Spanish scholarship accepts this figure. Certainly Eloy Díaz-Jiménez, who published the most complete body of facts about the life of the author of the *Libro de los exenplos* ("Clemente Sánchez de Vercial," *Revista de Filología Española,* VII, [1920], 358-68) accepted it, as do available histories of Spanish literature.

It is with scholars who are not Spanish that the divergences begin. In 1878, eighteen years after the publication of Gayangos' edition, Morel-Fatio published his text of the missing part of the *Libro de los exenplos* (*Romania,* 7 [1878], 481-526). He regarded the manuscript he used (Bibliothèque Nationale, Espagnol 432) as relatively complete, for it contained, as we have seen, the missing divisions under *a, b,* and *c,* as well as *exemplum* number 216, also absent from the older manuscript; but he realized that the recently discovered manuscript, which for convenience we shall refer to hereafter as the Paris manuscript, lacked 18 of the *exempla* found in the older manuscript, hereafter to be called the Madrid manuscript (Biblioteca Nacional 1186). These missing *exempla* were numbered by Morel-Fatio in the Paris manuscript as follows: 234, 260, 283, 286, 289, 295, 296, 299, 300, 303, 340, 349, 368, 370, 371, 385, 386, and 387. Apparently, scholars overlooked his mention of this omission, and therefore the Paris text came to be called the complete text, and so it is known today. In passing, it might be well to state that there is no reason, save perhaps the scribe's haste to be done with his onerous task of copying, to explain why he failed to include the missing *exempla*. A careful reading of these omitted *exempla* as they appear in the Madrid text reveals no conformity as to the types of tales, and therefore one cannot show that he disapproved of any special kind of story and therefore omitted all such tales. The 18 missing stories are of many types—monkish tales, oriental apologues, medieval historical accounts, etc.

Morel-Fatio stated in the introduction to his edition (p. 483) that the author, Clemente Sánchez de Vercial, Archdeacon of Valderas in León, did not use the sources he cited at various points in the *Libro de los exenplos*, but translated into Spanish or paraphrased the original sources, using secondary materials. He believed that Sánchez had at his disposal some one of the many *alphabeta* of tales, that this *alphabetum* was itself a paraphrase, and in this way the *Libro de los exenplos* was put together; but Morel-Fatio was unable to point to any specific collection of tales that could have served Sánchez in this way.

As we have seen, Morel-Fatio found in the Paris manuscript 71 divisions lacking in the Madrid text. Adding the 71 to the number edited by Gayangos, 395, he actually first arrived at the number of 467. From him Menéndez y Pelayo took the figure and disseminated it among scholars in Spain. Morel-Fatio also remarked that all the translations of the Latin maxims were in rhyme.

His greatest contributions to this area of research were his editions of the 71 divisions not found in the Madrid text and his discovery of the author of the *Libro de los exenplos*. This last appeared in a brief dedicatory passage that appears immediately before the first of the alphabetical divisions and reads as follows: "*Muy amado fijo, Johan Alfonso de la Barbolla, canonigo de Ciguença, yo* CLIMENTE SANCHES, *arcediano de Valderas en la iglesia de Leon, te inbio ssalud en aquel que por su precioso sangre nos rredemio. Por quanto en el libro que yo compuse para tu enformacion, que puse nombre* Compendium censure, *en fin del te escrevi que proponia de copilar un libro de exenplos* por a.b.c. *e despues rreduzirle en romance...*" Once the name Clemente Sánchez had been discovered, Morel-Fatio was able to identify him and to date the composition of the *Libro de los exenplos* between 1400 and 1421.

J. D. M. Ford (*Old Spanish Readings*, New York, 1939, pp. 165-66) summarized the findings of Menéndez y Pelayo and Morel-Fatio and lamented the lack of a critical edition and of a comparative study of the *Libro de los exenplos*. He also stated that professor M. A. Buchanan of the University of Toronto was preparing such an edition. In the most recent listing of Buchanan's publications (Jack H. Parker, "Publications of Milton Alexander Buchanan," *Hispanic Review*, 20 [1952], 325-32) there is no reference to an edition of the *Libro de los exenplos*, and both Professor Parker and Mrs. Buchanan have stated that a careful search never turned up any indication that professor Buchanan had ever progressed beyond the planning stage of such an edition.

A. H. Krappe, who studied the backgrounds of Clemente Sánchez' work ("Les sources du *Libro de los exemplos*," *Bulletin Hispanique*, 39 [1937], 5-34), like Morel-Fatio, saw no original sources behind the *exempla*, and could suggest no secondary work that might have furnished Sánchez with his materials. He did, however, consider the prose in the book as superior to contemporary French, Italian, and Latin, listed the numbers of those *exempla* taken from the *Disciplina Clericalis* (number 9, 12, 24, 30, and 31), and offered no opposition to the statements of previous writers that the collection of tales contained 467 *exempla*.

What has been reported to this point is, in essence, all that has been said about the *Libro de los exenplos*, aside from J. T. Welter's treatment (*L'Exemplum dans la littérature religieuse et didactique du Moyen Âge*, Paris, 1927) and the study of T. F. Crane (*The Exempla of Jacques de Vitry*, London, 1890, pp. ciii-cv). Welter's book lists also the cited sources of Sánchez and shows how the *exempla* in the *Libro de los exenplos* can be fitted into types (p. 105), and Crane studies it in the general development of the *exemplum* in European literature. My classification of the *exempla* according to the *Motif-Index* of Stith Thompson (*Motif-Index of Mediaeval Spanish Exempla*, Knoxville, 1949) does no more than list the motifs in *El libro de los exenplos* together with those in a number of other medieval collections of tales. [AUTH. Stith Thompson's *Motif-Index of Folk Literature. New, Enlarged, and Revised Edition*, 4 vols., Bloomington, 1955-58, includes all the motifs listed by me.]

A good deal, therefore, still needs to be done: there is no study of the style of Clemente Sánchez' book of *exempla*; no one has published a syntactical study, although Charles Javens is at present making one as his doctoral dissertation at the University of North Carolina [AUTH. His dissertation was finished in 1965 and is available for study: *A Study of Old Spanish Syntax: The Fifteenth Century*]; a vocabulary study in the form of a recently completed doctoral dissertation has been prepared by Louis Zahn for the same institution, but it has found no publisher [AUTH. In fact, it has now been published in its entirety as the *Vocabulario etimológico documentado* to my own edition]; no one has published an account of the distribution of the *exempla* under the classification or types suggested by Welter; still lacking is a comparative study; and worst of all, there is no published critical edition [AUTH. Since this statement was made I published *El libro de los ejemplos por a. b. c.*, Madrid: CSIC, 1961. *This is what is alluded to in the next sentence as being in manuscript form.*].

Having recently completed an edition of the *Libro de los exenplos* (405 double-spaced typed pages), I believe that Clemente Sánchez' book merits a great deal of careful study. I see in Sánchez' prose a stage in the development of Spanish writing, believe that the vocabulary contains a large number of words not yet recorded as Spanish, and feel that the themes set down by Sánchez indicate a wider knowledge of classical antiquity than has been suspected in fifteenth-century letters. While editing the *Libro de los exenplos*, I have made certain observations somewhat at variance with previous remarks and have arrived at a few conclusions not yet made known. What follows, therefore may perhaps best serve as a kind of introduction to these findings, for I hope in subsequent articles to develop some of them more lengthily and carefully.

1. One of the first things I noticed was the mistaken number of the *exempla*. Perhaps a new number is no great contribution to knowledge; and yet, if we are to know the *Libro de los exenplos*, the number of its tales should at least be given correctly. Careful reading of the book reveals that it has a good many more than 467 tales. It is true that there are 467 alphabetical divisions—395 in the Madrid text and 71 in the Paris. But not all the alphabetical divisions are limited to a single *exemplum*. The first division in the manuscript edited by Morel-Fatio (*Abbas primo debet se quam alios iudicare*) contains not one, but three separate *exempla*, in illustration of the Latin maxim. Each *exemplum* has a different set of characters and locale, and each is introduced by certain introductory

phrases common to the *Libro de los exenplos*. After the first tale appears the break that introduces the second. It reads *"Otrosi el abbat que llamauan Joseph pregunto..."*; the third *exemplum* is introduced by *"Otro flayre dixo a aqueste abbat Pastor...."* In the very first alphabetical division, then, three appear. Alphabetical division number 63 in Morel-Fatio's text contains no less than five separate *exempla*, all of which are quite concise, but are nonetheless individual tales. A list of all the alphabetical divisions so divided into separate *exempla* would be too long to present here, but it may be stated that of the 72 alphabetical divisions given by Morel-Fatio, 42 contain more than one tale; of the 395 divisions indicated by Gayangos, 55 represent more than one *exemplum*. In other words, in Morel-Fatio's edition 91 separate *exempla* exist, and not 72, a difference of 19; in Gayangos' text there are 451 and not 395, a difference of 56. The combined manuscripts embody not 467, but 542, that is 75 more *exempla* than anyone has hitherto counted.

Perhaps those who arrived at the erroneous computation should not be blamed too much. They followed a common enough practice in dealing with medieval texts. Many of us have done the same, have counted, that is, the divisions or titles in a manuscript without examining what each contained. Haven't most of us been telling our students that Don Juan Manuel's *Conde Lucanor* contains 50 tales? I have been saying so for years, in error, for number 27 of the *Conde Lucanor* has two separate and distinct stories, giving the book actually 51. [AUTH. See my *"El Conde Lucanor* Contains Fifty-Three Stories and no Fewer," the twelfth essay in this collection, originally published in *Romance Notes*, 24 (1983), 59-64. And quite recently, I have been reminded that in Part V of *El Conde Lucanor* appears a fifty-fourth enxiemplo. I have written an article that will apear in the *Festschrift* honoring Joseph H. Silverman to be published in this same series, called *"'Enxiemplo de un cavallero que fue ocasionado et mato a su señor et a su padre': Enxiemplo 54 in El Conde Lucanor."*] Conversely, the *Libro de los engaños*, which scholars have told us contains 24 stories, has only 23, for one of its 24 divisions is not a separate story at all, but is only a part of the frame-story of the book. Lastly, the *Libro de los gatos*, the number of whose tales seems not to have been mentioned except by Crane (p. cvii), who reported that it had 58 *exempla*, has instead 65 separate stories.

It seemed important to give credit where it was due and to report that the *Libro de los exenplos* is a much richer repository of tales than some had suspected, broadening the scope of medieval thematology considerably.

2. Of less importance, but still worthy of some comment, is the matter of the poetry in the *Libro de los exenplos*. Generally, when speaking of the poetry in this book, scholars mean the Spanish verse (?) translations of the Latin maxims. They do not mean the one long passage written in *cuaderna via* which is found in *exemplum* number 225 of the Madrid text as edited by Gayangos. This passage is simply a close copy of a similar sequence in the *Libro de Alexandre*. We can, therefore, lay aside all mention of this passage and concentrate upon the translations of the Latin maxims. Beginning with Ticknor and reading all the scholarly comment about the *Libro de los exenplos*, one finds references to the verses that translate the maxims into Spanish. Morel-Fatio, Menéndez y Pelayo, Amador de los Ríos, Díaz-Jiménez, Krappe, all speak of rhyme or imply that the lines are in verse. Indeed, both Gayangos and Morel-Fatio even presented the translations of the maxims in verse form in their editions, lending weight to the statement that they are all verses; but actually in the manuscripts it is rare to find these Spanish translations so written. It would appear that the scribes of both the manuscripts, in an effort to save paper, wrote as close to the edge of the righthand margin as possible, carrying over a word or so when necessary to the following line. Seldom, therefore, can one find two lines that resemble couplets. For example, in the Paris manuscript one reads *"El abbat conviene a los malos bien fazer"* (fol. lv, col. 1) written in one line. However, if an editor breaks a running line at the point in it where a word appears that will rhyme with the last word in the line, then he can show rhyme and set the line up as though it were a couplet. For example, *exemplum* number 2 in the Morel-Fatio's text was edited by him as follows: *"El abbat primero sus pecados deue ver, / Que los de los otros rreprehender."*

Number 217 in the Madrid manuscript offers these lines according to the edition of Gayangos: *"Al santo que miraglo face, / Vana gloria non le place."* But by no stretch of the imagination or of editorial ingenuity can the following be made to rhyme: *"El abbat primero deue a ssi mesmo, / Que a los otros juzgar"* (Morel-Fatio, no. 1).

A good many of the maxims in translations can be made to appear as couplets in assonance instead of full rhyme: *"Quien al ciego animas encomienda, / Es locura magnifiesta"* (Morel-Fatio, no. 64), *"Qui da todo lo suyo ante su muerte, / Merece que le den con mazo en la fruente"* (Gayangos, no. 50) is another example of rhyme.

A list of those that have assonance, rhyme, and no rhyme at all would be too long to give here. Let it suffice to say that most of the maxims in translation have full rhyme or near full rhyme, that over 40 are in assonance, and that a good dozen are not poetry of any sort. Probably Clemente Sánchez never intended that all be in rhyme.

3. Certainly it would not be feasible to present here a complete comparative study of the *Libro de los exenplos*. But since those who have written about Sánchez' use of sources or of his failure to use originals have differed so widely, it seemed worthwhile to examine a few and to let a little light in upon the subject after the passage of so many years. The reader will recall that Amador de los Ríos and Menéndez y Pelayo believed that Sánchez used the cited sources and that Morel-Fatio and Krappe were of the opinion that he did not. In an effort to verify or refute the matter of actual use of the sources by Clemente Sánchez I have examined certain of the passages in question, comparing carefully all the citations of Valerius Maximus (Sánchez cited this Latin author more than 25 times) with Sánchez' Spanish version. All except three appear to be translations of the Latin, and even the three that may not be are fairly close. Sánchez employed dialogue in the exact places where the original Latin used it, he gave the events in the stories cited in the exact sequence of their appearance in the Latin, and he named the books and chapters in Valerius Maximus which he followed. The same is true for the *Disciplina Clericalis* for the several citations from Gregory the Great in his *Dialogues*. The very first *exemplum* in the *Disciplina Clericalis* appears in the *Libro de los exenplos*, no. 17 of the Morel-Fatio text [AUTH. as well as my own]. The Spanish closely follows the Latin, using dialogue when the Latin used it, employing parenthetical expressions where they were employed in the Latin. Those interested in making their own comparisons will find a convenient reference in A. González Palencia's edition of the *Disciplina Clericalis* (Pedro Alfonso, *Disciplina Clericalis*, Madrid-Granada, 1948, pp. 6 and 97 respectively, for the Latin and Spanish versions).

Conclusive proof that Sánchez used all his cited sources can only come after all have been carefully compared. The one offered below can do no more than illustrate the closeness of the Latin and the Spanish:

Valerius Maximus	Clemente Sánchez
Demosthenis quoque astuti mirifice cuidam ancillae succursum est, quae pecuniam depositi nomine a duobus hospitibus acceperat, ea conditione ut illam simul utrisque redderet. Quorum alter, interjecto tempore, tanquam mortuo socio squalore obsitis, deceptae omnes nummos abstulit. Supervenit deinde alter et depositum petere coepit. Haerebat misera in maxima pariter et pecuniae et defensionis penuria, jamque de laqueo et suspendio cogitabat. Sed opportune Demosthenes ei patronus affulsit: que ut in advocationem venit, "Mulier," inquit, "parata est depositi se fidere solvere: sed nisi socium adduxeris, id facere non potest. Quoniam, ut ipse vociferaris, haec dicta est lex, ne pecunia alteri sie altero numeretur.	Demostenes, filósofo, fué homme de maravillosa sabidoría e accorrió á una mujer que era en gran pesar e necesidad, en esta manera. Dos homes que posaban en su casa diéronle en guarda una cuantidad de dinero con esta condicion: que lo diese á amos y dos en uno, et non al uno sin el otro. Dende á poco tiempo el uno dellos vino e dijo que su compañero era muerto, e con engaño rescibió los dineros de la mujer, e dende a poco vino el otro e demandaba lo que dejara en guarda e depósito. E la cuitada mujer lloraba, que non tenía el dinero nin quien la defendiese, e ya non pensaba sinon de la muerte. E Demostenes fué a juicio por su abogado, e dijo: "Esta mujer presta stá de pagar lo que recebió en depósito, mas non lo puede facer por muchas voces que dés, salvo si trajeres tu compañero; ca la condicion fué puesta que non se diese el dinero al uno sin el otro." (Gayangos, no. 6)

4. The function which the *Libro de los exenplos* was intended to serve has likewise been the subject of divided opinion. Gayangos and Amador de los Ríos did not consider the *exempla* of Sánchez as having been collected for preachers, for they did not know the author. It was Morel-Fatio who first wrote that they were intended for sermons, like so many of the *alphabeta* (introduction, p. 483). Then Menéndez y Pelayo agreed with his statement (p. 169), and to this day most scholars continue to hold this opinion. But Crane (p. cv), who knew the authorship, realized that Sanchez' book might be a great deal more than another alphabetized collection of monkish tales. In them he saw something approaching recreational narratives.

What was Sánchez' own comment as to function? He had only this to say, that he put together a book of *exempla* by a.b.c. and rendered it into Romance for the pleasure (he used the word *solaz*) of his friend Johan Alfonso de Barbolla, and for those who did not understand the

Latin language. From this statement and from the fact that scholars knew that most of the many Latin *alphabeta* served preachers as sources for sermon-tales, comes the belief that Sánchez compiled his *exempla* for this purpose. The author of the *Libro de los exenplos* did not say so, as we have seen. It is quite possible, of course, that his *exempla* may have been used for the background of sermons, since it was arranged alphabetically and since it was written in Spanish, but it is likely, too, that it had another function. Perhaps Sánchez intended it to be a volume of entertaining, as well as of edifying stories, as was true in the case of the *Gesta Romanorum*.

If Sánchez aimed his tales at preachers, then he acted in defiance of at least one of the councils of the Church (that of Salzburg, 1386) and in the face of a wave of criticism of sermon-tales. Many of his *exempla* fall into the class of those considered harmful at Salzburg, and later at the councils of Sens (1528), Milan (1565), and Bordeaux (1624), especially when such stories were told from the pulpit. But if Sánchez offered merely a collection of pleasant or interesting stories aimed at the general reader for his amusement and edification, then he was not liable to charges leveled against unseemly sermon-stories. From what we know of the life of Clemente Sánchez, Archdeacon of Valderas (see Díaz-Jiménez, pp. 359-66), it seems unlikely that he would have gone against the current of ecclesiastical law. He was a man deeply interested in correcting clerical abuses and in enlightening ignorant priests. Witness his *Sacramental*, a tract that carefully informed the clergy about the Holy Scriptures and attempted to instruct them in the proper regard for the sacraments. Read the facts gathered by Díaz-Jiménez, many of which appear in *España Sagrada*, and see how faithful and pious a servant of God this Clemente Sánchez was. It is difficult to believe that such a man would have compiled a collection of tales that his Church could have considered harmful to the pulpit of the times.

The more I contemplate the *Libro de los exenplos* and ponder its function, the more the belief grows in me that Clemente Sánchez de Vercial intended his collection of *exempla* to be a book of interesting tales, that he arranged them alphabetically because this had become almost the pattern for books made up of stories, and that he appended moralizations to most of his tales because it was the fashion to do so, even though the moralization was at times quite pointless. Certainly many of Sánchez' moralizations have no real connection with the *exempla* they accompany. But books were supposed to edify the reader, and Sánchez, like Don Juan Manuel, followed the current of offering a moral with his stories. But had Don Juan Manuel and Clemente Sánchez intended nothing more than didacticism, they would have hardly written such lengthy tales, would have hardly concentrated upon polish and literary excellence and style. They hoped, no doubt,— and Don Juan even said so—, that their *exempla* would lead men to a better and moral life. Why not? The desire to teach was one of the forces that characterized their times. But surely it was not the only force behind their writing. The very length of some of their stories would seem to prove the point. One of Sánchez' *exempla* (number 332 of the Paris text) runs to 224 lines in the manuscript (folios 128v, col. 2 through 130v, col. 1). This compares in length and development of plot with the longer tales of Don Juan Manuel and with those in the *Gesta Romanorum*. Furthermore, the *Libro de los exenplos* uses old themes in a refurbished form, just as did Don Juan Manuel, and introduced themes not employed in the other collections of tales. Sánchez' book may turn out to be one of the important connections between the literatures of the ancients and the writings of the late Spanish Middle Ages.

[AUTH. In collaboration with Dennis P. Seniff I am preparing a second edition with updated bibliography, sources and parallels, and Louis Zahn, who provided the etymological lexicon is emending it, so as to see it published again in the same volume. We believe that this edition will also be published by the Consejo Superior de Investigaciones Científicas.]

Note

* Reprinted from *Hispania*, 50 (1957), 179-86.

King Alfonso's Virgin of Villa-Sirga: Rival of St. James of Compostela*

URING THE SECOND HALF of the thirteenth century King Alfonso X seems to have undertaken to belittle the shrine of St. James at Compostela. Such a course of action is more understandable in later times when such writers as Mariana went so far as pen what we now regard as downright vilifications of the saint.[1] During the reign of Alfonso, however, the reasons are not so clear, and there is a need for more definite study as to why this king wrote, or caused to be written, verses that seem to belittle Santiago, the Patron Saint of Spain.

Generations of Spanish kings had revered the shrine of St. James. Indeed, medieval Europe had from the early ninth century, when the body of the saint had been discovered in Galicia, held his tomb in reverence and veneration. Untold thousands of pilgrims had marched out of Paris by the Rue St. Jacques to make their way through Orleans, Tours, and Pamplona to the city of Santiago de Compostela. Long after the death of King Alfonso (he ruled 1252-1284) pilgrims made the long journey. St. James remained Spain's patron and the battle cry of Spanish armies even in the time of Charles V was *"Santiago, y cierra España."*

King Alfonso X was certainly not ignorant of the popularity and attraction of St. James. The King's own history, the *Crónica General*,[2] relates the facts concerned with the siege of Coimbra by Ferdinand III, his father, when St. James' aid alone was enough to overcome the city. Both Alfonso and Ferdinand must have realized, as their ancestors had realized earlier, that Santiago was a kind of focal point of resistance during the long years of the Reconquest. Without the belief in St. James, sent down from heaven to champion their cause, many Spaniards might have slipped out of the orbit of Christianity and into that of Islam. Indeed, even with the saint's protection, the influence of the East and of Moslem beliefs was strong and traces of the influence may still be seen in Spanish customs and folkways. Américo Castro[3] even suggests that Spanish Catholicism has been to some degree colored by aspects of Islam. But that is another story.

One has a good right to wonder, in view of St. James' status in medieval Europe, what could have led a king to question his greatness and to belittle the efficacy of his cult in the Iberian Peninsula. Why had Santiago fallen from grace with the King of Spain? Had Alfonso decided, as some have suggested, to attempt to curb the political influence of the Francophile monks of Cluny who had become entrenched along the Way of St. James?[4] Cluny owed allegiance to the royal house of France, and King Alfonso may have feared the widespread influence of this Benedictine brotherhood. Could Alfonso have looked with disfavor upon the clergy at Compostela who refused to abide by clerical regulations set up in Rome, who avoided the tonsure, dressed in brilliant colors, lived lives not seemly and disregarded official decretals?[5] It is known that in Compostela there existed a feeling in ecclesiastical circles that no allegiance was owed to Rome. And what of the hordes of foreign pilgrims, many of whom were the riffraff of the roads and cities? Did Alfonso regard Compostela as a den of iniquity that drew to Spain great multitudes of undesirables?

During the reigns of Ferdinand and Alfonso long strides had been made in regaining territory from the Moors. The great cities of Cordova and Seville had surrendered. The province of Murcia had been captured. Could King Alfonso have thought that the need of St. James as a warrior saint had run its course? Or had certain mystical experiences of the royal family and of Alfonso personally, in which the Holy Virgin figured, caused the king to belittle the saint?[6]

We may never know the answers to these questions. But we know that Alfonso X carried a miraculous image of the Virgin on his saddle when he rode into battle; we know that he believed that the Virgin had intervened in his behalf when he was ill;[7] and we know that he called himself her troubadour and caused to be written in her honor a remarkable and extremely valuable book, the *Cantigas de Santa Maria* (Canticles of Holy Mary).[8] Indeed, many scholars suspect that the king actually composed a number of these songs. It is among these *Cantigas* that one may find some interesting facts that illustrate the rivalry between the shrines of the Virgin and the shrine of St. James. King Alfonso's views, as stated in the *Cantigas*, are unmistakable.

The *Cantigas* are, as most scholars know, a great compilation of miracles of the Virgin, written in verse and set to music. In the better codices full-page sets of illuminated miniatures accompany the songs,[9] and these pictures are an important step in the development of Hispanic art and may be regarded as one of medieval Europe's great art works. The music of the *Cantigas* has attracted the attention of such musicologists as Higinio Anglés, Willi Appel and Julián Ribera.[10] Sociologists and historians find the *Cantigas* a vast and rich repository of daily living, actually portrayed in a multitude of phases. Folklorists and thematologists are beginning to realize how great a reservoir of motifs and themes these songs contain.[11] In the four hundred-odd poems, written in Galician-Portuguese (the favorite vehicle of lyric verse in Spain during the thirteenth and fourteenth centuries)[12] there is a whole world preserved in words, music and picture.

At least three of the *cantigas* seem to belittle the efficacy of the shrine of St. James. *Cantiga* 218 bears the following title or explanatory caption written in prose: *Esta é como Santa Maria guareseu en Vila-Sirga*[13] *un ome bõo d'Alemanna que era contreito.* After this appears the first stanza which reveals that the shrine of the Virgin there was the site of miracles.

> E dest en Villa-Sirga
> miragre mui fremoso
> mostrou a Vírgen, Madre
> de Deus, Rey grorioso,
> et entr' os seus miragres
> é d'oyr piadoso
> de que ela faz muitos
> nobres et mui preçados.

The canticle then goes on to relate that a rich merchant of Germany fell ill and was paralyzed completely, that his feet and his hands were contracted and twisted:

foi tan mal parado,
per que ficou tolleito
d'anbos et dous lados
. . . .
foi end' atan maltreito
que de pees et máos
de todo foi contreito.

He persuaded some pilgrims who were about to depart on the
pilgrimage to Santiago de Compostela to take him with them, although they did not wish to do so. After the long trip they deposited
him before the altar of the saint and the man received no cure. What
was even worse, he suddenly went blind. At this the pilgrims who
had carried him from Germany decided to leave him!

el quando en Carron foron
ar cego o acharon,
et de o y lexáren
todos s'acordaron;

The spot in which they had left him was not far from the church
of Our Lady of Villa-Sirga, and as the poor man lay weeping, the
Virgin heard him. She cured him of his paralysis and of his blindness,
and he returned to Germany to sing her praises:

mas a Madre
do que da agua uynno
fez, ouue d'él mercée
et oyú seus braados.
. . . .
o oyú et saóu-o
como mui poderosa,
e póis a poucos dias
foi-sse para ssa terra
por prazer da que nunca
se mercée én serra;

The *Cantiga* ends with a stanza in which the listener is advised to
visit the shrine at Villa-Sirga and to make offering there. *Cantiga* 218,
then, shows that an afflicted man went to Compostela, prayed, and
was not heard: in the Virgin's shrine at Villa-Sirga his prayers were
answered.

Cantiga 253 continues the praise of Villa-Sirga to the discredit of Santiago de Compostela. The title or explanatory caption here reads as follows: *Como un remeu de França que ya a Santiago foi per Santa María de Vila-Sirga, et non pod' én sacar un bordon de fero grande que tragía en peedença.*

A certain Frenchman sinned and as a penance was sent to the shrine of St. James by his abbot:

> recebeu en peedença
> que fosse logo guisado
> pora yr a Santiago,
> ca lle mandou seu abade.

He was to carry a twenty-four pound staff of iron all the way and was to place it on the altar. On the way he passed through Villa-Sirga and he asked the people about the place. In their answer one can read something of King Alfonso's sentiments about the shrine there:

> —Alí chaman Vila-Sirga
> logar mui maravilloso
> en que muito bon miragre
> sempre faz et saboroso
> a santa Vírgen María,
> Madre do Rey poderoso;
> et a eygreia é sua
> et derredor a erdade.

The man calls upon the Virgin for aid, as he is weary of the iron bar. At this prayer the bar falls to the ground and breaks into two parts. Neither the pilgrim nor anyone else can lift it. He prayed for assistance to the Virgin of Villa-Sirga who made the bar weightless:

> solto de ssa peedença,
> pois que lle tolleu tan fera
> carrega que él levava
> do ferr' e de ssa maldade.

As can be seen, he recovered his bar. He hastened on then to Santiago de Compostela and carried out his pilgrimage, but he was thereafter a greater devotee of the Holy Virgin than of St. James:

> Des í log' a Santiago
> foi conprir sa romaría;
> et pois tornou a ssa terra

serviú muy ben todavía
en quanto uiueo de grado
á Vírgen Santa María.

These two miracles—*Cantigas* 218 and 253—give some indication
of the preference of King Alfonso for the shrine at Villa-Sirga.
Number 278 goes even farther. The very title is a little story in itself:
*Como hua bõa dona de França que era cega, ueó a Vila-Sirga et teue y uigia, et foi logo
guarida et cobrou seu lume; et ela yndo-se pera sa terra, achou un cego que ya en
romaría a Santiago, et ela consellou-lle que fosse per Vila-Sirga.*

This miracle took place at a time when the Virgin was beginning
to work miracles at the little shrine:

Esto foi en aquel tenpo
que a Vírgen começou
a fazer en Vila-Sirga
miragres, por que sãou
a muitos d'enfermidades
et mortos ressocitou;
et porend' as gentes algo
começauan d' í fazer.

The blind French woman went first to Santiago where she received no cure: "mas a vẽ-ll'assý que no sãou de sa ida / que sol podesse
veer." On the way back to France she stopped at Villa-Sirga and received
her sight. Later on the road she met a blind man traveling toward the
shrine of St. James and she advised him not to go there, but to stop at
Villa-Sirga where there was a better chance of cure. The woman is
definite in her criticism of Santiago as a miracle-working shrine:

E contou todo seu feito
cómo fora con romeus
muitos pera Santiago,
mas pero nunca dos seus
ollos o lum' ý cobrara;
mas póis a Madre de Deus
ll'-odera en Vila-Sirga
pelo seu muí gran poder.

The blind man gave up his attempt to reach Compostela and made
his way to Vila-Sirga where he called upon the Mother of God and
was given back his sight: "et pois foi en Vila-Sirga / fez ssa oraçon et
uyú; / ca non quis Santa María / en o ssar detẽer."

One could argue that the *Cantigas de Santa María* were written to laud the miracles of the holy Virgin, but such an argument does not explain satisfactorily why it was necessary to laud these miracles by belittling those of St. James, Spain's patron. In the four hundred-odd songs it is not the practice to criticize or cast aspersion on other shrines. Only St. James's shrine at Santiago de Compostela is the object of such aspersion.

Villa-Sirga was apparently, in the mind of King Alfonso, a favorite shrine, and Evelyn Procter has listed fourteen *cantigas* that relate miracles performed there.[14] But other shrines were also the sites of miracles: Puerto de Santa María, which was settled by Christians sent by King Alfonso who also built its church, was the site of twenty-four miracles in the *cantigas*; Salas in Aragon was the site of seventeen; Terena in Portugal has twelve; and there are occasional miracles in other places, such as Montserrat with no more than six. The shrine of Our Lady of the Pillar in Saragossa is not mentioned, a strange fact, for the Virgen del Pilar has always been in the minds of Spaniards, one of the most important, if not the most important of all. One might hazard the guess that since the founding of this shrine was a kind of collaboration between the Virgin and St. James, Alfonso thought it unwise to use it as the site for miracles. After all, the Blessed Virgin appeared at Saragossa, in the first century the city of Caesar Augusta, to St. James who had been carrying on there his missionary activities. It was she who reminded him that she had asked him to build a shrine to her in that part of Spain in which he had made the largest number of converts (there were eight men converts). Saragossa was that place and there at the Virgin's direction St. James constructed the shrine, which has since become one of the most important in all the Spanish-speaking world.

Pilgrims to Compostela continued to flow into Spain, and as we have seen, the cult of St. James survived into the twentieth century. The beginnings of its decline, however, seems to have been inaugurated much earlier. Strange to say, it seems that King Alfonso the Wise laid the foundations of this decline.

Notes

* Reprinted from *Middle Ages—Reformation—Volkskunde, Festschrift for John G. Kunstmann*, Chapel Hill: University of North Carolina Press, 1959, pp. 1-8.

1 Padre Mariana stated that the tales of St. James were *"cuentos de viejas."* Quevedo in his *Su espada por Santiago*, however, defended the belief in the saint. In 1618 Pope Paul V, at the insistence of the Carmelites, decreed that St. Theresa was co-patron of Spain with St. James. Américo Castro (*España en su historia*, Buenos Aires, 1948, p. 182) states that *"los salones favorecían a la Santa y las masas, al Apóstol".*

2 R. Menéndez Pidal, *La Crónica General de España* p. 488a, as cited by Américo Castro, *op. cit.*, p. 135.

3 *Ibid.*, 183.

4 See Georgiana G. King, *The Way of St. James*, New York, 1920, for an extensive treatment of the pilgrimage route and its history; see also Américo Castro, *op. cit.*, 107-52.

5 Américo Castro, *op. cit.*, 169.

6 Twenty-eight of the *Cantigas de Santa María* relate miracles performed by the Holy Virgin for King Alfonso or for members of his family or friends.

7 *Cantiga* 209 is notable. Its title reads: *Como el rey Don Alfonso de Castella adoeçeu en Vitoria e ouu' hũa door tan grande, que coidaron que moresse ende; e posseron-lle de suso o liuro das Cantigas de Santa María et foi guarido* (How the king Don Alfonso grew ill in Vitoria and had a sickness so grave that they thought he would die; and they placed upon him the book of the *Cantigas and he was cured*).

8 *Cantigas de Santa María*, ed. Leopoldo A. de Cueto, Marqués de Valmar, 2 vols. (Madrid, 1889). All citations of miracles by number refer to this edition. [AUTH. I had not yet seen the edition of Walter Mettmann. His second volume, which contains *Cantigas* 218, 253, and 278, appeared after the publication of this article.]

9 The codices that contain the full-page sets of miniatures are Escorial MS. T.I.1 and MS. Banco Rari 20, formerly II.I.2 13, of the National Library of Florence.

10 Higinio Anglés, *La música de las Cantigas*, II, (Madrid, 1943); Julián Ribera, *La música de las Cantigas*, (Madrid, 1922).

11 I have finished a Motif-Index of the *Cantigas*... [AUTH. This motif-index was unfortunately lost several years ago, and a new one is being prepared by William R. Davis of Mercer University at my suggestion].

12 Three great books of songs written in Galician-Portuguese have been preserved containing some 2000 songs by 200 poets: *Cancioneiro de Ajuda* (ca. 1280); *Cancioneiro da Vaticana* (mid-14th century) and *Cancioneiro de Colocci-Brancuti* (mid-14th century).

13 Villa-Sirga lay a few miles off the Way of St. James and was quite close to Carrión de los Condes. The village today is called Villa-Alcázar de Sirga.

14 Evelyn Procter, *Alfonso X of Castille*, Oxford, 1951, 29.

More on the Rivalry Between
Santa Maria and
Santiago de Compostela*

N AN ARTICLE ENTITLED "King Alfonso's Virgin of Villa-Sirga, Rival of St. James of Compostela" [AUTH. The preceding article of this collection] I treated an interesting aspect of the curious competition between the shrine of the Blessed Virgin at Villa-Sirga and the great shrine of pilgrims at Santiago de Compostela. This competition would last for centuries, and even such a notable as Quevedo would involve himself in it. But what took place beyond the thirteenth century of King Alfonso X el Sabio is another story and will not fall within the confines of this article. The article cited pointed out that though Alfonso owed a debt to St. James for certain victories, as did his father St. Ferdinand, who ruled as Ferdinand III, for some reason not apparent as yet, the Learned King in his *Cantigas de Santa Maria* produced what we can only regard as belittlement of the cult of the saint. Could King Alfonso have thought that the need of St. James as a warrior saint had run its course? Or had certain mystical experiences of the royal family and of Alfonso personally, in which the Virgin figured, caused the king to belittle the saint?

The *Cantigas*, as most scholars know, is a great compilation of miracles of the Blessed Virgin, written in verse and set to music, and, in two of the codices, illuminated by miniatures of unusually fine quality and rich detail.[1] These pictures, let me say in passing, form an important step in the development of Hispanic art, the longest and most varied of medieval Spanish poetic anthologies, the most copious outpouring of different melodies, and the corpus par excellence of the techniques of narrative art.[2] In the four hundred-odd poems, for the most part of the relation of miracles, but nevertheless important, too, in this anthology of Marian hymns, lies a whole world of medieval story, music and picture.

The original article revealed that at least three of the *Cantigas* seem to belittle the efficacy of the shrine at Compostela.[3] In *Cantiga* 218 whose title or explanatory caption is written in prose, and of course, in Galician-Portuguese, as are the poems themselves, we read: "Esta e como Santa María guareceu en Vila-Sriga un ome bõo d'Alemanna que era contreito"[4] 'This is how Holy Mary healed in Villa-Sirga a good man from Germany who was contorted.'[5] In the miracle we read that the German, helped by his countrymen, indeed carried to Compostela by them, was placed before the altar of the saint, prayed there, and departed not only healed but even blind. His companions decided to abandon him, and he was desperate until some pilgrims told him he had best get to the shrine of Our Lady of Villa-Sirga where fine miracles were worked and often. Since he had been abandoned not far from there, he managed to arrive and pray. Of course Our Lady heard him as he wept and cured him of both his paralysis and his blindness. The verses tell how grateful he was:

> o oyu et sãou-o como mui poderosa, por que quantos y eran foron maravillados. Razon an de seeren seus miragres contandos... E pois a poucos dias foi-sse pera ssa terra por prazer da que nunca sa mercee enserra.

Cantiga 253 was seen also to discredit the saint. Its title actually gives a thumb-nail summary of the miracle: "Como un remeu de França que ya a Santiago foi per Santa Maria de Villa-Sirga, et non pod' en sacar un bordon de fero grande que tragia en pẽedença" 'How a pilgrim from France on the way to Santiago through Santa María de Villa-Sirga, was unable to pick up a very large iron staff which he carried as a penance.'

As he passed through the town dedicated to Our Lady, he questioned the inhabitants about her shrine, and they told him this—and we can read into the lines a great deal of Alfonso's feelings for one of his favorite shrines:

> «Ali chaman Vila-Sirga, logar muy maravilloso, en que muito bon

miragre sempre faz e saboroso a Santa Virgen Maria, Madre do Rey poderoso; e a eygreja e sua é derredor a erdade.»

The pilgrim suddenly had to drop the bar, for it had grown too heavy. It even broke in two, but his faith in Our Lady restored it, and he was able to pick it up and carry it to the saint's altar as the penance his bishop had required. Naturally, this experience changed his life as the denouement reveals:

Des i log' a Santiago foi conprir sa romaria; e pois tornou a ssa terra, serviu muy ben todavia enquanto viveo de grado a Virgen Santa Maria.

Lastly in *Cantiga* 278 the king disparaged Compostela even more. The very title here is a little story in itself: "Como hũa bõa donna de França que era cega, vẽo a Vila-Sirga et teue y vigi-li-a, et foi logo guarida et cobrou seu lume; et ela yndo-se pera sa terra, achou un cego que ya en romaria a Santago, et ela consellou-lle que fosse per Vila-Sirga." We read that a blind French woman went to Compostela but was not cured.

Mas hũa dona de França, cega, per quant' aprendi, romỹa a Santiago foi, mas aveo-ll' assi que non sanou de sa ida que sol podesse ceer.

On the way back to France she stopped at Villa-Sirga[6] and Our Lady gave her back her sight. She met a blind man on the way to Compostela and her advice to him, which was taken, reveals her opinion of the power of the saint, and, I believe, what Alfonso's opinion was also.

E contou todo seu feito, como fora con romeus muitos pera Santiago, mas pero nunca dos seus ollos o lum' y cobrara, mas pois a Madre de Deus llo dera en Vila-Sirga pelo seu mui gran poder.

The blind man gave up his hopes of a cure from St. James and besought Our Lady of Vila-Sirga who cured his blindness.

Only St. James's shrine receives such criticism from the Learned King's *Cantigas de Santa Maria*. I believed at the time of the writing of the original article that several reasons may have existed for this disparagement of Compostela. Downright devotion to Our Lady, kindled by his belief that she had actually given him succor and cured him when the physicians failed to and when he was at death's door, may be the entire explanation.[7] But is it not possible that to insure a larger

clientele of pilgrims he attempted, through belittlement of the saint's
shrine, to draw off pilgrims from the great pilgrimage and lead them to
the shrine at Villa-Sirga which he wanted to make great?[8] Or had he
asked St. James for assistance and failed to receive it?

Be that as it may, Alfonso in another way downgraded the saint by
actually pilfering one of his more famous miracles, one so famous as to
appear in the great Marian collections of Aimeri Picaud's *Codex de
Compostel* as well as in the *Legenda Aurea* and the *Speculum Historiale*, not to
mention its pictorial presentation in a stained glass window at Toulouse. One wonders at his temerity in what he caused to be written,
set to music and illuminated in the *Cantigas de Santa Maria*. The miracle
attributed to the saint across some good part of Christendom would
surely have been recognized for what it was, and those who heard or
read or saw the illustration would have realized how Alfonso had
removed the saint and inserted in his place Our Blessed Lady. It is a
very graphic and remarkable example of the king of adaptation
recommended by St. Augustine when he made it clear to his disciples
that one could profitably and ethically convert a pagan story into a
Christian exemplum.[9] Such revision and substitution in the cases
Augustine had in mind can be understood better than the deliberate
alteration of the miracle of one saint, here St. James, so as to make the
people believe it had been done by another, that is St. Mary.

The version of the miracle found in the *Cantigas* follows in fairly
close detail that of the earlier cited collections of miracles in Latin. But
from the outset, and even in the title of *Cantigas* 175, "Como Santa
Maria livrou de morte un mancebo que enforcaron a mui gran torto, e
quimaron ũu herege que llo fezera fazer" 'How Holy Mary freed from
death a youth whom they hanged in great error, and burned a heretic
who had caused it to be done,' we see the Virgin replacing the saint.

From the very beginning, then, Our Lady gets the credit for saving
the youth's life. The story runs that a father and his young son travel
toward Compostela as pilgrims and reach Toulouse where they lodge
at an inn, whose owner is a heretic. Unseen by anyone, he hides one of
the inn's silver goblets (in the Latin versions it is gold) so as to
incriminate the youth. He waits until the boy and his father are on the
road and then sends the bailiffs after him. The boy is searched and the
goblet found. On the spot he is sentenced and hanged from the
gallows. The cruel innkeeper even accompanies the minions of the law.
The verses in which he accuses the youth are moving:[10]

Tan toste que o acharon, o erege que seu era jurou por aquele vaso e que llo furtad' ouvera o moço que o tragia; e a jostiça tan fera foi de sanna, que tan toste diss': —Este moç' enforcade.

The lad is then hanged, and his poor father continues his pilgrimage to Compostela where he prays before the saint's altar as he had vowed he would do. Then he goes back to retrieve the body of his son from the gibbet.

Now in the miracles of Santiago, written and illustrated in stained glass and on paper, it was St. James who kept the young man alive while his father went to the famous shrine. It seems no more than natural that this should be, for the father of the youth had started a long pilgrimage in honor of the saint, and had actually carried it out, losing his son in the process. But in the *Cantigas de Santa Maria*, as has been pointed out, it is the Virgin who saves him. And in the miniatures one can see her as she lets his feet rest on her hands as he hangs from the gallows. The king so liked this miracle that he had it illuminated with two full pages of miniatures, a rarity in his *Cantigas*. It is as though he not only wanted to change the miracle to make it one of Our Lady's, but even wanted to emphasize it by giving it twice the pictorial coverage he gave nearly all the other miracles.[11]

In the earlier versions St. James supported the youth's body for several weeks: in the *Cantigas de Santa Maria* the Virgin stands beneath the gibbet and supports him for three whole months:

E pois sse calad' ouveron, contou-lles todo seu feito com' estedera na forca tres meses todos aeito, u a Virgen o guardara, e a verdade do prieto lles disse, rogando muito:—O erege mi chamade...

The two pages of miniatures are among the most artistic in the entire corpus of the *Cantigas*.[12] As is true in all but one of the pages of illumination, six panels, each with its own caption, narrate the events. Panel 1 shows the two pilgrims, father and son, making their way, dressed in the characteristic garments and headgear of pilgrims, through a mountainous and forested area. Panel 2 is filled with action, for at the left we see one event, the innkeeper hiding the cup in the youth's traveling bag, while at the right sit the father and son eating their supper. Panel 3 shows the innkeeper dispatching the bailiffs after the pilgrims who have departed. We can actually see them both to the right, separated from the scene to the left by a small hill and a tall tree. This technique of multiple action in one panel is common in the

Cantigas, as indeed it is in earlier Spanish manuscripts and in many in other countries. Panel 4 shows the bailiffs riding hard after the pilgrims, one holding a mace in front of him, while the two pilgrims look back in fright, their hands expressing it quite adequately. Panel 5 narrates visually the finding of the cup in the sack, the innocent youth pleading, his father on his knees, hands joined in prayer, and the bailiffs surrounding them both. Panel 6, the last in this page, shows a strange scene. The boy hangs by the neck from the gibbet, his hands bound behind his back, and beneath him stands Our Lady in her heavenly robes, her crown, and the usual halo behind her head. Her outstretched palms support the youth, for his feet rest upon them. Behind her an angel stands. The father kneels on the earth, hands joined in prayer, and gazes up at his son whom he apparently believes is dead. The constabulary march off with their spears resting on their shoulders.

The second page is no less vividly illustrated. In panel 1 we see the father kneeling before the altar of St. James in Compostela. Golden arches and columns and golden lamps decorate the church, and on the altar are lavish candlesticks, candles, and a chest holding, no doubt, a relic. In panel 2 we see the father after his three months absence kneeling again under the gibbet and behind him an angel, while another angel stands behind the Virgin who still supports the son on her outstretched palms. The boy looks down and speaks to his father:

E u el assi chorava, diss' o fillo: —Ome bõo, padre, e non vos matedes, ca de certo vivo sõo; e guarda-m' a Virgen Santa, que con Deus see no trõo, e me sofreu en sas mãos pola ssa gran caridade.—

In panel 3 we see the father who has rushed to the city, explaining what has happened. His arms and hands expressively show the depth of his emotion. Two mounted lawmen sit on their steeds and listen, their hands also indicative of their feelings, in this case amazement. One of the father's hands points in the direction of the gallows, to be seen in the next panel. In panel 4 we see much activity. Mounted men sit on their horses to the left of the gallows. Another mounted man with a sword is severing the rope, while men on foot, their arms around the youth's waist, lower him to the earth. His father kneels and prays. No longer needed, the Virgin has disappeared.

In panel 5 we see the father and the son confronting the heretic, while a great many people stand by. Three men armed with spears stand at the left and three at the right of the scene, lending, with their weapons, a very artistic touch. And in the last panel the innkeeper gets his just deserts. A bonfire burns, and in it we can see him bound and sitting in the flames, his face a mask of terror and pain. A group of citizens stands to the left and another to the right watching. One man at the left seems to be admonishing him.

We can now add a fourth *Cantiga* to the three which have been showed as disparaging the shrine at Compostela. This last—if it is the last, as subsequent research will eventually show—is a different and more devious and indirect kind of belittlement of St. James. Since it was given more or less official sanction by a powerful and learned king, it, like the other blows struck at the saint's repute as a miracle-worker, might have been telling indeed. The entire matter is very intriguing, for it can lead to many suggestions about the entire character of King Alfonso, his philosophy, his very religiosity.

Notes

* Reprinted from *Crítica Hispánica* 1 (1979), 37-43.

1 The two manuscripts which contain a wealth of narrative art in their miniatures are Escorial T.I.1 which contains 194 full pages of illumination, and Florence, Biblioteca Nazionale, MS. Banco Rari with its 90. For a complete treatment of the four manuscripts see Evelyn S. Procter, *Alfonso X of Castile, Patron of Literature and Learning* Oxford: Clarendon Press, 1951, p. 24.

2 Richard P. Kinkade and I have completed the first of four books on the iconography of medieval Spanish literature, this one dealing with narrative art in miniatures of which the *Cantigas de Santa Maria* form a substantial part [AUTH. Now published as *Iconography in Medieval Spanish Literature*, Lexington: The University Press of Kentucky, 1984].

3 Walter Mettmann, *Alfonso X, O Sábio, Cantigas de Santa Maria*. Coimbra: Acta Universitatis Conimbrigensis, 1959-72, 4 vols., is the text from which all citations are made. [AUTH. In the first article on the shrine at Compostela and Alfonso's belittlement of it, the edition of Cueto was used.]

4 Each *Cantiga* has a title which is intended to be a very brief summary. More minute summaries appear in the form of captions above each of the six panels in every page of illuminations.

5 Many diseases are cured by the Virgin in the miracles of the *Cantigas*. There is need for more study in this area, for in it there are quite possibly unique mentions of maladies. The Virgin cures the sick, the deformed, the lame, the halt, and the blind, as well as the possessed, and she resuscitates the dead. She also cures animals—hawks, silkworms, bees, etc.

6 Villa-Sirga is today Villa-Alcázar de Sirga near Palencia.

7 Several *Cantigas* relate the Virgin's personal assistance to Alfonso. The

one which may have moved him most occurred during a protracted illness when he was near death's door and when none of the remedies suggested by the court physicians was of avail. It was only when he had a copy of the *Cantigas de Santa Maria* placed on his chest, as he lay in bed, that he was cured. *Cantiga* 206 relates this miracle, and it can be seen in miniature 119 v of Florentine codex. [AUTH. See our *Iconography*..., color plate 32.]

8 It is believed that Gonzalo de Berceo wrote the three saints' lives as propaganda to persuade those who had made pledges to the monasteries where the saints' bodies lay buried to meet their pledges.

9 Another example of a *Cantiga's* adaptation from a previous story is number 42 in which a young German about to play batball places a ring on the finger of the Virgin's image to protect the ring from harm. In the twelfth century in France a story in Latin relates that a young ball player placed his ring on the finger of a statue of Venus. Either Alfonso knew the Latin tale, or found it in some manuscript he used as a source for the *Cantigas*, or perhaps found it current in Spain, already changed from Venus to the Virgin. [AUTH. The twentieth story alluded to is Prosper Mérimée's *La Vénus d'Ille*.]

10 We are not told why the heretic worked to destroy the youthful pilgrim. The motif is, of course, almost as old as literature. Holy Scripture introduced it in the story of Joseph in Egypt, when he had valuables placed in the traveling bags of one of his brothers as they left for home.

11 For a discussion of this miracle of St. James in French stained glass see Émile Mâle, *The Gothic Image—Religious Art in France of the Thirteenth Century*. Reprinted in 1958 as a Harper Torchbook (New York: Harper and Row), pp. 327-28.

12 These two pages of illumination, like nearly every page in the *Cantigas de Santa Maria*, offer wonderful opportunities for the study of daily life, custom, and affairs of the thirteenth century. See my "Daily Living as Presented in the Canticles of King Alfonso the Learned." *Speculum* 33 (1958), 484-89 and my "Folklore in the *Canticles* of Alfonso X." *Southern Folklore Quarterly* 23 (1959), 175-83 [AUTH.] both are reprinted in this volume].

Cuaderna Vía and Its Appeal*

ERCEO'S FAVORITE POETIC METER must in itself have been attractive to his public. We can assume, I believe, that it had popular appeal and was successful, for otherwise surely he would not have written all his works in *cuaderna vía* during many years of his life. Had he discovered that this verse form was badly received, he would surely have turned to some other form, since others had been tried and accepted. No innovator—and to some considerable extent he was an innovator in the use of *cuaderna vía* and may have been its inventor—would subject his audience to a poetic medium unpleasing or irritating or boring to that audience. Since in all probability Berceo read his works aloud to groups of illiterate people, he would quickly have detected any lack of enthusiasm, would have changed his poetic style and would not have penned thousands of lines in a medium unpleasant to his public.

Cuaderna vía was not to the medieval audience, whether literate or illiterate, a poetic medium dull, disagreeably monotonous, sing-song, or otherwise without poetic quality. Indeed, Berceo's *cuaderna vía*, and of course the even more skillful *cuaderna vía* of the Archpriest of Hita in the fourteenth century, must have been heard with delight and can be read with delight today. Were this not so, the two poets who strove most actively to attract the people's interest and affection would not, could not, have composed their thousands of lines in this medium. The same can be said of Chaucer, whose *Canterbury Tales* could not have been monotonous in their own meter to that poet's contemporaries and are not monotonous to the literary today.

Proof of enthusiasm for Berceo in our own times can be found in the writings of some of the most accomplished of modern poets. Rubén Darío himself (1867-1916), that sweet singer, included in his

Prosas profanas a warm and loving poem, "A Maestre Gonzalo de Berceo." It merits inclusion here in the original, for it makes Berceo and his poetry emerge sparkling alive and nostalgically bedewed with some of that poet's own humanity and tenderness:

> Amo tu delicioso alejandrino
> como el de Hugo, espíritu de España;
> éste vale una copa de champaña.
> como aquél vale un "vaso de bon vino."
>
> Mas a uno y otro pájaro divino
> la primitiva cárcel es extraña,
> el barrote maltrata, el grillo daña;
> que vuelo y libertad son su destino.
>
> Así procuro que en la luz resalte
> tu antiguo verso, cuyas alas doro
> y hago brillar con mi moderno esmalte;
> tiene la libertad con el decoro
> y vuelve como al puño el gerifalte,
> trayendo del azul rimas de oro.

Manuel Machado (1874-1947) composed his poem to Berceo in the *cuaderna vía* itself and entitled it "Retablo." Printed in his *Alma, Museo, Los Cantares,* it reads:

> Ya están ambos a diestra del Padre deseado,
> los dos santos varones, el chantre y el cantado,
> el Grant Santo Domingo de Silos venerado
> y el Maestre Gonzalo de Berceo nomnado.
> Yo veo al Santo como en la sabida prosa
> fecha en nombre de Christo y de la Gloriosa:
> la color amariella, la marcha fatigosa,
> el cabello tirado, la frente luminosa.
> Y a su lado el poeta, romero peregrino,
> sonríe a los de ahora que andamos el camino,
> y el galardón nos muestra de su claro destino:
> una palma de gloria y un vaso de buen vino.

Manuel Machado's brother, Antonio (1875-1939), in his *Poesías completas* included in honor of Berceo a piece entitled "Mis poetas." It depicts Berceo's work in darker hues, evoking less attractive vistas of the medieval landscape and spirit.

El primero es Gonzalo de Berceo llamado,
Gonzalo de Berceo, poeta y peregrino,
que yendo en romería acaeció en un prado,
y a quien los sabios pintan copiando un pergamino.
Trovó a Santo Domingo, trovó a Santa María,
y a San Millán, y a San Lorenzo y Santa Oria.
Y dijo: mi dictado non es de juglaría;
escrito lo tenemos; es verdadera historia.
Su verso es dulce y grave; monótonas hileras
de chopos invernales, en donde nada brilla:
reglónes como surcos en pardas sementeras,
y lejos, las montañas azules de Castilla.
El nos cuenta el repaire del romeo cansado:
leyendo en santorales y libros de oracion,
copiando historias viejas, nos dice su dictado,
mientras le sale afuera la luz del corazón.

And Enrique de Mesa, in his *Cancionero Castellano*, waxes ecstatic at the end of his poem entitled "El bon vino":

Para seguir mi camino
también olvidar deseo.
¡Oh Gonzalo de Berceo!
¡El bon vino!

The full rhyme of *cuaderna vía*'s quatrains has power. It catches the reader in its net and carries him along with force and sometimes with violence. Once entrapped, once caught up in the metrics and trained to march to the regular and unchanging cadence, once taught to expect each line in each quatrain to rhyme completely with each of the other lines, the reader surrenders to *cuaderna vía*'s spell and reads on tirelessly. Poets from time immemorial have learned to take advantage of what some regard as monotony, of what others prefer to regard as an acceptable and often as a vigorous flow and modulation. The *Kalevala*, Finland's national epos, written in eight-syllabled trochaic verse, partakes of somewhat the same monotony unjustly ascribed to *cuaderna vía*. A folk epic, composed for a rude and untutored people, this work had to attract and compel attention. Its composers understood the power of repetition and its tonal beat. A good idea of the *Kalevala*'s style and versification can be obtained from Longfellow's *Hiawatha*, which is a pretty true imitation of it:

Bright before it beat the water,
Beat the clear and sunny water,
Beat the shining Big-Sea-Water, etc.

The *Iliad* and the *Odyssey*, undying poems, varied little as they related in the unchanging six-footed measures of hexameter some of literature's greatest moments. No one saw monotony in the *Iliad* or the *Odyssey*. Of course hexameter's sameness lay in cadence rather than in rhyme, whereas in Berceo's medium both cadence and rhyme are repeated.

Latin hexameters, for example those utilized by Virgil in his *Aeneid*, can illustrate repetitive quality of ancient epics: Arma vi/ rumque ca/no Tro/iae qui/primus ab/oris.

Longfellow, to use this poet again as an example, wrote a form of hexameter, substituting accent for the quantity of the ancient epics. In *Evangeline* we find

This is the forest primeval. The murmuring pines and the hem-
locks,
Bearded with moss, and in garments green, indistinct in the twi-
light,
Stand like Druids of old with voices sad and prophetic,
Stand like harpers hoar, with beards that rest on their bosoms.

Monotony? Perhaps to some, but to nineteenth-century literate America definitely not.

And so Berceo, viewed by his contemporaries, no doubt seemed attractive. Continuance, flow, a kind of marching forward along a definite poetic path marked carefully by counted syllables, a definite break after the seventh, and full rhyme at the end of each line captured and moved the Bercean audience. Whether one chooses a narrative passage:

Maguer que fué el fuego tan fuert e tan quemant,
Nin plegó a la duenna, nin plegó al ifant,
Nin plegó al flabello que colgava delant,
Ni li fizo de danno un dinero pesant.
                                          (*Milagros*, quatrain 324)

or a descriptive passage:

Todos vestian casullas de preçiosos colores,

Blagos en las siniestras commo predicadores,
Caliçes en las diestras de oro muy meiores.
Semeiaba ministros de preçiosos sennores.

(Santa Oria, quatrain 58)

or a passage of didactic or instructional nature:

Conviene que catemos est sancto misterio,
En bien escodrinarlo non es poco lazerio,
Mas el que a David guió en est sallerio,
El nos dara conseio a est desiderio.

(Sacrificio, quatrain 241)

or a passage designed to exalt or glorify:

Sennora benedicta, Reina acabada,
Por mano del tu fijo don Christo coronada,
Libranos del diablo de la su çancaiada,
Que tiene a las almas siempre mala celada.

(Milagros, quatrain 910)

In no matter what context the poet guides his audience along a path so well marked and, indeed, so walled in, there is no escape until the poem ends.

Cuaderna vía, the fourfold way used by clerics like Berceo and Juan Ruiz a century after him, or by those who composed lengthy secular narratives like the *Libro de Apolonio*, was a successful and effective poetic medium for all varieties of subject matter.

Note

* Reprinted from my *Gonzalo de Berceo*, (New York: Twayne, 1971), pp. 35-41.

The Enigma
of Berceo's *Milagro XXV**

ERCEO'S MIRACLE XXV, known as "La iglesia roba-
da," in the *Milagros de Nuestra Señora*, diverges
greatly from the others and poses problems
which scholars have not solved. Apparently
Berceo did not include it in the original version
of the *Milagros*, but added it later for reasons he
never made clear, reasons which in themselves
are intriguing and which have evoked much
speculation. It is the only one of the twenty-five *milagros* which Berceo
did not take from the Latin collection of miracles which is known to
have been the source of the twenty-four he Hispanified in *cuaderna
vía*. As long ago as 1910 Richard Becker published his findings and
revealed that a manuscript in the Library of Copenhagen, known as
Thott 128, or else a manuscript identical to it, was Berceo's source,
and not several of the well-known repositories of miracles available,
such as the *Speculum Historiale*, the *Legenda Aurea* and the *Miracles de la
Sainte Vierge*.[1] Becker made it clear that Berceo's number XXV was not
in Thott 128. As recently as 1971 Brian Dutton studied the *Milagros*
against the background of the Copenhagen manuscript, transcending
Becker's study in details and readings of the texts, but he was unable
to do more, with respect to Number XXV, than surmise that it was
drawn by Berceo from a written source.[2] His supposition, like that of
Becker and of Solalinde,[3] is based upon the last two lines of quatrain
743 (907) ("el miráclo nuevo fuertment lo recabdaron, con los otros
miraclos en libro lo echaron") and the last half of the last line in 745
(909) ("como diz la cartiella").[4] But before one can accept this as
incontrovertible evidence of a written source, notwithstanding *cartiella*
and *libro*, some arguments to the contrary should be explored. Indeed,

Solalinde, before he had finished the preliminary essay for his edition of the *Milagros*, was obliged to conclude that Berceo might have used an oral source.[5]

So radically does XXV differ from the other twenty-four miracles —in content, in time, setting, tone, narrative technique, and the pattern of presenting miracles—that this miracle may well afford one of the only opportunities we have to study an original creation of Gonzalo de Berceo, or at least a creation not based upon a written source which would have confined the poet as he was confined when he Hispanified and versified the twenty-four Latin miracles. XXV may indeed be the "miraclo nuevo" Berceo labeled it.

Any scholar familiar with folk miracles will detect, if he studies XXV, elements of popular origin, and even of popular origin at the earliest stage of its development, when rough edges are present, when unnecessary, confusing, and unimportant details are included, much of which, had the miracle been rewritten or retold, would have been deleted in the interest of clarity and over-all narrative effect. The miracle as Berceo relates it has the ring of a report, or an account just as it happened, and not as generations of raconteurs would have altered it with an eye to improvement. The possibility that the poet was present when the events took place, or that he visited the scene of the miracle shortly after it had occurred, or had a verbal report soon after the occurrence, is a strong possibility. If any of this supposition is true, the originality of the miracle may reveal a great deal about Berceo's story-telling art that cannot be found in his handling and presentation of the known written sources.

Originality, of course, is not necessarily concomitant with narrative art. Nor is a story excellent simply because it stems from the folk. Milagro XXV as a narrative is inferior in structure to many of the other *milagros*. The reason probably lies in the antiquity of the others, for all of these were "old miracles" in that they had been written long before Berceo saw them, had been recast, perhaps again and again, had been culled of the irrelevant, and had been honed to an almost stark simplicity. Moreover, they had been fitted into the pattern characteristic of medieval miracles in which the concern for the didactic, pious message was as great as the artistic presentation. The "old miracles" belonged to the tradition of clerical brief narratives, they were considered literary by those who wrote them, and they were what people expected to hear or read. The pattern they followed was so well established that Berceo could not stray far from it as he composed his "new miracle."

Inferior to the other miracles or not, Number XXV reveals innovations on the part of the poet unlike anything he included in the twenty-four he drew from the Latin. One has the impression that Berceo, while not constrained by the strictures imposed by the plots and presentations of the written Latin miracles, was, though in a different way, guided by and even constrained by an oral account which caused some of the divergencies. He found that, free of the Latin versions, he could permit himself a certain kind of free rein and could pour into the account a great deal of the contemporary scene, much of local customs, and what appear to be personal observations with an eye to realism and fact; but at the same time this very freedom led to digressions which in some ways actually vitiated the cogency of the narrative.

The thirteenth century was an age of miracles and of the gathering and anthologizing of miracles, both in Latin and in the vernaculars. New miracles were actively sought and quickly committed to writing. Alfonso X, most probably while Berceo still lived, was producing the vast repository of Mary-miracles he named the *Cantigas de Santa Maria*.[6] The Learned King himself makes it clear that contemporary or "new miracles" greatly interested him and that he actually traveled on occasion to the scenes of miracles and at times even received gifts that were miraculous in origin.[7] Quite probably Alfonso employed people whose duty it was to gather and assemble contemporary miracles, since it is doubtful that he could have taken the time to ferret out the many which are unique in the *Cantigas*.[8] What more natural, then, than that Berceo would seize upon a miracle someone told him about or which he was lucky enough to have encountered among the rural folk to whom he ministered? If this is the case, if Miracle XXV was plucked by Berceo from the current and constantly evolving miracle lore of thirteenth-century Spain, then its breaking away from the age-old pattern is explained, as well as its suspected adherence to current and non-literary patterns.

The formula for most miracles is fairly standard. Early on the author sets the scene and introduces and characterizes the protagonists. The events leading up to the occurrence of the miracle follow a logical sequence. At the end, the virtuous are rewarded, the sinful punished or pardoned in a way that resolves all the elements of the conflict set up at the beginning. Number XXV, it will be seen, diverges from this pattern in unusual ways.

Number XXV begins, as do several others by Berceo, with the statement that he would like to relate another miracle which the Virgin accomplished. But the second quatrain seems to set forth concepts unusual to Berceo, if the poet is actually setting forth something hidden, as it is possible that he is. It has been suggested that 'li' in the second line of this quatrain means 'from her,' that is, 'from the Virgin.' Now 'li' can be so translated, and if it is, then the stanza simply means that one should be warned by the fate of the priest who stole the Virgin's wimple. If indeed this is the meaning of 'li,' then quatrain 704 (968) can be eliminated from the several elements used in my argument. My belief is that 'li' means 'from it,' that is 'from the miracle,' and if it does the argument is strengthened. But with or without this quatrain as evidence as to what I believe, the rest of the argument stands. The doubtful quatrain is as follows:

> Bien creo qe qui esti   miraclo oyere,
> no li querrá toller   la toca qe cubriere:
> ni la querrá por fuerça   toler lo que toviere,
> menbrarli deve esto   de mientre que visquiere. 704 (968)

If *li* means from it, that is, from the miracle, what is it that is hidden? Does Berceo mean that in the miracle there is something to be concealed from the audience? Something into which one must not delve into forcefully? If so, this is unlike the presentation of most miracles, since usually all that they contain ought to be clearly understood.

The third quatrain, without the possibility of denial, sets the miracle apart from the norm: the locale and the time are both Berceo's, and only in number XXV is this the case.

> En el tiempo del Rey   de la buena ventura,
> don Ferrando por nomne,   sennor d'Estremadura,
> nieto del rey Alfonso,   cuerpo de grand mesura,
> contó esti miraclo   de mui grand apostura. 705 (869)

Ferdinand III, grandson of Alfonso VIII, is the king mentioned. He ruled 1217-1252. It will be recalled that most authorities believe that Berceo was born around 1197 or '98 and that he died circa 1246, so

the miracle could quite easily have taken place during his lifetime and
that of King Ferdinand III.[9] Even if the king died before the miracle
occurred, and even though the death date of Berceo is uncertain,
none of this changes in any way the fact that Berceo and Ferdinand
were contemporaries. So when Berceo writes of Ferdinand as a king
"de la buena ventura," even if this phrase means, as some scholars
insist, that he was dead, it does not in any way indicate that the poet
and the king were not contemporaries. The setting of the miracle was
definitely in Berceo's Spain and not later and not earlier. In this Spain
that Berceo knew so well, stanza 706 (870) reveals that two robbers
left León to come to Castile. One was a layman, the other an
ordained priest 707 (871). They reached Çohinos, in the Valladolid
region of Castile, a village in the diocese, however, of León. Dutton
identifies Çohinos as Ceímos de Campos, Valladolid.[10]

> Movieronse ladrones   de parte de León
> de essa bispalía.   de essa regïón,
> unieron a Castiella   por su gran confusión,
> guïólos el dïablo   que es un mal guón. 706 (870)
> El uno era lego   en duro punto nado,
> el otro era clérigo   del bispo ordenado;
> llegaron en Çohinos,   guïólos el Peccado,
> el qe guió a Judas   fazer el mal mercado. 707 (872)

In the outskirts of the village stood a church dedicated to Our
Lady, 708 (872), and near it the cell of an anchoress. Now the priest-
thief from the outset is seen as a sinner of the worst ilk with an
unusual kind of wickedness. He differs from other clerical sinners in
the *Milagros* because he commits premeditated felony and breaks one
of the commandments, which later none of the clerical sinners in
Berceo's other miracles does. Priests and nuns in the *Milagros* are led
into sin by the devil or are caught off guard by lust or pride or some
other human frailty.[11] Some scholars even level the accusation at
Berceo that he allowed himself frequently and quite noticeably to
minimize the clerical vices and sins found in the Latin collection he
utilized.[12] In Miracle XXV this is certainly not the case. The priest-
thief is all bad. He breaks the eighth commandment, he had disgraced
his habit, has renounced his vows, or if he has not actually renounced
them, he sins in a more terrible way as a false priest. It is true that
Berceo writes that these robbers were led astray by the very devil

who led Judas to "fazer el mal mercado," a significant comparison, but even so the poet makes it very plain that thievery is the cleric's chosen profession. He has no virtue whatever, and in accordance with the format of miracles, he should receive the worst of punishments.

The thieves, having broken into the cell of the anchoress, sniff about looking for valuables, and with shovels dig here and there while the nun hides (709 [873]). They find little, for the anchoress has nothing except a very valuable piece of cloth. Berceo's only reason for mentioning this cloth would seem to be that the holy woman actually owned it, and he considered it as a detail in the story. It has no relevance to the account, and in fact, might even have confused the reader or hearer, since later another piece of valuable cloth, one associated with the image of the Virgin, is of great relevance.

Once the thieves had gathered up what the anchoress's cell contained, they turned to the locked church. Berceo skillfully paints their iniquity:

> Lo qe fue en la ciella   fue todo abarrido,
> malamente maneado,   en un saco metido;
> assaz era el lego   omne de mal sentido,
> mas de peor el clérigo   que más avié leído. 711 (875)

The robbers pry open the door of the church with shovels and ransack it. The details given in 714 (878) enable the poet to invoke outrage in the minds of his audience:

> Despoiaron las sabanas   que cubrien el altar
> libros e vestimentas   con que solien cantar:
> fue mal desvaratado   el precioso lugar,
> do solien pecadores   al Criador rogar.

Then they look greedily at the image of Our Lady with her Child and see the fine *toca* it wears. And, of course, the evil cleric, aware of the worth of sacred vestments, strips the headress from the image (717 [881]). It is a fine touch of characterization on Berceo's part to fix upon and develop the sacrilege and thereby make the cleric even more detestable. He who should have respected holy things, given his calling and his training, was the one to commit the profanation rather than the secular robber. He is the only person in the *Milagros*, clerical or lay, who desecrates an image of the Virgin. People familiar with the pattern of miracles would have expected him to be consumed by fire from heaven or suffer some other terrible fate.

The miracle occurs when the stolen *toca* or wimple wraps itself around the priest-thief's hand thus marking him as the culprit who removed it from the image [719 (883)]. Miraculous, too, is the strange witlessness that befell both robbers so that they were lost in the church and wandered about blindly.

Stanza 886 might lead some to believe that Berceo followed a written source, but reflection should allow for another supposition. He was well-educated and he knew church history and saintly legend. The reference to Theodora and Pope Clement need not imply that he did more than provide a comparison drawn from his store of knowledge.[13]

Andavan tanteando   de rencón en rencón,
como fazié Sinsinnio   el celoso varón,
marido de Teodora,   mugier de gran canción,
la qe por Clemens Papa   priso religïón. 722 (886)

The degree of detailed description in stanza 723 (887) is noteworthy, and is not common in the Latin miracles, although Berceo in some of the twenty-four he Hispanified often went far beyond the source and volunteered many details.

Los locos malastrugos,   de Dios desemparados
andavan como beudos,   todos descalavrados,
oras davan de rostros,   oras de los costados,
de ir en romería,   estavan mal guisados.

The depiction of the capture of the thieves and the rough handling they received after the anchoress had summoned help may reflect Berceo's personal witnessing of their capture or of similar arrests, and of the raw and ugly mob reaction to the desecration of a shrine.

Fueron luego venidos   gran turma de peones,
entraron en la glesia,   trovaron los ladrones;
manentráronlos luego   como vinién fellones,
darlis grandes feridas   con mui grandes bastones.

Dávanlis grandes palos   e grandes carrelladas,

coces muchas sovejo   e muchas palancadas;
levavan por los cuerpos   tantas de las granadas
qe todas las menudas   lis eran oblidadas. 725-26 (889-90)

The robbers were forced to confess—727 (891)—and to explain
how the Virgin had captured them. In 728 (892) and 729 (893) we
read of their sentencing, or at least of the sentence of death imposed
upon the secular thief: "sobre'l lego cativo prisieron mal consejo: /
alzáronlo de tierra con un duro vencejo."

The passages in quatrains 730-31 (894-95) might, at first glance,
seem to overburden or even to damage the plot's structure, since the
story does not need this incident. However, longer consideration may
lead to the conclusion that incidents like it were common in miracle
lore. Even had Berceo cared to rewrite or improve the miracle, he
might well have allowed it to remain.

Un calonge devoto   omne de sancta vida,
qe tenié so amor   en Dios bien encendida,
quando vío la toca   con la mano cosida,
dizié qe tal justicia   nunqua non fue oida.

Quiso el omne bono   de la toca travar,
en vez de la Gloriosa   el su velo besar,
mas al christiano bono   quísolo Dios onrrar,
despegóse la toca   adiesso del pulgar.[14]

After this digression from the mainstream of the plot, Berceo verily
breaks the miracle pattern one would expect him to follow. The
priest-thief's fate was not as simple to resolve as the secular thief's.
He had to be judged only in his own diocese. For nine whole
quatrains ([735-42 [899-906]) we read of clerical law and wonder why
Berceo gave so much space to it. He did nothing like this in any other
miracle, nor did his sources for the other miracles. Was he breaking
the pattern of miracle narration because he was reporting *all* of the
events surrounding the miracle, even when those events did not
contribute to the miracle's plot? The priest-thief should, according to
the formula of miracle lore, have been put to death or killed by divine
intervention, since he was a far greater sinner than his secular
partner. It may be that the entire sequence of the legal rights of the
criminal was included by the poet because he actually considered it as
part of what happened in the aftermath of the miracle. Had he

rewritten the miracle later, I believe that he would have omitted
these nine quatrains.[15]

Since the legal sequence may support the argument that Berceo
felt that he had to report all the facts surrounding the miracle, some
more detailed reference to these passages is needed.

The Leonese bishop of the diocese in which the profanation had
taken place came to Çohinos ("Dios lo quiso guiar") and found that he
had to deal with the problem (732a [896a]). He therefore took the bad
priest to his headquarters in the city of Leon. Once in the city of
Leon, the bishop states that he cannot judge the priest, having
learned that he is from another diocese, that of Avila.

> "Amigos,—dize el bispo,   —esto es aguisado,
> non es nuestro el clerigo,   nin de nuestro bispado:
> por nos non es derecho   que sea condenado:
> iudguelo su obispo,   su mercet, su peccado.
>
> Por del obispo de Avila   se es él clamado,
> clamóse por su clerigo   e de su obispado:
> iudgar ageno clerigo   por ley es vedado,
> podria yo por ello   despues ser reptado." 740-41 (904-05)

The bishop in León, before he sends the criminal to the bishop in
Avila, though he can actually do nothing to him, nonetheless sent
him off with a threat, one incidentally that he could hardly have
carried out, given the rights of priests already discussed. Perhaps the
bishop uttered the threat to make his people see that he did not
condone the crimes the man had committed, and if he did utter them,
then Berceo recorded them, again because he either heard the words
or was told what the bishop had said.

> Mas pongo tal sentencia   qe se açotado,
> qe si trovado fuere   en todo est bispado,
> sea luego pendudo,   en un árbol colgado;
> el qui lo perdonare   sea descomulgado. 742 (906)

The last, and one of the most striking violations of the miracle
pattern is the ending of the story. It is what modern fiction writers
refer to as a "walk-away ending," for it certainly does not resolve the
conflict and leaves the priest-thief's fate a mystery. Such an ending is
not to be found elsewhere in Berceo, and he must have so written it
because he did not know the fate of the thief and therefore could do
no more than offer a surmise about it.

Nunqua más lo veyeron   desqe lo envïaron,
en todo el bispado   nunqua lo testiguaron;
el miráculo nuevo   fuertment lo recabdaron,
con los otros miraclos   en libro lo echaron. 743 (907)

And how convincing, as to a written source, are the last two
lines? *Who* gathered up the new miracle and *who* put it in a book? In
what book? With *what* other miracles? Could not Berceo be talking
about his *own* book, his *Milagros de Nuestra Señora*? Might not he have
preferred to say, "they put it in a book," rather than "I put it in a
book?" Or could "they" not have taken the miracle which Berceo
versified and have put it in a book? How many scholars today have
said "they" published my article in such-and-such a journal?

As to the other reference to written form, "*como diz la cartiella,*"
how convincing is it? This reference does not prove that Berceo used
a written source, because we do not know to what *cartiella* refers.

Los malos qe vinieron   a fontar la tu ciella,
bien los tovisti presos   dentro en tu capiella;
al bon omne qe quiso   vesar la tu toquiella,
bien suelta gela disti,   como diz la cartiella. 745 (909)

When the poet mentions *cartiella*, he may refer to the miracle he
himself wrote. Or *cartiella* need not signify some written source
Berceo might have used. The word might even mean, in the way
Berceo used it, something like "proverb" or "saying," making quatrain
909 mean "You gave it to him, as the saying (the proverb) goes."

Miracle XXV is indeed a "new miracle" and even a roughhewn
miracle, as regarded from the technical narrative point of view. It
may even be regarded as a kind of poetic "first draft," composed on
the very scene of the miracle and at the very time it occurred, or soon
thereafter. All that Berceo saw or head about it he included in the
poem. Probably he never rewrote it or polished it. What he produced
is a story unhampered by the strictures of a *written* source, but
nonetheless conversely bound by an *oral* source which in its own and
yet different way was also binding, even though it permitted more
originality. Its innovations as well as its imperfections in narrative
technique and structure may reveal more of Berceo's artistry, excellent or poor, as a raconteur, than anything else he wrote.

Notes

* Reprinted from *Symposium*, 24 (1975), 361-70.

[1] Richard Becker, *Gonzalo de Berceo's* Milagros *und ihre Grundlagen*, Strasburg, 1910.

[2] Brian Dutton, *Obras Completas, II: Los milagros de Nuestra Señora*, London: Tamesis, 1971.

[3] Antonio G. Solalinde, *Milagros de Nuestra Señora* (Madrid, 1958).

[4] All quotations from the *Milagros* are taken from Dutton's edition.

[5] Solalinde, page xxiii, alludes to an oral source.

[6] Walter Mettmann, *Alfonso X, O Sábio, Cantigas de Santa Maria*, 4 vols., Coimbra, 1959-72.

[7] In *Cantiga* 18, for example, Alfonso goes to the church which contains two pieces of silk woven miraculously by silkworms and receives one as a gift from which is made a robe for the Virgin's image in the royal chapel.

[8] See my "A Medieval Folklorist," *Folklore Studies in Honor of Arthur Palmer Hudson* in *North Carolina Folklore* (Chapel Hill: 1965), pp. 20-23, also in this volume.

[9] Dutton, p. 209.

[10] Dutton, p. 209.

[11] In the *Milagros* as numbered, the sinners are ecclesiastics: I pride and defiance; II fornication; III stubbornness and impatience; VII fornication; IX impatience; X avarice and covetousness, XII vile speech; XIV monks sinned "grave sins"; XV cleric leaves order to marry; XX drunkenness and fornication; XXI abbess impregnated; XXV profanation and robbery.

[12] Solalinde, p. xxvi.

[13] Dutton, p. 209 publishes a Latin text of the story of Sisannio and Teodora and her conversion by Clement.

[14] The motif is common enough, ranging from the case in which only the hero chosen by God can perform the task (Arthur and the Sword Excalibur to Berceo's "bon omne.")

[15] Juan Ruiz, Archpriest of Hita (*Libro de Buen Amor*, quatrains 1144-50) also treats the rights of priests to be sentenced by their own bishops, but in a sequence in which such rights had a reason for being included.

A Re-Examination of
Don Juan Manuel's
Narrative Techniques:
"La mujer brava"*

HE BEST DEFINITIONS of what a short story should be more or less center upon a few salient requirements. Poe demanded singleness of effect, unity, and brevity. Don Juan Manuel generally, perhaps always, fulfills these needs. Almost all authorities include Poe's requirements and stress additionally the development of character and setting the plot. Again Don Juan Manuel's stories fulfill these qualifications, or so I shall try to prove it. A good short story has a conflict which the protagonist must resolve in some way. The protagonist, whether struggling with the forces of nature or society or with an individual opponent, at times gains the advantage; at other times he may have to yield to his foe. A good writer, by careful foreshadowing, gives his reader clues or perhaps only hints and subtle suggestions to help him to anticipate the outcome. He may even flatter the reader by planting suggestions so subtly that the reader believes he has, working with no assistance at all, guessed what will happen. But in the process of such hinting, suggesting, and guessing, the author must keep the reader unsure by the creation and even the maintainance of suspense. Finally, the author brings his reader to the decisive moment when suspense ends, and the protagonist wins his conflict—in other words, the climax of the plot is reached. Occasionally, in order to avoid too hasty an ending after the

climax, the author tapers the reader off with a last minute subplot which complements the resolution or outcome. Occasionally the resolution suggests what will happen in the lives of the characters long after the story ends. The old-fashioned "and they all lived happily ever afterward" is a form of this last, of course.

Let me state at the outset that all Don Juan Manuel's *exemplos* are short stories as we know this form of brief narrative today. His sources were many: fables, folktales, pious *exempla*, personal observations, in short, a large variety of brief narrative material. However, this does not mean necessarily that a fable as presented by Don Juan Manuel is the same thing as the Aesopian fable he started with. As María Rosa Lida, Menéndez y Pelayo and, quite recently, José Manuel Blecua point out, Don Juan Manuel could take the simplest brief narrative with the poorest structure, scene, plot and characters, and turn it into a well-rounded, well motivated, well structured, well-charactered, so to speak, and well-backgrounded masterpiece.[1]

This will be an attempt to examine carefully and in some detail the techniques employed by this author who, most of us believe, was the best Spanish short story writer before Cervantes. In essence I shall be redefining what others have said in a general way about the techniques which have been ascribed to Don Juan Manuel. Also, I believe that I can bring into new focus and illuminate the remarkable powers of this author that make him a spinner of tales far in advance of his times. In other words, I shall try to prove by illustration and to some extent by explication, not only *that* he was as good as the critics say he was, but also *why* he was that good.

Space will permit me to utilize only one story, "De lo que conteçio a un mançebo que casó con una mujer muy fuerte et muy brava," which is Number XXXV in *El Conde Lucanor*.[2] Most of the other fifty stories could have been used as the focal point of such a study as this. I chose "La mujer brava" for several reasons: it has a universally known plot; it is one of the best of the fifty-one stories; and it is so well-remembered that little need be said to revive it in most readers' minds. Then, too, it is not complex, it has no deep hidden meanings or existentialist undertones, and a critical interpretation of it such as this is feasible. Also it is a much studied story—except along the lines of narrative technique. Scholars have classified its motifs, and each of these appears in Stith Thompson's *Motif-Index*; comparative studies have been made by Knust and others; Chauvin links it with oriental traditions, and Daniel Devoto in a remarkably definitive bibliography has listed nearly all that has been written about it.[3] So in "La mujer brava" we have a straightforward, delightful little tale that can be summarized in a few lines. You will recall that a young Moor married a perfect shrew of a girl and gained ascendancy over her by killing three animals because they did not obey him and bring him water with which to wash his hands. This convinced the bride that he was insane and would kill her, too, if she did not obey him.

This story today has less to charm the feminine mind than it might have had in the fourteenth century when it was the style for women to play a submissive role. The few women who could read, and quite possibly the ones who could not and heard the story read aloud, believed that women should obey men.[4] Quite probably they resented women like the *mujer brava* who had been getting by with deeds no well-brought up woman should be allowed to get by with. We expect, however, that Don Juan Manuel was writing primarily for men anyway and did not let feminine opinion concern him much. In other stories he makes it plain that women knew that they were destined to eat humble pie in the divine scheme of things. In one story a lady would say a horse was a cow if her husband said so (Number XXVII). In another a lady pierced her own eye with a needle because her husband had lost his eye in a battle (Number XLIII).

The excellent structuring and superior narrative technique displayed in "La mujer brava" can now be examined in detail.

From the beginning Don Juan Manuel personalizes this story, in the same way he personalizes all the other stories. We read that a member of Count Lucanor's own ménage contemplated marrying a rich woman who had one terrible fault: she was a fierce and strong woman, a perfect shrew. Patronio, Count Lucanor's adviser, immediately engages the reader, as we all know, by confiding that he has knowledge of a similar case and how it was solved. The reader feels that he is about to read a factual account, one that has taken place in his own time, one that is not in some exotic place or era. Even if the reader recognizes this as a literary device, he is attracted by it. Since he quite probably has read the thirty-four proceeding tales, he expects a lesson, but the *mujer brava* is a contemporary problem and the lesson will quite probably be pertinent. Rapport is established by the narrator.

Another attraction, and a wise inclusion by Don Juan Manuel, is the background of the protagonist in Patronio's story. He is a young Moor. Now Moors in Don Juan Manuel's fourteenth-century Spain were developing more and more into attractive literary personages, exotic in dress and customs, romantic, intriguing, sympathetic.[5] Most Spaniards had seen Moors, from the brilliantly garbed emissaries sent into Castile by the kings of Granada to the more humble mudéjar artisans and farmers. There is, I think, something analogous here to the interest our own eighteenth- and nineteenth-century Americans had in the Indian nations. The Moor in Don Juan Manuel's time, like the Mohicans described by James Fenimore Cooper, had ceased to be implacable enemies and had become sympathetic literary figures. This syndrome had occurred sporadically long before the fourteenth century, indeed as early as the eleventh. One recalls that friendly and impressive Abengalbón who sheltered the Cid's daughter after the afrenta de Corpes. Soon the romancero would treat the Moor as a major literary figure, and not two centuries after Don Juan Manuel's time the literary Moor would reach his apogee in the Abencerraje.

The characterization of the Moor in "La mujer brava," who remains nameless throughout the story, is handled with greater depth than at first meets the eye. Graphically and with no more than a few firm strokes, made apparent through his thoughts and actions, this Moore's character emerges. The reader, with nothing else to work with, since the author offers nothing really descriptive, must flesh out this protagonist. He must draw upon his own observation of Moors or upon what he has read or heard about them. Requiring the reader to create his own idea of a character is, of course, recognized today as an effective narrative technique. The reader creates along with the author and he is flattered and pleased with the result. Modern writers admit that they attempt to have their readers visualize their protagonists. Once this has been done, the reader can make the literary figure move, speak, act and look like what the reader's own tastes demand.

The suggestions given by the author, as the young Moor plans his future, establish quick rapport with the reader. The author does not say that this young Moslem is up-and-coming, decent, clever (in that he sees a solution to his poverty), ambitious, and willing to take risks to improve his status: instead the young man's words and actions reveal all these qualities. The Moor himself establishes the conflict. His personality grows in magnitude as he acts. He respectfully refuses to accept the advice of his father, demonstrating a sense of independence and daring not expected in a member of a culture which highly esteemed parental authority. The reader assesses this Moor: really he is a remarkable young man; he is innovative, independent and wise beyond his years; moreover, he is all man and he is willing to try to tame an uppity and evidently ferocious young woman, a type who was anathema to every sensible male in the Peninsula, Mohammedan and Christian alike.

Don Juan, having made his reader establish rapport with such an attractive protagonist, begins to sow some seeds of suspense in the reader's mind. Can this young man really succeed? No one before has dared to sue for the Amazon's hand; the young man's father sees little hope of success; and most telling of all, the girl's own father, who should know her better than anyone, and who is most definitely anxious to marry her off, tells the young man's father: "—Par Dios, amigo, si yo tal cosa fiziesse servos ya muy falso amigo, ca vós avedes muy bien fijo, et ternía que fazía muy grand maldat si yo consintiesse su mal nin su muerte; et so çierto que, si con mi fija casase, que no sería muerto o le valdría más la muerte que la vida" (Blecua, p. 189).

Not a word of description, and yet the author imparts a strong characterization of the *mujer brava*. She is lethal by her own father's admission. Then the reader suddenly catches a glimpse of the father's character. He has a very tragic flaw and he must be unusual, too, in a way quite different from his daughter and her prospective groom. He is afraid of a woman! In a culture more male-oriented than even in Christian Spain, in a land where women lived in harems and wore veils, here was a father afraid of his own daughter!

Consider how Don Juan Manuel with almost no description, and only through impression and suggestion, has created three definite characters—not many-faceted characters, admittedly, but firmly drawn and with definite identities. As to background and atmosphere, the author with equal brevity and simplicity and wisdom has placed his characters in a setting which needed no explanation. After all, Moorish mores to Don Juan Manuel's contemporaries were facts of life. Kept apart, for the most part, from Christian Spain by the borders of their kingdom, they were nevertheless familiar figures. Spaniards knew Moorish customs, and the reader of this story would have felt put-upon to have such matters explained to him. Don Juan, therefore, flatters his reader's knowledge. The reader, may, without having it explained, savor the suspense in the very situation developing when

the bride and groom first see one another. Moors, who were betrothed, the reader will tell himself, seldom met until the day of the
wedding ceremony, and really not until after the ceremony, since both
bride and groom pledged their vows in separate places.[6] What will
happen, the reader wonders in suspense, when the two definitely
strong and opposing personalities confront one another for the first
time?

Don Juan Manuel's readers would not have wondered, as today's
readers may, as to how the *mujer brava* allowed herself to be married.
We are not told, as Shakespeare told his audience, that Kate, the
shrewish elder daughter, married so that her younger sister could
marry. But the people who read *El Conde Lucanor* would have known
that a Mohammedan woman unmarried was a woman disgraced. And
readers might well have surmised that the *mujer brava* wanted to escape
a perfect hell of a home life to answer the powerful challenge of having
a husband of her own to browbeat, just as she had browbeaten her
father. They would see that she wanted her own roost to rule. Any
puzzlement, then, about the reasons for her agreeing to marry is
resolvable.

Then Don Juan Manuel sets a truly suspenseful stage and creates a
remarkably tense situation. The conflict approaches its climax. The
two opposing wills are brought face to face for the first time. The
entire lives of two people are at stake. Suspense increases as the in-
laws depart in great misgiving, "cuidando que otro día fallarían el novio
muerto o muy maltrecho."[7]

And yet, even in a suspenseful situation, even when blood will
probably flow and death may result, Don Juan Manuel cleverly instills
into his story just the proper proportion of the humorous to titillate
his reader's wit and keep him from taking the story too seriously.

The sequence in the bridal chamber, like the best of typical
folktales, is divided into three adventures, and each task the young
husband has set himself to accomplish increases in magnitude. The
sense of progression is well-sustained. The reader, with the protagonist, encounters the first test, and shocked by its unexpected violence, is
eager to see what the next test will be, and the next. One can imagine
his betting with himself that the second and third test will be more
shocking than the first, and he is not to be disappointed.

Don Juan, in having the Moor kill the animals, takes cognizance
again of his contemporaries' knowledge of Moorish tastes and beliefs,

and he uses this to build a well-structured ascent to the story's climax. The first animal to die, because it does not bring water for his hands, is a dog. There is probably even an element of humor in this event since all Don Juan's readers surely knew Islam's scorn for the canine race. Is the young man faltering? Is he of poorer wit than the reader has been led to believe? Does he think a self-respecting Moorish damsel will be moved by the death of a mere dog? Why the Koran and Holy Scripture, too, mention no dogs except the curs that licked Lazarus' sores and devoured a certain shrew named Jezebel. A dog killed indeed! Nor is the damsel apparently impressed. The young husband must try again.

The second step makes more sense. The bride will be more disturbed by it. Cats in those days were altogether a different matter from dogs, even as they are today in Islam. The Prophet Mohammed himself revered cats and took his beloved tabby Muezza to paradise with him when he ascended. Royalty from Persia to India and from Cairo to Cordova thought highly of cats. The murder of the cat strengthens further the unusual qualities of the young Moor. In killing the cat he again breaks with tradition, probably finding it heartrending and even traumatic to kill this animal. Even his refusal to follow his father's advice about marrying such a fierce woman had been less difficult for him.

Even so, though the groom has defied almost mythic and racial traditions and transcended his own feelings of revulsion, and even though the bride must have been sufficiently shaken, she must not have showed serious signs of weakening. Why else would the groom have undertaken the third task, that of slaying his only horse? At this the bride, as well as all of Don Juan Manuel's readers, must have been stunned. All were familiar with a Moor's reverence for the horse above all things, keeping it inside his house or tent, as the story itself tells us, "El desque ovo catado a cada parte, et vio un su cavallo que estava en la casa." Indeed Christians in fourteenth century Spain, and for centuries earlier, had esteemed their horses, too.[8] Consider the Cid's Babieca. And all this is explicit in the very word in Spanish for gentleman or knight: *caballero*, and, of course, in the French *chevalier*.

No wonder the bride at last has to admit that her husband is a raving homicidal maniac and had best be humored. Don Juan Manuel catches her graphically in her terror and makes his readers conceive the depth of her fears, for she believed of a certainty that "esto ya non

se fazía por juego, et ovo tan gran miedo, que non sabía si era muerta o
biva" (Blecua, p. 191).

The suspense built up as the murder of animals progresses from
the worthless to the most valuable, then, is as notable and as well
developed as it could have been by any writer. The reader, of course,
almost from the outset, and certainly with the death of the dog, falls
instinctively into the folkloristic cadences of the three-fold sequence.
One murder means little, two not much, three fulfills the need for
balance. And yet, even as the author lays the pattern for the intensifi-
cation of suspense, he conversely, really inversely, points out to the
reader what is to happen without explicitly telling him what will. In so
doing he flatters the reader's intellect and powers of deduction, always
a good narrative hook. "I'll bet such and such will happen," the reader
tells himself, and when it does happen is pleased with himself. It is an
age-old as well as an ultra-modern psychological technique.

Suspense, also, as to the shrewish wife's character is injected, but
again the same deductions on the reader's part are called into play. Will
the bride break under her husband's sustained acts of violence? The
reader thinks she will, but he is not quite certain. She just might not.
He remembers how ferocious she has been in that she shows no signs
of weakness at the sight of the death of either the dog or the cat,
although the second death should have shaken her somewhat.

When the bride finally breaks, which has been expected all along,
the reader is flattered; he finds in her surrender a pleasant and warm
sense of masculine satisfaction. He sees settled the conflict between
tradition and the breaking of tradition. Moreover, the conflict between
the one man and the one woman stands for the conflict between all
men and all women which simply must be resolved in the male's favor.
Don Juan Manuel has succeeded fully both in the area of the *dulce* and
the *utile*. Man is supreme, not woman. How pleased the fourteenth-
century reader must have been! All wives and sweethearts had best
take heed. The bride abjectly brings water for him and he washes his
hands.

At this juncture the reader has a right to believe that he has
received resolution of the conflict, but the author seems to deny this.
There are yet other aspects of suspense to be savored for full
enjoyment. Actually, two more climaxes are to be experienced.

What will happen at bedtime, when the husband must lay aside the
sword with which he killed the animals? Can a would-be lover, hopeful

of a successful consummation of his marriage, continue to act toward his bride like a murderous maniac? Surely he must show tenderness at this important juncture. And what if the bride should guilefully decide to be complacent and willing to consummate the marriage? Spanish and Moorish literatures abound in books about the helplessness of man, once woman sets out to enmesh him in the oldest and most successful of traps.[9] Yes, there is cause for new suspense. Much is implied. Just maybe—but surely the author wouldn't really permit it— just maybe the fierce woman might turn the ultimate dominance of the male to her own advantage.

As always when such an intimate matter as sexual union must be discussed, Don Juan Manuel is succinct and proper. He leads quickly through a threefold set of progressions. The bride brings water for his hands, as we have seen. He demands to be served food. She serves it. She is utterly crushed: "Assi passó el fecho entrellos aquella noche, que nunca ella fabló, mas fazía lo quel mandava." And then in an implied third sequence they must have gone to bed, and the groom must have maintained his command of the situation. We read a stark little passage in which Don Juan Manuel ties up the loose ends and ends suspense. "Desque ovieron dormido una pieça," he states, using the same euphemism some use today, though I admit such propriety is rare indeed in modern literature. Yes, after they had "slept" a little, the groom issues still more orders to his bride, revealing that he has never for a moment relinquished the saddle into which he had vaulted. He orders her to let him sleep late the next morning, allowing no one to disturb his sleep, lest dire results occur.

And so the conflict between the two well-matched opponents is at last resolved and on a humorous note—for every one but the bride, that is. The next morning, when her parents and the groom's come in apprehension to gather up what might remain of him, the bride frantically warns them to be quiet lest her spouse arise from his bed and—but hear her exact words which are more expressive than any description. "Callad, sinon todos, también vos commo yo, todos somos muertos!"

The story of the *mujer brava* and her lord and master ends here to the satisfaction of all readers. How important is the *utile*! But how delectable the *dulce*! Then, by way of tapering off, Don Juan Manuel offers one last drop of honey to the readers' already sweetened cup. One last little conflict is inserted. Lo and behold that weakling, the bride's father, who has earlier gained our scorn, lo and behold that poor fool, this late in his own marital career, will try to get the upper hand of his own wife. "Of course," says the reader, "no wonder the girl was like she was. Shrewishness ran in the family."

The dénouement is foreseen, before the bride's father kills a rooster in a half-hearted effort to over-awe his wife, who laughingly makes it plain that he should have asserted himself earlier in their marriage.

The tale of the *mujer brava*, then, is a well-structured short story, if weighed in the time-hallowed scales employed to assay short stories. It is brief, unified and single in its effect. Poe would have been delighted at the way his rules for short story were followed, so long before he made those rules. Its setting is interesting and logical and makes the reader feel at home; the conflict, well developed and sustained, is resolved satisfactorily; the plot is skillfully constructed with the proper balance of suspense and suggestion, leading to the climax; the resolution is logical, and it even implies that the young Moor will live happily ever afterward, and that maybe his bride will, too, now that she knows her place.

The reader emerges refreshed and satisfied with the story and with his own appreciation of it. He understands perfectly why "don Johan lo tovo por buen exiemplo et fizolo escrevir en este libro et fizo estos viessos que dizen así:

> Si al comienço non muestras quien eres
> Nunca podrás después quando quisieres."

Notes

* Reprinted from *Hispania*, 58 (1975), 45-51.

1 Maria Rosa Lida de Malkiel, "Tres notas sobre Don Juan Manuel," *Romance Philology*, 4 (1950-51), 155-94; Marcelino Menéndez y Pelayo in *Obras completas* (Buenos Aires, 1946), pp. 149-59; José Manuel Blecua, *El Conde Lucanor o Libro de Patronio*, Edición, introducción y notas (Madrid, 1969), pp. 30-31 and 34-35.

2 See the editions of Hermann Knust and Adolph Birch-Hirschfeld (Leipzig, 1900) and that of Blecua cited in note 2.

3 Stith Thompson, *Motif-Index of Folk Literature: New Revised and Enlarged Edition* (Bloomington and Helsinki, 1955-58), motif T251.2; see the Introduction to the edition of Knust and Birch-Hirschfeld cited in note 2; Victor Chauvin, *Bibliographie des ouvrages arabes ou relatifs aux arabes*, II (Liège, 1897), 157; and Daniel Devoto, *Introducción al estudio de Don Juan Manuel y en particular de*

El Conde Lucanor. *Una bibliografía* (Madrid, 1971); Adolphe de Puibusque, "Le Comte Lucanor," *Revue Contemporaine* 2 (1852), 87-113, 218-46, 395-426, which last classifies the kinds of narratives this author sees as present in the work. [AUTH. Devoto's work cited above is no longer "definitive" since the bibliography on the subject is now greatly enlarged.]

4 A good many studies exist which relate Number XXXV to other writers: Ralph S. Boggs, "La mujer mandona de Shakespeare y de Don Juan Manuel," *Hispania*, 10 (1927), 419-22, indicates that Shakespeare was influenced by Don Juan Manuel; but few, in spite of the details cited, accept this today. Manuel Alcalá in "Don Juan Manuel y Shakespeare: Una influencia imposible," *Filosofía y Letras* [México], 10 (1945), 56-67, refutes the idea vigorously; Devoto, *op. cit.*, 426-34, presents numerous other studies.

5 Considerable attention has been given to the "oriental" element in *El Conde Lucanor*. For example, Diego Marín in "El elemento oriental en Don Juan Manuel: Síntesis y revaluación," *Comparative Literature*, 7 (1955), 1-14, sees oriental influence in stories, XX, XXI, XXIV, XXV, XXX, XXXII, XXXV, XLI, XLVI, and XLVII. Devoto believes that in a country like fourteenth-century Spain there was influence but that what there is of such influence Don Juan himself put into his stories, and did not take from the oriental literature of Spain. This seems to me to be a specious argument. Oriental influence, from whatever source or for whatever reason it is present, is still oriental influence.

6 See the remarks of A. González Palencia on Moorish marriage customs in "España musulmana," published in the *Historia de España*, II (Barcelona, 1935), 283, edited by Gallach.

7 This quotation in medieval Spanish, as well as all the others to follow, come from the edition of *El Conde Lucanor* by Blecua.

8 Readers may recall the value of the horse of Fernán González and the magnitude of the curse which the Caballero Cifar suffered in that any horse that he rode soon died. Medieval houses in Christian Spain had quarters for horses under the same roof with their owners. Even today in Santillana del Mar such houses can still be seen.

9 Don Juan Manuel's own uncle, Prince Fadrique, caused to be translated from Arabic the famous *Book of Sindibad* under the title *Libro de los engaños;* tales of deceitful women, wives included, are also to be found in *Calila e Digna*, translated, it is believed, at the behest of Don Juan Manuel's uncle, King Alfonso X, el Sabio; the famous *Disciplina Clericalis*, written ca. 1135 by the converted Aragonese Jew, Pedro Alfonso, contains stories of such women and few books were more read than this last. At least two of its stories, not about deceitful women, however, appear reworked in Don Juan Manuel's inimitable way, in *El Conde Lucanor*; and versions of other Arabic works, the *Thousand Nights and a Night* were also extant.

Don Juan Manuel's
El Conde Lucanor
Contains Fifty-Three Stories
and No Fewer*

 VERY CONTRIBUTION TO the history of literature, however miniscule, is important and should be made available to scholars and students. And, when the contribution is the correction of a mistake made by literary historians and by editors, it is still more relevant.

Spain's greatest medieval writer of brief prose narratives, Don Juan Manuel (1282-1348), included fifty-three different *exempla* in his famous *El Conde Lucanor*. Even so, to this day some of the most respectable histories of literature, as well as some of the best known editions and most detailed studies continue to state that there are fifty-one tales or *exemplos*. Students deserve to know the facts, professors who teach should convey the facts, and scholars who continue to research the book deserve to have the proper information before them, lest they, too, eternalize mistakes.

There is a reason, of course, for the number fifty-one. Don Juan Manuel himself divided that part of *El Conde Lucanor* which is usually read today, that is, the collection of *exemplos*, into fifty-one headings or divisions, each of which is labeled an *exemplo*. However, two of these sections or titles are dual in nature in that each contains two separate stories. It is difficult to understand how any one who reads these two sections, *Exemplos* 27 and 43, can fail to take cognizance of the two titles

104

in each heading, and, as he reads, fail to see that he is reading two separate accounts, each with its own plot, conflict, characters, and setting. Even the title of the two divisions should reveal this. In No. 43, whose title reads "De lo que contesçió al Bien et al Mal e de lo que contesçió a un omne bueno con un loco" [see Reinaldo Ayerbe-Chaux, *Don Juan Manuel: Libro del Conde Lucanor* (Madrid: Clásicos Alhambra, 1983), 383-93] a proper medievalist or expert in comparative literature, or folklorist, should recognize the story about Mal and Bien, since it appears also in *El libro de los gatos*, which is a translation/rendition of Odo of Cheriton's *Fabulae* or *Narrationes*, to name but two of its appearances. Readers ought to realize that the story of Mal and Bien has nothing to do with the second story about a madman and a sane bathhouse keeper.

Nor should a reader experience difficulty in seeing two separate titles, and therefore two separate stories, in number 27, "De lo que contesçió al emperador Fadrique et a don Alvar Fánnez Minaya con sus mugeres" (Ayerbe-Chaux, 263-88). Alvar Fáñez lived in the eleventh century and the Emperor Fadrique, whether he is Frederick Barbarossa (1123-1190), as some would identify him, or Frederick II of Sicily (1194-1250), as would others, lived much later. There is no connection between these characters.

Some will insist that the exact number of stories has no importance to literary studies. This writer argues that the number may be very significant. Don Juan Manuel may have wished to expand or stress the lesson which the two stories teach, so two tales may serve to emphasize the importance of the lesson; moreover, two stories may have been inserted to contrast the two types of characters—the "mythic" personified Good and Evil in one case and the down-to-earth, every day characters in the other narrations. Also Don Juan Manuel may have desired to delineate two psychological approaches to exemplify the problem set up in the two stories.

There is little need to explore all the editions of Don Juan Manuel's masterpiece so as to ascertain which was the first and which the last to fix the erroneous number fifty-one in the scholarly mind. The earlier the date, the more embarrassing it should be to the experts who are guilty of perpetuating it. Nevertheless, it seems worthwile to review briefly a few of the more important and influential studies and editions which continue to repeat the error. The edition of Pascual de Gayangos, found in *Escritores en prosa anteriores al siglo XV* in *BAE*, 51 (in all printings), lists fifty-one titles. Scholars may say as much as they please as to the critical excellence of this old volume, but even so one can be certain that across the years more students have read this version that any other. The famous edition of Hermann Knust, *Don Juan Manuel, El libro de los enxienplos del Conde Lucanor et de Patronio* (Leipzig: Dr. Seele and Co., 1900) also served to establish the error in the minds of more scholarly readers. The two best and most recent editions do not actually list two different tales under titles 27 and 43, but one at least makes it quite clear that each, indeed, contains two separate stories. This latter is that of Reinaldo Ayerbe-Chaux, alluded to above. The other by José Manuel Blecua, *El Conde Lucanor* (Madrid: Castalia, 1969; second edition, 1971; also in his *Obras completas* II, 1983) lists the usual fifty-one without giving any indication that two are present. Translators have varied. James York, *Count Lucanor or, the Fifty Pleasant Stories of Patronio* (Westminster, 1868) even reduced the number of tales to fifty. John E. Keller and L. Clark Keating, *The Book of Count Lucanor and Patronio* (Lexington: University Press of Kentucky, 1977), although they print fifty-one titles, at least indicate by arabic numerals in both 27 and 43 that two separate stories are present. Ian Macpherson in his *Juan Manuel: A Selection* (London: Tamesis Books, 1980) seems still unaware of the two extra stories. Daniel Devoto, *Introducción al estudio de Don Juan Manuel y en particular de El Conde Lucanor, una bibliografía* (Madrid: Editorial Castalia, 1972) is aware of the extra stories, but fails to stress the point, while Reinaldo Ayerbe-Chaux, *El Conde Lucanor, materia tradicional y originalidad creadora* (Madrid: José Porrúa Turanzas, 1975) makes the correct number quite clear, apparently to be overlooked even by such a scholar as Alan Deyermond in his *The Literary History of Spain: The Middle Ages* (New York: Barnes and noble, 1971) and in the more recent *Historia crítica de la literatura española al cuidado de Francisco Rico, I, Edad Media* (Barcelona: Editorial Crítica, 1980).

A brief résumé and treatment of each of the two titles which contain two tales seems profitable. In number 27, whose title appears above, what within the context of the story itself is there to indicate that Don Juan Manuel considered the duality of his account? As he begins to relate the *exemplo*, Patronio immediately confronts this duality, allowing Don Juan Manuel to drive home with emphasis that he is presenting two separate stories. "—Sennor conde Lucanor—dixo Patronio—, porque estos exemplos *son dos* (italics mine) et non vos los padría dezir *en uno*, contarvos he *primero* lo que contesçió al enperador

Fadrique, et *después* contarvos he lo que contesçió a don Alvar Fánnez"
(Ayerbe-Chaux, p. 265). Could Don Juan Manuel have made it any
clearer that he was presenting two entirely different tales? Later in the
same exemplo he wrote: "Mas a Don Alvar Fánnez contesçió el
contrario desto, et por que lo sepades todo commo fue, contar vos he
como contesció" (*Ibid.*, pp. 270-71).

Turning to the second title, number 43, we read, still from Ayerbe-
Chaux's edition (p. 384): "—Sennor conde Lucanor—dixo Patronio—,
esto que vos dezides *no es una* cosa, ante *son dos*, et muy revessadas [that
is to say, 'different'] la una de la otra. Et para que vos podades en esto
obrar commo vos cunple, plazerme ya que sopiéssedes dos cosas que
acaescieron: la una, que contesçió al Bien et al Mal; et la otra, que
contesçió a un omne bueno con un loco."

After the story about Bien and Mal, Don Juan introduces the second
story as follows: "Mas al omne bueno contesçió de otra guisa con el
loco; et fue assí" (*Ibid.*, p. 390).

This should be proof enough, but some will undoubtedly argue,
since each of the two stories in both 27 and 43 is narrated to exemplify
a single moralization, that the two are in reality a single story.
However, any one familiar with the current studies concerning narrative techniques and the elements of narrative structure will immediately realize that each of the four stories contains its own particular
plot, characters and setting.

The first of the pair of *exemplos* in 27 can be summarized as follows:
The Emperor Frederick married a woman whose personality and
character after marriage turned out to be those of a virago. Unable to
endure her contentiousness, Frederick went to the pope, but the
pontiff could not dissolve the marriage; however, he made an enigmatic statement, which was nevertheless clear enough to the emperor.
The pope said that he could not exact a penance until a sin had been
committed. Once home, the emperor tried in vain, as did his house-
hold, to change the empress's hateful ways. Failing in this, one day he
went hunting and took with him a supply of that venom used to
poison arrows. A part of this poison he left at home with the specific
warning to his wife, in the presence of many people, that she was not
to let any of it enter an open wound or sore. But, since his wife was
afflicted with an itch, he left her a portion of a curative ointment. The
perverse lady decided that the curative medication was not as good at
the one her husband had cautioned her not to use, so she rubbed that

into her skin and immediately died. This very complete story, containing the elements of brief narrative usually found in medieval tales, cannot be connected with the other *exemplo* in number 27.

The second, as complete as the first, relates that the aging Alvar Fáñez, companion of Mio Cid, wanted to marry one of the three young daughters of a friend. He tested each damsel by telling her of his drunkenness and violence and of certain unattractive habits which emerged after he had gone to bed. The two older girls refused to marry him, but the youngest accepted him, promised to conceal his secrets, and to endure even blows if he grew drunk and hit her. She stated that she would be honored to be his wife. This is, of course, the old motif of "patient Griselda," and some critics consider it a story in itself. However, Don Juan Manuel, taking actually another motif and adding it to the unhappy account of the marriage of Alvar Fáñez, makes this second motif become a part of the tale of happy marriage. Here the researcher many be tempted to decide that still a third story appears in number 27, and one can argue for this. Actually the incident of Alvar Fáñez, his nephew, and his wife which follows is but a continuation of Alvar Fáñez's married life, and hence can be regarded as part and parcel of number 27. Such a blending of two different stories can be found also in number 48, "De lo que contesçió a un omne bueno con un su fijo que dezía que avía muchos amigos" (Ibid., p. 429), so apparently Don Juan Manuel felt free to blend and shift motifs.

The second incident in number 27 relates that Alvar Fáñez's nephew visited him and his wife, and, seeing how he tried to please her in every way, he accused the old gentleman of being uxorious. To prove that Doña Vascuñana, the name given her by Don Juan Manuel, deserved such treatment, he went riding with her and the nephew, and when he saw mares, he said they were cows, and when he saw cows he said that they were mares. The nephew could not understand until Vascuñana, who was perfectly aware of what the animals really were, nonetheless decided that her husband knew better, and agreed with his designation.

The first of the two *exemplos* in 43 describes how Bien and Mal agreed to farm together. Mal deceived Bien, when they were raising sheep, into accepting the lambs, while Mal took the wool and the milk. When they raised swine, Mal took the piglets, while Bien had to be satisfied with the "wool" and the milk. When turnips were the crop, Mal got the roots, Bien the tops, and when it came to cabbages, Mal took the tops and Bien the roots. At last they married a woman and shared her as a wife. Mal demanded the parts below the waist, and Bien received the parts above it. When a child was engendered, of course, by Mal, Bien, at last cognizant of the wiles practiced upon him, refused to allow the child to suckle his part of the woman until Mal agreed to be subservient to Bien. This is a complete story, found in literature and folklore, and it cannot be regarded in any way as a part of the story which follows under the same title.

In this second story a bathhouse keeper was losing his income because a madman came every day to the baths and beat the customers as they bathed. To prevent this the owner stripped one day, entered the bath with a pot of scalding water and a cudgel, and when the madman arrived, he scalded him and beat him.

The first of these stories, that of Mal and Bien is "mythic" and "psychological," while the story of the madman is "practical" and "contemporary," and each story reveals the ways a somewhat common problem can be solved.

To sum up, there are fifty-three *exemplos* in *El Conde Lucanor*, unless one sees three rather than two in number 27, in which case there are fifty-four. There are certainly not fifty stories nor fifty-one. Therefore, those who edit *El Conde Lucanor*, those who write its history or study it in other ways, and those who translate it should all include the correct number of tales—fifty-three—in their works.

[AUTH. This article treats that part of Don Juan Manuel's *Conde Lucanor* which contains the *exemplos* which Patronio told to Count Lucanor. Recently I learned of still another *exemplo*, the 54th, which appears in Part V of this work (the Blecua edition, pp. 294-96). I am grateful to Dr. Brian J. Powell of the University of Hull for this information. For justification of the use of the round number "fifty," see Carlos Alvar, "Ay cinquenta enxiemplos," *Bulletin Hispanique*, 86 (1984), 136-41.]

Notes

* Reprinted from *Romance Notes*, 24 (1983), 59-64.

Another Look at
Exemplo 48 in
El Conde Lucanor:
"De lo que acontesçio
a uno que provava sus amigos"*

EINALDO AYERBE-CHAUX, our best *donjuanmanuelista*, calls number 48 "este complejísmo ejemplo."[1] Even his absolute superlative falls short, since this *exemplo* really goes beyond the pale of complexity. One is led to wonder how Don Juan concocted such a potpourri so at variance with all the other fifty-three stories in *El Conde Lucanor*. He seems to have been so deeply concerned with friendship, with stories which exemplify it, and with a tangled skein of an involved set of moralizations that he broke with the tenets of *exemplo* writing. Number 48 is unique among the fifty-three (some would say 54) tales. Actually Don Juan used the term *exemplo* loosely as he presented his titles, since in this case apparently he meant "chapters," and not individual and separate stories, because under certain *exemplo* headings two tales appear.[2] The unusual qualities are these: its author drew from at least four separate sources, and possibly from several others, some of which were, I believe, written, some oral, and some drawn from the author's memory of stories he had heard or read; unique, too, is the moralization which he put into the mouth of Patronio in the final preachment, since far more allegory or spiritual

interpretation is present than in his other *exemplos*, and since in it Patronio likens God the Father, Jesus, the Blessed Virgin, and the saints to characters in the *exemplo*, making Number 48 the most pietistic of all stories in *El Conde Lucanor*. In no other *exemplo* does Don Juan Manuel so freely move from borrowed source to borrowed source and from borrowed moralization to borrowed moralization, forcing materials together which had never been brought together before. Only in Number 48 does he lay so determined, although not always effective, a groundwork early in the *exemplo* for a preachment to follow. And only in Number 48 does he insert two completely extraneous and quite unnecessary incidents which, as will be demonstrated later, some scholars regard as unacceptable, absurd, displeasing, and even counterproductive. Perhaps Don Juan deliberately sought to be strikingly innovative, perhaps he was seduced by a subject dear to him, or perhaps he simply overextended his disquisition.

Most of the unusual qualities mentioned above do not belong to the tradition of *exemplo* writing. An *exemplo* by definition is a short piece of fiction free of ambiguity with a single moralization attached in order to teach a lesson. *Exemplos* were expected to be clear and simple in structure and uncluttered and uncomplex in presentation. Spiritual interpretations were often included, but their degree of complexity was generally low, since untutored people were expected to understand the moralistic lesson. Don Juan knew these requirements well, and in the rest of his stories he abided by them fairly closely. Indeed, so conscious of his audience's simplicity was he that in his Introduction he stated that to get the bitter pill of moralization down the public throat, the pill should be coated with the honey of pleasant narration.[3] Therefore, when he broke with the *exemplo*'s norms of composition, he made it possible for scholars in our own times to question and negatively criticize some of his works. Moreover, he seems to have unintentionally laid the groundwork for moralizations radically at variance with his didactic purpose in Number 48, and this may well have vitiated the lesson, as will be seen subsequently, because then, as now, people existed who were ready to pounce upon any serious piece of writing, even Holy Scripture, and read their own meanings into it.

Obviously Don Juan regarded the fictive part of each *exemplo*, with the possible exception of the enigmatic Number 48, as more important than the didactic part. After all, he was a literary man primarily, rather than a preacher. He knew his audience, and knew that many of the stories he presented in *El Conde Lucanor* had originally been turned into *exemplos* by the simple process of attaching moralizations to them.[4] He was confident that most of his public would accept sermonizing as a component of fiction, and indeed, that the erudites in his audience, especially the clergy, would expect it. Even so, he was daringly innovative in Number 48. The sources he blended were well known and even famous in his time. Therefore, he must have realized the risk involved in altering them and in blending them into an unfamiliar and untraditional whole.

A summary of the content of Number 48 will be helpful here to point out how the author deviated from his sources or transformed them, possibly injecting his own original ideas and incidents. A father tells his son to make many friends, and the son reports that he has acquired ten who would die for him. To test these ten a slaughtered pig is put into a sack. The son then goes to each of his friends to beg him to bury the body of a man whom he says he has killed. All refuse, although some offer to pray for him, while others will accompany him to his execution and attend his funeral. The father then sends the son to his own half-friend, who buries the sack in his garden under his cabbages. Later, to test the half-friend a second time, the father tells his son to slap him in the face in public. The half-friend accepts the insult, and his only protest is offered when he tells the son that he has acted improperly and that for no reason will he, the half-friend, uncover the cabbages in his garden.

The father next sends the son to ask help from his own whole-friend, and because people had seen the youth carrying the sack from friend to friend, the young man was accused of a murder which "por aventura" had taken place. the whole-friend, in order to save him from death, orders his own son to claim guilt and sacrifice himself in his place on the gallows. After this, in the lengthy moralization Patronio spiritually spells out the complex lesson.

Probably there are four sources of Number 48, although possibly there may have been more. First Don Juan Manuel follows the events in *Exemplum 1 of the Disciplina Clericalis* of the twelfth-century Aragonese *converso*, Pedro Alfonso, one of the most widely disseminated repositories of *exempla* in the Middle Ages, proven by its more than sixty extant manuscripts distributed from Iceland to Istanbul. The *Disciplina Clericalis*, then, would have been at Don Juan's elbow as he wrote his *Conde Lucanor*; even so, another book, and one contemporary with his own, *Castigos e documentos para bien vivir*, sponsored by his cousin Sancho IV, followed the story in the *Disciplina*, and indeed, this version of the tale by Pedro Alfonso more closely parallels Number 48 than does the *Disciplina*'s story itself, so Don Juan felt the influence of both, *Disciplina* and *Castigos*. Clearly he knew the *Disciplina*, either in the original Latin or in the version produced by Sancho in *Castigos*. The second series of events found in *Exemplum* 2 of the *Disciplina*, which is entirely separate from Pedro Alfonso's first *exemplo*, with a different milieu and different characters, was also followed in a general way by Sancho in *Castigos*.

To me this very possible dependence upon the *Disciplina* and *Castigos* indicates literary influence; however, it cannot be denied that Don Juan might not have allowed the stories in the work of Pedro Alfonso and of Sancho to shape his writing of Number 48. He could have heard the account he offers, which seems to be a blending of the *Disciplina*'s *Exempla* 1 and 2 and reworked by Sancho, in some oral form and could have remembered it as he wrote his version in his *Conde Lucanor*.

Second, as has been pointed out, Don Juan adds the empty offers made by the friends to excuse themselves from helping him at the risk of their own lives. His audience would quickly have identified the general source of those promises, since they appear in all versions of the widely disseminated "Story of the Three Friends."[5] In that well-known *exemplo* a young man has three friends, two of whom he treats honorably, one shabbily. In his dire need the favored, but faithless friends console him with some of the promises mentioned in Number 48 when the son approaches them to ask them for help. A careful comparison of this sequence with the various versions available— *Barlaam e Josafat*, the *Scala Coeli*, and the *Gesta Romanorum*, to name but three—cannot lead to an exact identification, although at a first glance at Number 129 of the *Gesta*, which combines the "Story of the Three Friends" with Number 1 in the *Disciplina* in such a way that the three friends are tested with the pig in the sack, one might be led to believe that identification is possible. Even though Don Juan Manuel might well have used this combination, I am certain that he did not, so closely does he follow the exact details of Pedro Alfonso's story as found in Sancho's version. Probably in the case of the tale of the Three Friends Don Juan did not utilize a written source at all, but instead drew on his memory of a version or versions which he did not have before him as he wrote Number 48. The promises found in all the probable sources are much more detailed and lengthy than the rather brief promises inserted by Don Juan Manuel. This should not surprise scholars, since he habitually condensed incidents and even entire sequences, sometimes going so far as to encapsulate a novelesque piece into an *exemplo*, as he did in Number 19, "De lo que contesçio a los cuervos e los buhos," a longish piece he took from *Calila e Digna* (either from a written source or possibly from an oral one or from his own memory, though the latter supposition seems unlikely, given the amount of detail from the original which parallels the content of Don Juan Manuel's version).[6]

For a third source one suspects again the influence of the *Disciplina Clericalis*, this time for the motif of the self-sacrifice of the whole-friend's son.[7] The story in Pedro Alfonso's work is too complex to outline here, but in it a friend claims guilt for a murder his friend has been accused of committing, and he is prepared to die for it. Since Don Juan followed detail by detail the events of *Exemplum* 1 of *Disciplina Clericalis*, it seems logical to surmise that he also drew from *Exemplum* 2 or from Sancho's retelling of it. The plot is the same in the *Disciplina* and in Number 48 of *El Conde Lucanor*, and, of course, of the story in *Castigos*: a man is falsely accused of murder (under different circumstances) and his friend states that he, and not the accused, is guilty of the crime. One might wonder whether or not Don Juan had in mind Jesus' self-sacrifice to save mankind, which is similar, but which lacks, of course, the elements of accusation of murder found in the *Disciplina* and *Castigos*. At any rate, Jesus' sacrifice, which He endured at His father's command, is brought into Patronio's final preachment.

So far, then, Don Juan was influenced, I believe, by the *Disciplina Clericalis*, directly or through *Castigos*, in one case, probably in two, at least by association, and by the story of the Three Friends and their promises.

Still a fourth source, this one probably written, must now be listed along with a fifth unidentifiable source, unless this latter is not a source at all but rather comes from Don Juan's creative imagination. These are the incidents of the slap and of the sacrifice of the whole-friend's son, and they are important in any criticism of Number 48, since scholars of note have been outraged by them, and three critics, including the present writer, see negative connotations inadvertently created by Don Juan Manuel.

The fourth possible source is a story found in Chapter 39 of *Castigos e documentos para bien vivir*. Consider its content and how it excels Number 48 in several ways.[8] This is the incident of the slapping of the half-friend. Many readers today, although they fully understand the efforts which Don Juan made to reveal the lengths to which a friend would go to prove friendship for another, nevertheless find the incident of the slap counterproductive and poorly motivated. Quite probably some readers in Don Juan's own time entertained the same sentiments. To every reader, whether medieval or modern, the father and the son are callous, cruel, and unreal. However, the son's final reasons for slapping his benefactor in Sancho's version must be regarded as realistic and well-motivated. Here the son was unwilling to slap the half-friend. "Father," he said, "may God not wish that I do such a deed to one who demonstrated so much love for me." The father turned to him and said: "I will curse you and you will have no share in my possessions if you will not do it." The good son took it so hard that he began to grieve and weep, saying that he would prefer to die rather than do such a thing. The father became so enraged that he commanded him to leave his house immediately. And since the guests were beholden to the father, they said: "Son, do what your father orders." Then the son with great shame went up to the good man and slapped him in the face.

In passing it should be noted that here we have one of the many good examples of character development in medieval literature, an element which is often denied by scholars. Character development, we all know, is one of the most important factors in fiction. Books like the *Libro de buen amor*, with its finely drawn Trotaconventos, Endrina, and Don Melón; *Cavallero Zifar* with its remarkable Ribaldo and the even more remarkably developed Grima; and Don Juan Manuel's own shrew wife and her young husband, belie the accusation of the lack of good characters as opposed to stock characters.

If medieval readers, like moderns, reacted negatively to the incident of the slap, like us they would have been outraged even more by the incident of the whole-friend's son's self-sacrifice. Don Juan's desire to create the epitome of boundless friendship is far too contrived here, leading Juan Bautista Avalle-Arce quite rightly to state that the transcendental interpretation by Patronio is the driving force behind the structure of Number 48; but even so I believe this force is not enough to compensate for the downright unreality of this incident.[9] It offended surely the sensitivities of medieval readers as it offends our own, and the argument that people in Don Juan Manuel's times were so inured to the harshness of life that the actions of the father and his son would not seem callous, seems specious: great literature depends upon a set of everlasting human values, as pertinent in ancient and medieval times as they are today. These values are the threads which hold together the fabric of literature and, indeed, of the morality of the human soul. What offends us, as we read this story most probably offended Don Juan's audience as well. It would have offended pagans too, for surely ancient Greeks and Romans, and the ancient peoples of the Far East would have reacted as we do today. No culture can tolerate ingratitude.

But the slap is nothing as compared with the self-sacrifice of the whole friend's son. While we cannot cite critics from Don Juan's times, we have important critics in our own. Ángel Valbuena Prat states that in the sacrifice of the whole-friend's son Don Juan "lleva la abnegación del buen amigo a un grado absurdo y cruel," and goes on to say that "desde el punto de vista humano la historia es inaceptable."[10] Salvatore Battaglia also finds the incident absurd and unviable, and goes so far as to suggest that some one other than Don Juan Manuel had inserted it. He regards the incident as completely counterproductive.[11] Kenneth R. Scholberg is also offended by the self-sacrifice, but he excuses it, writing that "from the human point of view the story is unacceptable. It is only with the inclusions of what the author termed the 'spiritual' interpretation that the *exemplo* becomes meaningful."[12]

This leads us to the possible negative or counterproductive effect engendered by this incident. We all know that a great deal of medieval literature, although not as much as some scholars insist, contained double meanings, sometimes referred to as *sic et non*.[13] This purposeful ambiguity, ascribed especially to the *Libro de buen amor*, hardly seems acceptable in a seriously moralistic work like *El Conde Lucanor*. Possibly the last thing Juan Manuel wanted to do was lead his audience from the path of morality, or, as Juan Ruiz did, offer a dual moral lesson. Therefore, the kind of negative reaction the two extraneous incidents could have produced might have dismayed him greatly. And yet lessons quite at variance to the pietistic one he stressed could have been derived by some fourteenth-century people, if we can accept what our fellow scholars tell us about medieval man's propensity to see all manner of hidden meanings, *double-entendres*, and typological interpretations—especially in Don Juan's contemporary, the Archpriest of Hita. Such remarkably imaginative or, if you prefer, so remarkably perceptive folk as these, would have sniffed out quickly any possibility of the presence of recondite, coded, or otherwise concealed meanings in *El Conde Lucanor*.

If one studies the kinds of lessons offered by Patronio in the other *exemplos*, one soon realizes that most belong to that realm of morality which emphasizes the importance of cleverness, of practical and pragmatic wisdom, of how to avoid being cheated or taken advantage of, of getting ahead of other people. These lessons smack of the wisdom literature of the East, so well represented in the *exemplos* in *Calila e Digna, El libro de los engaños,* and *The Thousand Nights and a Night.* Even though Don Juan rarely teaches deliberate deception, sometimes he does, for example, in *Exemplo* 19 about the crows and the owls, traceable through *Calila e Digna* all the way back to the Hindu *Panchatantra.* Indeed, even Don Juan's story of Don Yllán, the necromancer of Toledo, as does his *exemplo* 35 about the *muger brava,* recommends deception of a special kind. Since most of the *exemplos* in *El Conde Lucanor* are of eastern provenance, might not some of his audience have seen an ambiguous *non* in Number 48 to counterbalance the intended and clear *sic*? If so, then the *exemplo* could be counter-productive, teaching, along with the virtues of friendship, the bitter and practical lesson that it pays to be opportunistic and inconsiderate even of one's friends, willing to exploit them to prove one's point, and callous about the effects of the favors asked of them. The father can be seen to have so exploited both the half-friend and the whole-friend.

Still another negative lesson could possibly have been derived by Don Juan Manuel's readers or by those who heard his stories read aloud, at least by those amazingly sagacious and practically clairvoyant members of medieval society at whom writers such as Juan Ruiz are said to have aimed their works. Four citizens, the father and the son and the whole-friend and his son, deliberately break the law of God and of man when they pervert evidence in court so as to bring about the execution of an innocent young man merely to enable the selfish father to prove the friendship of his whole-friend.

This idea of negative lessons in *exemplos* leads to another point worthy of consideration yet never considered, insofar as I can discover. Can we be certain that all medieval people read or listened to the moralizations attached to stories, even to Don Juan Manuel's stories? Most audiences of written works, since they were illiterate, had to hear the works read aloud or recited. Would they have always been exposed to the moralizations found in books? Did all professional or nonprofessional story readers or storytellers include moralizations? Would not many such performers have deliberately omitted or curtailed moralistic lessons? If this idea is viable, then some audiences might never have been aware of Patronio's lengthy transcendent preachment. If so, then such audiences would not have received the clarification intended by Don Juan Manuel which would have mitigated the effect of the *non* found in the incidents of the slap and the self-sacrifice of the whole-friend's son. Quite probably some people, for one reason or another—the reader's or teller's desire to present only the story and no moralization, or the audience's own proclivity to skip the lesson—simply did not receive any instruction. What of the audience made up of Spanish Jews and Muslims, of whom there were many? What of people who were nominally Christian or who gave short shrift to doctrinal matters and wanted mainly to be entertained by interesting stories? Those who missed Patronio's preachment might well have regarded Number 48 as counterproductive, might have misinterpreted it entirely, insofar as moralization was concerned, or might have regarded the contrived plot and conflict as too unrealistic. If many students and scholars today so regard this *exemplo*, it is reasonable to believe that many in the Middle Ages entertained the same sentiments and opinions. Medieval writers, preachers, and entertainers surely must have been aware of the varied composition of their audiences, and such awareness might have guided them as they wrote. If so, we today should take this into consideration. After all, King Sancho's version offered no transcendental or spiritual interpretation, but only an explanation by the father as to why he tested his friends, proving, it would seem, that the tale could be told without a pietistic explication.

It comes down to this, when all is said and done. If one sets out to examine Number 48 as a piece of literature, i. e., as a short story or *exemplo*, and attempts to understand its narrative techniques, one finds a great deal which can be questioned and criticized: too many motifs and incidents blended into a confusing mélange; the accumulation of materials sufficient for a *novella*, rather than an *exemplo*; the compressing or compacting of such materials into the brief space required by an *exemplo*; the inclusion of two extraneous and dubious incidents, which in the Middle Ages might well have led to unintentional conclusions on the part of the audience, and which, indeed, today may lead to such conclusions, and all for the sake of an involved and pietistic preachment.

Notes

* Reprinted from *La Corónica*, 13 (1984), 1-9.

1 *Don Juan Manuel: Libro del Conde Lucanor, edicion, estudio y notas* (Madrid: Editorial Alhambra, 1983), p. 429, n. 330.

2 Various editions contain 50 or 51 *exemplos*. Since numbers 27 and 43 each contain two separate stories, with different characters and chronological periods, there are truly 53 in that part of the five-part book which we read for their *exemplos*. See my "Don Juan Manuel's *El Conde Lucanor* Contains Fifty-Three Stories and No Fewer," *Romance Notes*, 24 (1983-84), 59-64. I must now add still another *exemplo* one not found among the usual group in Part I of Don Juan's collection of *exemplos*, but in the *5a* Parte (Blecua's edition, 294-96). Dr. Brian J. Powell of the University of Hull reminded me of this fact in a recent letter written long after the appearance of the above-mentioned article in *Romance Notes*.

3 *Lucanor*, ed. Ayerbe-Chaux, p. 63, lines 45-53; and in translation by L. Clark Keating and myself, *The Book of Count Lucanor and Patronio: A Translation of Don Juan Manuel's* El Conde Lucanor (Lexington: University Press of Kentucky, 1977), p. 41.

4 People tend to forget that an *exemplo, exemplum,* or moralized tale is just as much a brief narrative as those narratives—one has the right to call them short stories—which were written or told without a moralization attached. The same story, not considered an *exemplo*, becomes one by the simple process of attaching a moralization to it. For intensive study of the *exemplum* see Salvatore Battaglia, "L'esempio medievale," *Filologia Romanza*, 6 (1959), 45-82. His remarks to the effect that the *exemplum* is a narrative genre in itself with its own laws and that it is not an embryonic tale or perhaps a story which exemplifies the steps in an evolutionary stairway of narration (p. 70) is of importance to any investigation of medieval short story. Even so, he falls short of labeling the *exemplo* a full-fledged short story, as I maintain it usually is, repeating my point with the statement that the brief narratives considered short stories are *exemplos*, with the addition of a moralization and of possibly other characteristics of the *exemplo*. More recently John England has recapitulated the importance of *exemplos* in medieval Spain and has studied hitherto unexplored facets of structure in Don Juan Manuel's stories: see "'¿Et non el dia del lodo?': The Structure of the Short Story in *El Conde Lucanor,"* in *Juan Manuel Studies*, ed. Ian Macpherson (London: Tamesis, 1977), pp. 69-86.

5 The versions which are extant and which were no doubt available to Don Juan Manuel were, according to Ayerbe-Chaux, who lists them all and either translates them or reprints them in the original language in his *El Conde Lucanor: Materia tradicional y originaldad creadora* (Madrid: Poarrúa Turanzas, 1975), pp. 358-76: *Barlam y Josafat*, the *Exempla* of Jacques de Vitry, the *Fabulae* or *Narrationes* of Odo of Cheriton, the *Gesta Romanorum*, and the *Scala Coeli.*

6 See my "From Masterpiece to Résumé: Don Juan Manuel's Misuse of a Source," in *Estudios literarios de hispanistas norteamericanos dedicados a Helmut Hatzfeld con motivo de su 80 aniversario* (Barcelona: Hispam, 1974), pp. 41-50 [AUTH. which

follows this study].

⁷ The sources of the first story in the *Disciplina Clericalis* and of the second are believed to be of Eastern origin. There is a Sanskrit version of the Three Friends (though its events are concerned with only two) in the *Kathāsaritsāgara (Ocean of Streams of Story)* by Somadeva: see *The Ocean of Story*, trans. C. H. Tawney (London: Charles J. Sawyer, 1936), V, pp. 87-88. As far as I am aware, this version has not been noticed by Juan Manuel scholars. For a chart of the possible sources of the Story of the Half-Friend, see the article of Charles P. Wagner, "The Sources of *El Cavallero Cifar*," *Revue Hispanique*, 10 (1903), 5-104, which also aids in the tracing of the sources of the Three Friends, the Test of Friendship, and the Story of the Two Friends. Pages devoted to the Half-Friend are 78-83 with a stemma between 82 and 83.

⁸ This sequence can be found in note 2 of Pascual de Gayangos's edition, *Castigos e documentos del rey don Sancho*, in *BAE*, 51, pp. 157-58; Agapito Rey published the same passage from MS *C* in his edition of *E: Castigos e documentos para bien vivir ordenados por el Rey don Sancho IV*, Indiana University Humanities Series, 24 (Bloomington: Indiana University Press, 1952), p. 166, n. 8. [AUTH. Dennis P. Seniff and I are preparing a new edition of *Castigos e documentos* for the Hispanic Seminary of Medieval Studies at the University of Wisconsin, with publication possible by 1988.]

⁹ Juan Bautista Avalle-Arce, "Una tradición literaria: El cuento de los dos amigos," *NRFH*, 9 (1957), 1-35.

¹⁰ *Historia de la literatura española* (Barcelona: Gustau Gili, 1946), I, p. 182.

¹¹ Salvatore Battaglia, "L'esempio medievale," pp. 36-37.

¹² "A Half Friend and a Friend and a Half," *BHS*, 35 (1958), 187-98.

¹³ Readers will recall that upon the foundation of *sic et non* in the *Libro de buen amor* much modern scholarship rests.

From Masterpiece to Résumé: Don Juan Manuel's Misuse of a Source*

ENERALLY ACCEPTED IS the belief that Don Juan Manuel was always successful in reworking, refurbishing or otherwise improving his sources. One only has to read his Number XI about Don Yllán, the magician of Toledo, or Number XXV, "La mujer Brava," to be convinced. But there are cases, even among some of his better known tales, which are exceptions to the rule. One is Number XIX, "Exemplo de los buhos et los cuervos," and it is a remarkable case of the opposite, that is, it reveals that he could take an excellently structured story and reduce it to one far from its original excellence. Daniel Devoto seems not to have understood this when he wrote "Pocos ejemplos permiten apreciar tan exactamente las características del arte narrativo de don Juan Manuel como éste, cuya fuente literaria inmediata (y probablemente única) es el capítulo VI del *Calila y Dimna.*"[1] To Devoto brevity and unity seem to mean all, and in Chapter VI of *Calila* he saw little of either. Perhaps Don Juan Manuel wished to accord it in *El Conde Lucanor.*[2] It would be analogous what caused him to sacrifice so many of the elements of narrative technique that have made many of his stories famous. Also it would have been exceedingly difficult to adapt the almost novel-length "De los cuervos e de los buhos" in *Calila* to the limited space Don Juan Manuel wished to accord it in *El Conde Lucanor.*[2] It would be analogous to what would result if one reduced one of the longer *Novelas ejemplares* of Cervantes to three pages. Indeed, what Don Juan Manuel wrote, as compared to the story in *Calila,* is a kind of résumé or abridgement.

First of all he must have decided to omit the extraneous material, as Devoto considered the eight stories he mentioned (actually, there are nine), so as to "sacar un cuento limpio."[3] But the loss of the nine *exemplos* detracts from the structure of the story in Don Juan Manuel's book. Each of these interpolated tales contributes to the over-all progression toward the climax, and each plays a definite role in that progression.

Then, as a further effort to achieve brevity, Don Juan sacrificed the development of character, the use of dialogue, the buildup of suspense, the establishment of rapport with the reader by taking him into his confidence and flattering his ego by leading him, through implication, to feel that he knew what was going to happen, but only after much intellectual activity on the reader's part.

With these thoughts in mind, let us now turn to the investigation of Don Juan Manuel's failure to improve upon his model, primarily by evaluating what it was that made the model, Chapter VI of *Calila*, as excellent as it is. In the process of this investigation it is inevitable that the reader must observe that I am of necessity pointing out that before Don Juan Manuel's time there existed in Spanish literature a brand of brief narrative not inferior to the *exemplos* of the acknowledged master, Don Juan Manuel. This is not an original concept. Menéndez y Pelayo himself in his *Orígenes de la novela* had realized the quality of some of the tales in *Calila e Digna*. So had Amador de los Ríos in his *Historia crítica*.[4] But since literary criticism of the past has a way of losing ground, and when a book like *Calila e Digna* is rarely read carefully and sympathetically by our generation, its literary excellence needs re-examination; moreover, no one, insofar as I have been able to determine, has actually investigated the structuring employed by the nameless translators who so skilfully rendered the Arabic *Kalilah wa-Dimna* into Castilian. This study, then, will attempt to make two concepts clearer: that Don Juan Manuel sometimes did not adapt his models as artistically as he might have; and that such earlier works as *Calila* were in no way inferior to the work of the raconteur whose *exemplos* most scholars consider to be the most artistic and literary tales written in Spanish before and in his times.

Number XIX of *El Conde Lucanor*, like all Don Juan's *exemplos*, is personalized by its introduction in which Count Lucanor (understood to be Juan Manuel himself) asks advice of his counselor, Patronio, and is answered by a story in which a similar problem is resolved. In this it excels Chapter VI of *Calila*, for the earlier work opens in a less personal fashion in that the counselor begins his narrative in answer to his monarch's request that he tell a story of a man "que se engaña en el enemigo que le muestra humildat" (3295). However, once the plot is unfolded by the narrator, the technique of *Calila* is superior. Patronio baldly states that..."los cuervos et los buhos avían entre sí grand contienda, pero los cuervos eran en mayor quexa" (120:15 ff). No individual crow is mentioned, and no specific owl. The passage reads as though it were a part of some bestiary or zoological tract. It continues in the same impersonal tone: "Et los buhos, porque es su costumbre de andar de noche, et de día estar escondidos en cuebas muy malas de fallar, venian de noche a los árboles de los cuervos albergavan et matavan muchos dellos, et fazianles mucho mal" (120: 17 ff.).

How different and how refreshing and compelling are the opening lines of the same story in *Calila*! The reader learns that certain crows lodged by night in a mighty tree and that they had a king. (Don Juan Manuel never mentions a king of the crows), and that nearby was a large cave inhabited by the king of the owls and his people. "E por la grand enemistad antygua que es entre los cuervos e los buos salio una noche el rrey de los buos con su compaña e fue a dar sobre los cuervos en el arvol donde estavan asosegados syn miedo algunos. E ferieron e mataron tantos dellos e fueronse en su salvo" (3303-07). This version, in addition to mentioning a particular crow, the king, tells the reader that owls attacked on *una noche*, not just "by night," and that the crows were *asosegados syn miedo alguno*. The crows lodge in *un arvol muy grande*, not simply *en arboles*, while the owls dwell *en una cueva muy grande*. The reader of *Calila* is able to identify with these particular crows, for the author has, in a few choice words, told him a great deal about them.

Don Juan Manuel continues, still impersonally: "Et passando los cuerbos tanto daño, un cuervo que avía entrellos muy sabidor, que se dolía mucho del mal que avía reçevido de los buhos, sus enemigos, fabló con los cuervos sus parientes, et cató esta manera para se poder vengar" (120:21).

Calila allows dialogue to carry the entire burden of the narrative for many lines, since the king of the crows asks each of five privy-counselors for his assessment of the problem and his solution of it. The reader, on learning that there are five counselors, is primed to expect five plans and his interest is aroused; moreover, he will be permitted to catch a rare glimpse of what takes place at the courts of kings and to savor conspiratorily, as it were, the most secret of deliberations. Matters royal, diplomatic, military (all confidential) will be discussed. The reader is flattered, even as his interest is sharpened. He is expected to understand such affairs and he is determined to meet the author's expectations of him. The milieu of the court of a king is always a good show and it always enhances the dramatic quality of any story. Even the words *poridat* and its plural *poridades*, are mentioned, intensifying the deep atmosphere of secrecy. So great is the secrecy to be that not even the royal counselors are to be permitted to be privy to it. "—E señor,—" says the wisest counselor "—las poridades han lugares sabidos, e ay poridades que pueden saber muchos e otras que non han de saber mas de dos; e yo non tengo por bien que en esta poridat non sean mas del rrey e su privado" (3401-05).

The reader is hooked. He is part and parcel of the confidential parley of the king and his most trusted counselor in a very star chamber of classified information. Rapport is strongly established between reader and author. Indeed rapport between the reader and the crows is beginning to burgeon.

It is in these early sequences of the story in *Calila* that the interpolated tales appear. Each was inserted for the explicit purpose of strengthening the plot of the story of the crows and the owls, and so as to conduct the reader more surely and more entertainingly to its dénouement. Unity, therefore, far from suffering damage, is intensified. The reader is not conducted in haste, as he is in Number XIX, but is led carefully along, his mind focused upon the advantages and disadvantages of the various plans, and yet free to wonder as to the outcome of the war between the two tribes of birds. He must await the outcome, although he is artfully led into the temptation of trying to predict it; the author is certainly not going to drop the outcome in the reader's lap all of a sudden, as Don Juan Manuel drops it. Nothing is done hastily or spontaneously: every part must fall into place at a proper time. It goes without saying that techniques such as these create suspense and sustain interest. In the process, and as a part of the process of unfolding the story of the crows and the owls, the reader is given the extra dividend of some delightful little stories. Also in the process he is forced to divide his thoughts into two spheres: one part of his mind enjoys the *dulce* of the interpolates tales, while the other part is never allowed to forget that great events are in progress and that much lies between the interpolated story in progress and the climax of the primary narrative. The inserted stories, then, deserve at least some attention.

The first, which is told to the king by the wisest of his counselors, is intimately linked with the plot, since it begins to make the reader understand why the owls and the crows are such bitter enemies. The reason is that the crows prevented an owl from being elected king of the birds. But before the reader reads of this, he must read two other tales inserted into the interpolated story. The first, related, incidentally by a crow in the first interpolated tale, tells how a clever rabbit tricked some elephants into retreating from the rabbits' community by making them believe that they were in danger from the moon. This is the first of a skilfully presented progression of tales, each of which advocates strategy based upon deceit. The reader, as he reads these tales illustrative of the victory of the weak over the strong through deceit, wonders if the wise crow of the narrative can equal or excel the strategy of the characters in the interpolated tale. The reader wonders, too, since the story was inserted into the main plot, if the trick of rabbits, or some version of it, will be the stratagem employed against the owls.

The second tale, also omitted by Juan Manuel, tells how a *gato religioso* agreed to judge the case of a weasel and a rabbit, and cleverly caught and ate them both by lulling them into too close proximity. Thus the second progression of deceit is presented. Can this be the answer, the reader wonders, to bring about the defeat of the owls?

At this juncture the crow counselor returns to his plotting with the king in the campaign of the war against the owls. Battle is out of the question, he believes. Only *arte* can save the day. To prove this he tells the king an additional story. In this tale three tricksters each tell an *omne religioso* that the deer he has bought is really a dog, and thereby persuade him to give it to them. Would a stratagem based upon obfuscation suffice to destroy the owls, the readers wonders, and finds himself still in suspense and uncertainty?

Note, then, that four tales have been told to the king—the reason for the enmity of the crows and the owls, the one about the elephants and the rabbits, the one about the weasel, the rabbit and the pious cat, and lastly, the story of the gullible owner of the deer. Apparently none of the four varieties of deceit is to be the solution of the problem. The reader therefore turns to the wise crow and waits to see what he will propose.

Don Juan Manuel, unwilling to digress into interpolated tales, even though their inclusion would not have been a useless digression, allows his crow to launch his plan point blank: "Et la manera fue ésta: que los cuervos le messaron todo, salvo ende un poco de las alas, con que volava muy mal y muy poco. Et desque fue assi maltrecho, fuesse para los buhos et contóles el mal et el daño que los cuervos le fizieran"... (120:27). Thus and quickly Don Juan Manuel's reader learns what the strategy is to be. The *utile* is attained in a minimum of words.

In *Calila* we progress in a more deliberate way and we savor more deeply and more pleasurably the events as they occur. The *utile* of the lesson is subordinated to the *dulce* of the narrative itself.

In *Calila* a considerable amount of characterization is now developed. The crow who is to become a spy plots carefully and describes his plan graphically. "E tengo por bien, señor, que te fagas sañudo contra my con tu mesnada toda, e que me mandes picar e feryr e mesar fasta que me bañe todo en sangre, e que me mandes echar al pie del arvol donde nos venieron feryr, la cabeça e la cola toda mesada, e que te vayas tu e tus mesnadas dende a tal lugar..." (3568-73).

Don Juan Manuel passed so swifly from his crow's stratagem to his arrival at the cave of the owls that the reader was hardly conscious of any transition at all. Not so *Calila*: the crow reached the owls in a very different way, one that adds much to the development of his character, already skilfully growing in the hands of the author. We read that the other crows flew to safety, that the owls attacked by night, finding all the crows gone; we read of their disappointment and of the imminence of their return to their base; and then we read of the wounded crow's remarkable *arte*, of his skill in histrionics. "E desde el cuervo que estava echado al pie sentio que non le avian visto, começo de gemir e dar bozes por que le viesen por non perder su trabajo e peligro en que era puesto. E a las bozes e gemidos que dava sentieronle algunos de los buos e fezieronlo saber al rrey, e fueron a el por le preguntar por los cuervos. E levaronle ante el rrey e preguntaronle que quien e donde era o donde eran los cuervos" (3579-84).

The picture of this crow spy, plucked, bleeding and moaning, is graphic. More and more he emerges as a formidable antagonist of the owls and as a protagonist with all that the word implies. But Don Juan Manuel, as he hurried his version along, failed to take advantage of such characterization.

His character in *Calila* grows in stature as he is brought before the owl king for interrogation. When asked why the crows mistreated him, he has a logical answer prepared, one obviously not concocted on the spur of the moment. He is a convincing spy. He told the owl king: "—Yo soy fulano, fijo de fulano, e los cuervos son ydos de aquy fuyendo, e myrad qual me pararon.— Dixo el rrey: —Commo tu eres uno de los mas pryvados del rrey de los cuervos e del su consejo, ¿qual fue el pecado o la ocasyon porque te fezieron eso?— Dixo el cuervo: — Mio malfecho me lo fizo.— Dixo el rrey: —¿Qué fue eso?— Dixo el cuervo: —Señor, ya sabedes commo la otra noche pasada venistes vos e vuestras conpañas sobre nosotros e nos fezistes gran daño. El rrey de los cuervos llamo a consejo e yo le di por consejo que non le consejava lydiar con los buos, porque eran mas fuertes e mas rrezios que nosotros salvo que nos sometiesemos a vosotros . . . E menospreçiaron my lealtad, a pararonme tal commo tu vees" (3585-3603).

Don Juan Manuel wastes no time on a consultation between the owl king and his counselors, although he does mention that one, who was wiser than the others, urged the execution of the crow and when his advice was not take, departed for safer lodgings. But in *Calila* the reader is again allowed to see a king and his advisers in action. To balance the four interpolated tales told in the court of the crows, four tales are inserted at this juncture. Again suspense is developed, again the reader is made to feel that he is privy to classified consultations. Moreover in *Calila* another character is developed with skill and vitality. He is an owl, Cassandra, and the perfect foil in intelligence, wisdom, and patriotism for the crow spy. Even the interpolated tales told by the other owl counselors contribute to the strength of character found in the wisest of the owls, because the tales also lead the reader to see the owls in an unfavorable light. The stories are not as pertinent to the problem of the crow spy as they should be, and I hazard the guess that this was by the deliberate intent of the author to make the owls seem stupid and unsympathetic.

The wisest of the owl counselors, however, tells two stories to convince his people that the crow is indeed a spy and should be put to death. Both stories are pertinent, since one reveals the danger of untrustworthy people in positions of trust, and the other proves that all creatures will under stress return to their native habits and characteristics.

Even the owl king is given character and personality. He is depicted as a proud and stupid creature, unwilling to listen to good advice,

seduced by wishful thinking, and repeatedly the reader sees that he
"non tornava cabeça" when the wise owl gives him advice.

Without mentioning an owl king Don Juan Manuel tells his readers
"Quando los buhos esto oyeron" [the crow's promise to betray his own
people], "plógoles mucho, et tovieron que por este cuervo que era con
ellos era todo su fecho endereçado, et començaron a fazer mucho bien
al cuervo et fiar en todas sus faziendas et sus poridades" (120:36 ff.).

In *Calila* the crow spy, to convince his captors, offers to be burned
so that he may be reincarnated as an owl, a chancy offer to make and
one that further enhances the strength of his character. Don Juan
Manuel has none of this.

At last, when the crow's feathers have grown out, Don Juan
Manuel tells his readers: "Et desque las péñolas le fueron eguadas, dixo
a los buhos que, pues podía volar, que yría saber do estavan los cuervos
et que vernía dezírgelo porque pudiessen ayuntarse et yr a los estroyr
todos. A los buyos plogo mucho desto" (p. 121:11 ff.).

In *Calila* the reader receives a more detailed account. "E al cuervo
plogo mucho aquello que oyo e honrravanle todos fasta que engordo e
le creçieron sus plumas, e myro e aprendio toda su fazienda con los
buos; e sopo dellos lo que querian fazer. E un dia saliose a furto, e fuese
adonde estavan los cuervos, a aparto al rrey..." (3816-20).

The reader knows that the climax is near. Don Juan Manuel as
usual in this particular tale, sweeps his reader along rapidly, and the
dénouement comes as no surprise. There is not even anything unusual
in the end of the owl menace. The crows... "fueron a ellos de día
quando ellos non buellan et estavan segurados et sin reçelo, et mataron
et destruyeron dellos tantos porque fincaron vençedores los cuervos de
toda sus guerra" (121:21 ff.).

The death of the owls in *Calila* is novel indeed. The crow spy
unfolds a wonderful plan to his king. He says that the owls are lodged
in their cave near a place where there is a great deal of dry wood. "...
e nos levemos quanta podieremos en los picos e pongamiosia en la
boca de la cueva do ellos yazen de dia. E ay çerca ay cavañas de
ganados, e yo arrebatare dende fuego e ponerlo he baxo la leña; e
aventaremos todos con nuestras alas fasta que lo ençendamos el
fuego; e se aprenda la leña e con el fuego e con el fumo moryran todos
quantos buos ay estan... e fueron muertos todos los buos; e
tornaronse todos los cuervos salvos e seguros a su lugar" (3827-35).

Don Juan Manuel's story has ended, but in *Calila* there is a kind of assessment of the matter by the king of the crows and his spy. Although the conflict has been resolved, as a good story should resolve it, the author tells his reader what the spy thought in the days of his captivity, how he assessed the owl king, and how he regarded his only worthy opponent. The owl king was a fool, he tells his own king. And to drive the point home he tells one last story which deals with a foolish king of the frogs and how he allowed himself and his people to be destroyed. The story ends in *Calila* in praise of the one wise owl. "Entre todos ellos non falle ome que fuese de rrecabdo salvo aquel que consejava my muerte; e todos los otros eran de muy flaco e mal acuerdo e de muy poca ynvisidat, nin myravan cosa en my fazienda commo quier que los consejava, e dezia fartas cosas aquel que consejava my muerte; e nunca le querian creer nin ser obediente nin entendieron su mal maguer que farto ge lo dezia aquel" (3843-50).

The ending in *Calila* is unusually natural and unexpected. The crow spy's respect for his enemy is touching. The story ends on a sincere and very human note.

In summation it can be said that although Don Juan Manuel narrated the story of the crows and the owls found in Chapter VI of *Calila e Digna*, and though he managed to tell a brief and unified story, his product is less literary, less entertaining, and less artistic than his model. He did not exercise his well-known skills in characterization, since not one of the crows or owls is accorded more than the few lines required to identify him. His model with little description, save for a few masterfully structured concepts, created two quite strong characters—the crow spy and the owl Cassandra—and two other characters who at least have personalities well enough depicted to be considered as good supporting characters—the crow king and his counterpart among the owls. None of these four is many-faceted, admittedly, but all four are possessed of definite identities.

Don Juan Manuel devoted little attention to atmosphere, local color and background. The crows live in trees, the owls in caves. One senses always an oppressive determination to condense, abbreviate, and narrate in the most sparing of tones.

This effort at condensation destroys many opportunities for suspense and the establishment of rapport with readers; it removes the pleasing and interest-catching progression so lauded by Devoto, Puibusque, and Cirot, namely "...y lo que interesa sobre todo en él es su desarrollo 'dramático,' en el sentido teatral del vocablo..." Don Juan fails in XIX to do what Devoto praises in *exemplo* VI of *El Conde Lucanor:* "... divide la acción, retarda el desenlace, va disponiendo sus afectos en series progresivas."[5]

Lastly, the very element of conflict so necessary in plotted stories is downgraded by Don Juan where in *Calila*, the two strongest characters, the crow spy and the owl Cassandra, face one another and epitomize the conflict of the entire story; in Don Juan Manuel, if they ever saw one another face to face, the reader is not told so.

Number XIX in *El Conde Lucanor*, then, is simply a well-written résumé, whereas its model, Chapter VI of *Calila e Digna* is an artistically developed story. The reader emerges from number XIX with the feeling that he has been instructed with a lesson applicable to a life-situation, but he does not come away with the pleasant glow produced by one of the prince's delightfully structured and personalized *exemplos*.

Notes

* Reprinted from *Estudios literarios de hispanistas norteamericanos dedicados a Helmut Hatzfeld con motivo de su 80 aniversario*, Madrid: Hispam, 1975, pp. 41-40.

1 Daniel Devoto, *Introducción al estudio de Don Juan Manuel y en particular el Conde Lucanor: una bibliografía*, Madrid, 1972, p. 403.

2 The editions used are: José Manuel Blecua, *El Conde Lucanor*, 2nd ed. (Madrid, 1971), and Robert W. Linker's and my *El Libro de Calila e Digna* (Madrid, 1967). All citations from *Exemplo* XIX are from Blecua, page and line; all citations from *Calila*, Chapter VI, refer to the line numbers of our edition.

3 Devoto, *op. cit.*, 404.

4 M. Menéndez y Pelayo, *Orígenes de la novela*, I (Santander, 1948); J. Amador de los Ríos, *Historia crítica de la literatura española*, I (Madrid, 1861).

5 Devoto, *op. cit.*, 403.

Folklore in the
Cantigas of
Alfonso el Sabio*

HE STRONG TIES linking folklore and literature have long been recognized and studied. The science of folklore with its techniques for classifying motifs and types of tales has clearly delineated some of the relationships between literary and popular traditions. Indeed, these classifications reveal that vast areas of universal literature —and this includes the writings of known authors—stem ultimately from the folk. It is known, too, that a kind of reciprocity is active between literature and folklore, for the folk borrows from erudite tradition and in due time absorbs these borrowings completely. Sometimes it is even possible to trace a perfect cycle: a folktale, in some writer's hands, becomes a literary tale; this literary tale, borrowed by the folk, again becomes a folktale.[1]

The period of classification of folktales, legends, myths, etc. has recently attained new heights with the publication of Stith Thompson's New Enlarged and Revised Edition of the *Motif-Index of Folk Literature*.[2] Therefore, the time is ripe for carrying out studies aimed at showing the elements of folklore in great works of literature. Who knows, even today, the actual folkloric content of such masterpieces as *Don Quijote, The Canterbury Tales, The Decameron*, or the works of Rabelais?

The present essay will attempt to examine and to discuss the elements of folklore in one of Spain's great medieval books, the *Cantigas de Santa María*, written under the patronage of King Alfonso X, "el Sabio." These poems need only a brief introduction, for they have been the subject of much study by students of musicology, art, literature, archaeology, and sociology. The *Cantigas* were written at the command of the Learned King and assembled in lavishly illustrated volumes. Alfonso himself is quite probably the author of some of the poems, for he appears in a number of them as do members of his immediate

131

family. Each *Cantiga* relates a miracle of the Blessed Virgin. Each contains the musical notation that makes it possible to sing the miracles.[3] And in the codices the songs are accompanied by full-page sets of beautifully colored and illuminated miniatures.[4] The *Cantigas* belongs to erudite poetry in thirteenth-century Spain and were written not in Castilian, but in Galician-Portuguese, a tongue regarded by cultured people as more apt for lyric verse and for song. It should be added that the *Cantigas* were also intended for singing in church, and indeed, the king in his last will and testament provided for the safekeeping of his *Cantigas* and stated that they were to be sung on the feast days of Our Lady. "Otrosí mandamos," he wrote, "que todos los libros de los *Cantares de loor de Sancta Maria* sean todos en aquella iglesia do nuestro cuerpo se enterrare, e que los fagan cantar en las fiestas de Sancta María..."[5]

All this places the *Cantigas de Santa Maria* well within the limits of learned tradition, of even polished erudite tradition, and one might well be permitted to wonder what the *Cantigas* have to do with folklore, or what folklore has to do with the *Cantigas*. Can one prove that elements of true folklore exist in these songs?

The answer is very definitely in the affirmative. The *Cantigas* of the Learned King literally abound in folklore. One is almost tempted to state that no single piece of medieval literature outstrips the *Cantigas* in this respect. Of great importance and special interest to folklorists is the fact that in addition to mention of folklore, these are actual illustrations of many of its aspects. These pictures, incidentally, contain the basis for most revealing studies of medieval life in many of its phases; that they contain remarkable portrayals of medieval folkways goes without saying.

Three hundred and fifty-three separate miracles exist in the *Cantigas de Santa María*, but more were included, to judge from the tables of contents of the codices.

The problem of treating the folklore in the *Cantigas* is not one easy to solve. The only attempt to date is that of F. Calcott,[6] who in his study, *The Supernatural in Early Spanish Literature*, devoted to the *Cantigas* only an investigation of purely supernatural aspects and the folklore surrounding these aspects. Calcott's study is most enlightening and it traces medieval Spanish folk beliefs in some detail and even goes so far as to attempt a classification of such beliefs. Scholars who wish to pursue other areas of folklore in the *Cantigas*—for example, folk speech, folk arts and crafts, folk music, folk medicine, etc.,—would do well to study the researches of Calcott.

The present study will deal for the most part with the actual folk motifs found in the miracles; however, other less easily defined folkloristic elements merit mention, and some attention must be accorded these. In a book-length study now in progress about the way of life in thirteenth-century Spain the writer will devote considerable space to folklore. For the present, the following remarks may to some degree suffice.

1. General Folklore in the *Cantigas*

In addition to the actual folk motifs in the *Cantigas de Santa María,* many aspects of general folklore appear. Medieval Spanish folkways, customs, laws, beliefs and superstitions, etc., form the background of many of the miracles, and these are often depicted in the miniatures. *Cantiga* 42[7] is concerned in part with a ball game—one that closely resembles a baseball game—and the miniatures show this game in progress; in *Cantiga* 144 there is a thirteenth-century bullfight which was held in celebration of the marriage of a wealthy man's daughter; black magic is an element of *Cantiga* 125, and in the illustrations appears the magic diagram drawn by the protagonist to protect him from the host of demons he has conjured up; *Cantiga* 129 depicts clearly an old folk belief concerning the theft of a communion wafer to be used in a charm to work witchcraft.

Strange superstitions are common; *Cantiga* 128 shows how a woman made a waxen image of a child to be presented to the Virgin Mary so as to insure the healthy birth of the mother's expected baby; in number 87 of the Florentine Codex, which is number 209 of the Ms. B.1.2 (formerly E 2), the unillustrated but almost complete ms. of all the *cantigas,* King Alfonso is seen obtaining cure from a deadly fever by touching a copy of his *Cantigas* in much the same way that the folk believes a cure is obtained by touching the Holy Bible; *Cantiga* 319 tells of the use of enchantment in a futile attempt to cure a case of rabies.

Jewish customs are cited with frequency; in *Cantiga* 107 the Jews of Segovia try a young Jewess who has professed a desire to accept Christianity, after committing a sin and as a punishment cast her from a high cliff; a Jewish child in *Cantiga* 4 unwittingly receives the Holy Sacrament given to the pupils in a school and is thrust into a furnace by his irate father; *Cantiga* 12 focuses attention upon the Jewish custom of crucifying an image of the Saviour.

King Alfonso and his court poets seem to have taken great interest in miracles whose backgrounds and characters were popular. Certainly a large number of the songs deal with the middle class and even with the peons. Local shrines—some apparently quite insignificant—are the scenes of miracles, and the poets of the *Cantigas* may justifiably be called early *costumbristas*.

2. Folk Motifs in the *Cantigas*

The richest deposits of folklore in the *Cantigas de Santa María* lie in the stories of the miracles. The motifs used by the Learned King and his poets are quite varied as to subject and stem from many sources, some of which have not been traced. Mussafia, one of the earliest to attempt to trace the sources, believed that the King began by using the well-known miracles found in the standard collections, such as the *Miracles* of Gautier de Coincy. He stated that 64 such well-known miracles are numbered in King Alfonso's first one hundred *Cantigas*; 17 in the second one hundred; 11 in the third; and only 2 in the fourth one hundred.[8] Solalinde felt that no such positive listing as this should be given, but he agreed that the *Cantigas* made use of the better known miracles at first.[9] Perhaps after a rather selective compilation the king and his collaborators found it necessary to use miracles not found in the collections, or perhaps they decided that Spanish miracles were actually preferable. Be that as it may, local Spanish miracles gained increasing favor as the *Cantigas* were set down. After all, Spaniards in all periods of writing have evinced great interest in their own affairs and their own customs and folklore, and the fact that they did so in the thirteenth century is not really strange.

Miracles of the Virgin and of the saints belong to that body of narrative considered to be well within the realm of folk tradition. We know them as saints' legends, and Spain is especially endowed with them. Such accounts have been admirably treated by Stith Thompson in an essay in *Folklore Américas* entitled *"La Leyenda"*.[10] Many of these tales have greatly enhanced the very development and evolution of world narrative. Scholars believe that most miracles of this variety originated with the folk, gradually made their way into ecclesiastical circles, and finally became the property of religious literature. Some, of course, came from the minds of the clergy and were borrowed by the folk, thus participating in the kind of reciprocity mentioned earlier in this study. The more moving and emotional miracles, those with universal appeal, and those which for undetermined reasons were among the most cherished by Christians, formed the core of the great collections of miracles. By the middle of the thirteenth-century such collections had appeared in many lands, and some existed in Spain before the *Cantigas* of King Alfonso. Latin was the usual vehicle for these miracles, but vernacular versions existed as exemplified by the *Milagros* of Gonzalo de Berceo or the *Miracles* of Gautier de Coincy.

A. Motifs Borrowed Directly from Other Works

R. S. Boggs has pointed out very effectively the prevalence of folk motifs in literature.[11] The very *raison d'être* of the *Motif-Index of Folk Literature* is predicated upon this fact. The substratum of folk motifs beneath the miracles in the standard collections, therefore, must be considered. The standard miracles, included in the great erudite collections, like most stories of this kind, seem to belong to popular tradition in their original form. This means, of course, that when the Learned King and his collaborators used these standard miracles, they were indeed using folk motifs. But since the miracles were in their eyes traditional narratives believed to be true and not fictional, the writers of the *Cantigas* were not admittedly using folkloristic materials. The fact that each of the stories probably originated in some distant and remote past and sprang from the people, probably never entered their minds. As students of folklore we today, in our modern wisdom, may say that the motifs in the standard collections go back to the folk; but we cannot accuse the Learned King of dipping directly into folklore when he dipped into the works of such a writer as Vincent of Beauvais. When the writers of the *Cantigas* played the role of folklorists they did so in their use of miracles of a very different sort—the miracles gathered in Spain from local shrines and from the larger churches, too, but miracles that were Spanish and probably current among the folk.

A few of the *Cantigas* taken from the standard collections should be mentioned. *Cantiga* 42 is the story of a young man who placed his ring on a finger of the Virgin's image and saw the stone finger close upon the ring. This tale enjoyed great popularity during the Middle Ages and was related in several languages. Folklorists know it as the motif of the statue bride, and Thompson cites it as T367 "Young man betrothed to a statue." Matthew Paris, Gautier de Coincy, and Vincent of Beauvais used it. It appeared in the *Alphabetum Narrationum*, the *Legenda Aurea*, the *Gesta Romanorum*, the *Scala Coeli* and the *Kaiserchronik*, although in the last three the statue was that of Venus and not of the Blessed Virgin. Scholars believe that the motif came from the folk, that it was first told about the statue of Venus, and that it finally drifted into the orbit of Our Lady's miracles. The story *is*, then, a folktale, but by the time it came into the hands of the Learned King it belonged to erudite and clerical traditions.

The same may be said of *Cantiga* 74 which tells of an artist who liked to depict the devil as a most hideous creature. The fiend appeared to the painter and threatened him, later causing the scaffolding on which he was standing to fall to the floor. The painted likeness of Our Lady supported the artist until he could be rescued. By the time Alfonso used this story it had long been the property of the standard Latin collections.

Scores of such well-known motifs could be cited. As we have seen, they all, or nearly all, were originally of folk creation, but to the writers of the *Cantigas* they were not folklore. Listing more of this variety will not strengthen the argument that the king utilized popular tales in his book.

B. Borderline Cases—Alfonsine Versions of Literary Tales or of
   Popular Tales?

Miracles of real popular background can be cited, and will be later; however, there are borderline cases which demand some study. Are these miracles of true folk origin or are they pseudo-folktales, reworkings of well-known stories from such books as the Bible or from the writers of classical antiquity? It is difficult, if not impossible to determine whether some of these sprang from the folk or from the minds of the writers of the *Cantigas*. A few, told in briefest summary, will suffice to illustrate this problem.

Cantiga 241 is an excellent example. During the festivities on his wedding day a young man leaned from a window to wipe out a wine glass. Losing his balance, he fell several stories to the street and was injured mortally. Even when he was taken up, broken and dying, his mother refused to give up hope. She had him carried to the altar of the Virgin where, in response to her prayers, he was healed completely. This story, it will be noted, is a close parallel to that of Eutychus (Acts 20: 9-12) who likewise fell from an upper window and who was restored to life by St. Paul. Is the version of the *Cantigas* a reworking of the story of Eutychus? If so, whose reworking? An erudite poet's or that of a man of the people?

Number 193 is another case in point. A merchant is bound and thrown overboard by his fellow passengers. Three days later sailors on another ship passing that way see him under the water and haul him up. He has survived in a bubble beneath the waves. Similarities between the *Cantiga* and the story of Jonah are obvious.

Cantiga 167 bears a resemblance to the resuscitation of Lazarus, and number 236 has as its subject the miracle of walking upon the water.

The *Cantigas* contain also what appear to be reworkings of stories from other works of literature. *Cantiga* 98 tells of invisible forces that prevent a wicked woman in Valverde from entering a church, reminding one of how St. Mary the Egyptian was so prevented from entering the Church of the Holy Sepulchre.

Cantiga 103 relates the story of a pious monk who listened for three hundred years to the song of a little bird, although to him it seemed no longer than a moment.

Surely *Cantiga* 369 is a Spanish version of the tale known to folklorists as "the Ring of Policrates." A wicked *alcalde* in Santarén hired two men to deceive a devout woman. One man was to buy barley from her, leaving as security a ring of the *alcalde's*; the other was to steal the ring. So it was done, and the woman was at the *alcalde's* mercy. But the thief had dropped the ring into the sea, and when the woman's daughter cleaned a fish that evening, she found it.

All these and many others belong to popular traditions, and all have lived for ages in erudite writing.

C. Genuine Folk Motifs in the *Cantigas*

The most interesting of all the varieties of miracles in the *Cantigas de Santa María* are those that appear to be original to Spain and to have been drawn directly from the lore of the people. Of these the most famous and long-lived is probably the story of the Jewess Marisaltos. This miracle is still told in Spain and in Hispanic America. A rather poorly executed picture of one of its scenes can be seen today on the wall of the cloister of the Cathedral of Segovia near the niche which is said to contain the remains of the Jewess. The painting shows Marisaltos falling from the clifftop from which she has been hurled by her Jewish executioners, and the Virgin can be seen saving her from her death. In King Alfonso's *Cantiga* 107 the identical events are described, and the miniature shows the miraculous rescue of the Jewess.

Peculiarly local miracles are common in the *Cantigas*. Some are quite earthy and bear the definite stamp of agricultural life. Gautier de Coincy would have turned up his erudite nose at such tales, but King Alfonso included them in his *Cantigas*. Such stories belong to the realm of folk belief about poisonous reptiles and insects. Wherever people are ignorant of natural history—as farm folk so often are—this kind of tale originates. The writer of this article heard almost an identical version of the story next to be told, minus the Blessed Virgin and the Spanish setting, from the mouth of a farmhand in Kentucky in 1955. *Cantiga* 138 renders it thus: a woman "felt" that a serpent had somehow got inside her. Warned by a voice to go to the shrine of Our Lady she went there, beheld a vision of the Virgin who told her to go to Cádiz "where Jesus is" if she hoped to be rid of the snake. The woman went to the Cathedral of Cádiz and knelt before an image of Jesus, whereupon she vomited up a red snake.

In Toledo, according to *Cantiga* 99, a lovely girl put her finger into the ear of a deaf-mute and drew out a hairy worm. The man regained his hearing. Later the Virgin showed a wise priest how to restore his speech.

Cantiga 315 relates the miracle of a woman whose child, placed in standing wheat while the mother helped with the harvest, swallowed a head of wheat. The babe's belly became so swollen that his mother thought he had swallowed some poisonous insect. She hastened with the child to the shrine of Our Lady of Atocha at Madrid. After she had prayed, she undressed the infant and found that the head of wheat had worked its way out between the child's ribs.

In Ciudad Rodrigo a priest drank a poisonous spider in a goblet of wine. He prayed to the Virgin to help him, for the spider had traveled about inside his body and had caused him great anguish. He could feel it in his forearm scratching him painfully. In answer to his prayer, the Virgin caused the spider to make its way out of his arm, leaving the priest unharmed.

Cantiga 18 sings of some very remarkable silkworms. A woman of Segovia, whose livelihood came from the production of silk, found her silkworms dying of disease. She promised the Virgin a robe for the image in the church, but forgot to give the robe. The worms wove two garments. One was given to the image, and King Alfonso took the other for his private chapel.

A furrier (*Cantiga* 49) in Terrena never honored the Blessed Virgin.

One sabbath day he held a needle in his mouth, so as to leave his hands free, and the needle miraculously became stuck in his throat. For days he was in agony and no doctor could help him. At last, he had himself carried to the shrine of Our Lady and there he prayed and fell asleep. While he slept he coughed up the needle.

Literally scores of Spanish miracles appear in the *Cantigas*,[12] making this work of the Learned King and his collaborators one of the richest sources of medieval folklore. Only a few have been adequately studied, however. When all aspects of folklore—folk arts and crafts, folk music, folk medicine, folk beliefs, etc. have been examined and evaluated, our knowledge of the Middle Ages and our understanding of those times and of the people who lived then will be greatly extended.

Notes

* Reprinted from *Southern Folklore Quarterly*, 23 (1951), 175-83.

1 See my "El cuento folklórico en España y en Hispanoamérica," *Folklore Américas* XIV (1954), No. 1, p. 5 [AUTH. This is the first article in this collection.].

2 Stith Thompson, *Motif-Index of Folk Literature, New Enlarged Revised Edition*, Bloomington, 1955-58.

3 Higinio Anglés, *La música de las Cantigas II* (1943), the musicologist's is the most authentic study; see also Julián Ribera, *La música de las Cantigas*, 1922; Expériences Anonymes of New York has produced an excellent long-play recording of several of the *Cantigas* sung by the countertenor, Russell Oberlin.

4 Escorial MS T.I.1 (also known as E I) contains 212 pages of miniatures; Florence, Biblioteca Nazionale MS Banco Rari 20 (formerly entitled II. 1. 213) has 93 miniatures; in Escorial MS B.1.2 (E 2) there are miniatures in which are seen musicians with their instruments. J. Guerrero Lovillo, *Las Cántigas de Santa María, Estudio arqueológico de sus miniaturas*, Madrid, 1949, reproduces in black and white all the miniatures of MS T.I.1.

5 J. Guerrero Lovillo, *op. cit.*, p. 19, cites this part of the final testament of King Alfonso.

6 See F. Calcott, *The Supernatural in Early Spanish Literature*, New York, 1923, for a classification of the miracles according to their contents. A. F. G. Bell, "*Las Cantigas de Santa María* of Alfonso X," *MLN*, 10 (1915), 338-48, also attempts classification.

7 The numbers of the *Cantigas* are cited according to the enumeration of the Marqués de Valmar's edition, *Cantigas de Santa María de Don Alfonso el Sabio*, Madrid, 1889, 2 vols. [AUTH.] It is now possible to use the full-color edition which reproduces the Escorial manuscript: *Cantigas de Santa Maria: Edición facsímil de Códice T.I.1. de la Biblioteca de San Lorenzo de El Escorial, Siglo XIII.* Madrid: EDILAN, 1979, 2 vols., although Walter Mettmann's edition remains the scholarly standard.]

8 The studies of Mussafia, which attempt to trace the sources of the *Cantigas*, are included in the edition of the Marqués de Valmar, Vol II.

9 A. G. Solalinde, "El códice florentino de las *Cantigas*," *Revista de Filología Española*, 5 (1918), 175-76.

10 Stith Thompson, "La leyenda," *Folklore Américas*, 12 (1952).

11 R. S. Boggs, "Folklore in Literary Masterpieces of the World," from *Miscelánea de estudios dedicados al Dr. Fernando Ortiz por sus discípulos, colegas y amigos*, Havana, 1955.

12 I am now preparing a motif-index of the *Cantigas*, and am able to report that there are many motifs not listed in the *New and Enlarged Motif-Index* of Stith Thompson. [AUTH. This work is now being carried out by William R. Davis of Mercer University.]

Daily Living
as Presented in the
Cantigas of Alfonso el Sabio*

ING ALFONSO X of Castile needs no introduction
to mediaevalists. His contributions to the writing
of history—*Estoria de España* or *Primera Crónica
general* and *General Estoria*[1] are well known; the
many translations from the Arabic done at his
command, such as *Los libros del saber de astronomía,*
the *Lapidario,* and the *Libro de ajedrez, dados, y tablas*[2]
made themselves felt abroad as well as in Spain
during the Middle Ages and even into the Renaissance; his legal code,
Las Siete Partidas,[3] became one of the most widely distributed geograph-
ically of all legal codices, and even helped to shape to some extent the
laws of the United States of America. Less known, however, is a work
of literary merit, *Las Cantigas de Santa María,*[4] often referred to in English
as *The Canticles of Holy Mary.*

Those mediaevalists who have studied the *Canticles*—and their
number is small, even when one takes into consideration the Spaniards
themselves—know that in the pages of the four extant codices lies
some interesting and extremely valuable information. The *Canticles* are
unique in a number of ways and offer a variety of materials not found
elsewhere. Musicologists consider these songs important to the development of music and regard the illustrations of musicians and their
instruments (MS. B.1.2. or E.2 of the Escorial) as one of the best of
such illustrations surviving from the Middle Ages. Students of Folklore, thematology, and comparative literature recognize the *Canticles* as
a rich mine of motifs and themes, some of which appear nowhere else.

141

Historians and sociologists are looking to the songs to solve certain problems of history and for a better understanding of daily life in the thirteenth century. Professor Evelyn S. Procter of St Hugh's College, Oxford, in discussing the Canticles,[5] points to a number of historical facts established by mentions made of them in these songs. The history of Spanish art, and to some extent of mediaeval European art, rests upon King Alfonso's songs. Professor José Guerrero Lovillo of the University of Seville has recently published a brief, but enlightening treatise upon the rise of the art of miniatures in Spain[6] in which he traces the influence of French miniature art upon King Alfonso's artists and shows how the Spanish techniques and concepts then blossomed into something quite different from the original French models.

By and large, however, mediaevalists have overlooked what the Canticles have to offer, at least insofar as daily living is concerned.

Las Cantigas were composed by King Alfonso X, or by his order, to record the miracles of the Blessed Virgin. They were written, it should be remembered, in Galician-Portuguese and not in Castilian. During Alfonso's time, and indeed for many years after, this tongue was considered most apt for the composition of lyric poetry. Castilian, for the most part, was used for narrative poetry and, of course, for works in prose.

King Alfonso liked to refer to himself as "Our Lady's Troubadour." He must have devoted a great deal of time to the Canticles. Apparently he had the great collections of miracles of the Virgin examined, for many of his canticles seem to have been taken directly from such collections as those of Vincent of Beauvais or Gautier de Coincy. As the composition of the Canticles continued across the years of Alfonso's reign, the standard miracles no longer sufficed and more and more miracles of native vintage were inserted. Evelyn Procter lists those miracles said to have occurred in the Spanish and Portuguese shrines of the Virgin in Puerto de Santa María, Salas, Villa-Sirga, Terena, and Montserrat.

In all there are 353 miracles in the four surviving manuscripts of the Cantigas. Any larger number given fails to take into account the fact that certain miracles are duplicated from manuscript to manuscript and even in certain single manuscripts. They are presented in one manuscript in three different media (Escorial MS.T.I.1), that is in verse, in music, and of great importance to those interested in the mediaeval way of life, in remarkable miniatures. This codex contains full-page sets of miniatures, each divided into six panels. In each of the panels can be seen one of the major events in the miracle so illustrated. The animals, people, angels, demons, and saints are depicted, in the opinion of most artists who have seen them, with great fluidity and spontaneity of movement. Their dress and actions reveal a great deal. The backgrounds upon which the characters move, however, are much more revealing as to the life of those times.

Another codex of the *Canticles* (MS. Banco Rari 20, formerly II.I.213) of the National Library of Florence also contains miniatures, although its ninety pages of these illustrations fall far short of those found in the above-mentioned tomes of the Escorial. Furthermore, many of the miniatures were never finished, and some are no more than the preliminary sketches. However, this very incompleteness has contributed to knowledge. Students of mediaeval art can see in these unfinished miniatures a great deal about the manner in which the pictures were made. Some scholars, Professor Guerrero Lovillo among these, believe that the miniatures were the work of several artists and that there may have been a kind of production-line procedure in vogue at that time. The Florentine codex, incidentally, contains no music, although space was left for it; however, the canticles of this codex appear in another and larger codex (B.1.2, or E2) with music, and therefore the music for these songs is not actually missing.

The state of preservation of all four codices is remarkable. It is immediately apparent that great care has been accorded them. Indeed, King Alfonso so loved the songs that he made provision for their safekeeping in his last will and testament. Guerrero Lovillo cites the passage in his archaeological study of the *Canticles*.[7] "Likewise we order," reads the testament, "that all the books of the *Songs in Praise of Holy Mary* be in that church where our body will be buried, and that they cause them to be sung on the feasts of Holy Mary. And if that one, who may inherit what is ours according to law and our will, should desire to own these books of the *Songs of Holy Mary*, we command that he give for them good payment to the church from which he removes them so that he may own them with our grace and without sin."

When Philip II had the *Canticles* removed from Seville's cathedral, where Alfonso was buried, he provided good custodians in his library at the Escorial, and to this day the *Canticles* remain in almost perfect preservation.

The *Canticles* contain such a wealth of material concerning daily life in mediaeval Spain that one hardly knows where to begin. Some of the miracles took place in cities, and the miniatures in this case show an amazing amount of detail as to the life in streets and plazas, in churches, in palaces, or in private homes. Professor Guerrero Lovillo's archaeological study contains all 195 miniatures from MS.T.I.1., reproduced in black and white rather than in the beautiful colors of the original. One can, therefore, refer to these reproductions in a discussion of individual canticles.

Canticle IV is very valuable. It shows a school in progress, with the children seated on the floor listening to their teacher reading from a book. After the class the scholars took communion, and all this is clearly seen in the miniature. According to the story of this miracle, a Jewish pupil received the holy wafer from the image of the Virgin on the altar. For this his father, a glass maker, cast him into the furnace used in this trade. The details of the furnace are clearly visible, as are those of the meal of the Jewish family when the child tells his parents about having received communion.

Canticle XXV shows the establishment of a money-changer; XXVIII depicts a city under siege by Moors, with siege machinery, men in armor, and many of the weapons of war; XXXI takes place on a farm, and there is a good deal of detail as to vehicles, managers, and farm animals; XXXIII is one of several canticles relating storms at sea and offers remarkable pictures of ships; XXXIV tells of a Jew who threw a picture of the Madonna into a latrine, and the arrangements as regards such facilities are clearly shown; gamblers and all that takes place in a tavern appear in LXXII; one sees an artist at work on a scaffold high in the nave of a church in LXXIV.

The two examples of miniatures presented here were chosen almost at random, but they will, it is hoped, give some idea of what the pictures were like. Both come from the manuscript of the Escorial (T.I.1). In their full color, with gold and silver illumination, these, like all the miniatures, are naturally much more impressive if seen in color.

Canticle XVIII is one of some twenty-five that contain just beneath the pictures a kind of summary in Castilian of the Galician-Portuguese poem. It is quite possible that King Alfonso planned such a summary for the entire set of miniatures. If such was the case, the plan was not carried out.

This canticle concerns itself with what may be regarded as one of

Canticla XVIII: "Como a moller rogou Sancta Maria que lli gardass' os gusanos de seda e que lli daria end huna touca."

the popular miracles of the Alfonso the Learned, one drawn, surely from Spain's own folklore. We read that a woman whose business was the production of silk in the city of Segovia appealed to the Virgin when the silkworms were afflicted with some sort of disease. Each section or panel of the page, it will be noted, bears a kind of caption describing, in Galician-Portuguese, what is taking place. The three bands of miniatures are to be viewed from left to right. In the first panel the woman can be seen kneeling before the altar of the Virgin. In her hand she extends a tray filled with sick worms. The caption ("How the woman prayed to Holy Mary that if she would save the worms she would give her a robe") plainly explains what is taking place. The woman is wearing a characteristic garment, one seen in many of the miniatures, and even on this page in the fourth and fifth panels where other women appear. The altar design is in tile, but the altar cloth, which repeats the design that frames the entire page, bears a fringe at its lower extremity and is therefore a cloth and not ceramic. The chapel is of simple design with little in the way of decoration save the pattern in tile and cloth already mentioned.

In the second panel one can see the woman leaving the chapel. Some time has passed, and according to the caption, she has been remiss as to her promise ("How, being before the altar, she remembered the robe she had promised to Holy Mary, and she was in grief because of it").

Panel three shows us the woman after she has hurried home to begin the promised robe ("How the woman returned home and found that the wilkworms were weaving the robe"). In the fourth panel we see her with a number of Segovians whom she has summoned ("How she went out into the street to call the people, and the worms began to weave a second robe"). The woman then took one of the robes, in the fifth panel, and went with it to the chapel ("How the woman gave to the priests that robe which the worms had made").

The final panel ("How King Alfonso took one of the robes for his own chapel") shows the king with some of his courtiers, standing in the church with the robe in his hand. The king's appearance in the miniatures is frequent, and he apparently preferred to have himself depicted as a young man, even though before all the canticles had been written and illustrated, he was past middle age.

Note in the third panel the silkworms upon the frame where they were kept. The mulberry leaves can just be seen in the illustration. In the colors of the original they are clearly visible. The frame with the worms is painted at right angles to the viewer, for the artists wanted the worms to be seen distinctly, and had the frame been shown horizontal to the floor, they could hardly have been seen. This technique, incidentally, is followed in the *Libro de ajedrez, dados y tablas (Book of Chess, Dice and Backgammon)*, in which all the game boards appear at right angles so that the moves can be easily seen.

A close examination of the silkworms will show how realistically they are portrayed, except, of course, for their size, which is entirely out of proportion to the woman. This magnification was necessary if the worms were to be seen.

Of passing interest, at least, is the image of the Virgin and the Child Jesus. No mention is made in the canticle of its having moved or changed its position in any way. A casual glance will show that the image in the first and second panels (those in the first band at the top) is different from the two pictures of the image in the last two panels. At the top the Virgin holds the Child quite close to her face, a little closer in the second panel than in the first, almost as if she were about to kiss him. In the last two panels the Child is sitting placidly with his arms in his lap, and his head is not pressed to the Virgin's at all. There is even another difference in the last two panels: at the left the Virgin's right hand rests upon her knee and her left hand is on the shoulder of the Child; in the right and final panel her left arm is thrown completely around his shoulders, indeed her hand seems to be covering his left shoulder, while her hand extends to his lap. This phenomenon is repeated many times in the miniatures.

Canticle CVII is another taken from the Spanish scene, and again the city is Segovia. The story survives today in Spain among the folk. A large and poorly executed picture of one of its incidents may be seen painted alfresco on a wall in the cloister of the Cathedral of Segovia near the niche labeled as the resting place of Marisaltos, heroine of the miracle.

According to the canticle, Marisaltos, who earned this sobriquet from the leap she made, was a young Jewess who yearned to be a devotee of the Virgin. In the first panel we see her under arrest ("How they seized a Jewess of Segovia who had fallen into error"). She was sentenced by her people in the second panel ("How they led her to be hurled down from a peak that was there"). In the background stands the great Roman aqueduct which, strangely enough, the artists have painted not with Roman arches, but with the well-known horseshoe arch of the Moors. No one, by the way, has explained this mistake, although it has been suggested that Alfonso's artists did not see the aqueduct and drew it from a description, or perhaps saw it and did not draw it until enough time had elapsed to permit the error they made in its depiction.

Panel three shows the Jewess falling toward the earth from the high peak ("How they cast her down and she was not hurt because she called upon Holy Mary"). In panel four she has landed safely ("How she arose unharmed praising Holy Mary greatly"). Above her in the sky the Virgin extends a hand downward. In panel five the Jewess speaks to the Christians ("How she entered the church of Holy Mary and related the miracle to the people"). In the last panel one can see Marisaltos sitting in the font as the priest showers her with baptismal water ("How that Jewess was made Christian").

This page of miniatures is more detailed than the one dealing with the miracle of the silkworms. Much of the city can be seen in the first panel, as well as in the second; windows, the barbican, arched doorways, roofs with characteristic tiles, the aqueduct, the costumes of Marisaltos' compatriots with their exaggerated Semitic features, seen again and again in the miniatures.

Note the tree in the background and the flowers on the mountainside, some of which have been identified as flowers that still grow in that region of Spain. The altar, again covered in tile, and the elaborate altar cloth are worthy of note, and quite different from the ones depicted in Canticle XVIII.

After Alfonso's death Spanish miniatures, according to Guerrero Lovillo, passed into decline. Certainly none in the following century, or even in the next, equalled those of the *Canticles*. Indeed, none, insofar as regards the portrayal of daily life, has been found to compare with them. When all the miniatures in the codices of the Escorial and of the National Library of Florence, as well as the codex that presents the musicians and their instruments, have been thoroughly studied, we will have a considerable amplification in our concepts of what the life of man was in the second half of the thirteenth century.

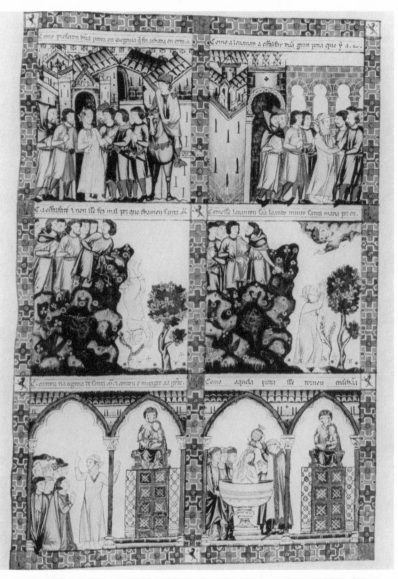

Canticle CVII: "Como preseron huna judea en Segovia qie foi achada en erro."

[AUTH. See the color facsimile, *Cantigas de Santa Maria. Edición facsímil del Códice T.I.1. de la Biblioteca de San Lorenzo de El Escorial, Siglo XIII*. Madrid: EDILAN, 1979, which is a work of art in itself, with color reproductions of great beauty and authenticity. For a complete transcription of the prosifications see James R. Chatham. "A Paleographic Edition of the Alfonsine Collection of Prose Miracles of the Virgin," in *Oelschläger Festschrift* (Estudios de Hispanófila, 36, Chapel Hill, 1976), pp. 73-111; and Anthony J. Cárdenas. "A Study of Alfonso's Role in Selected *Cantigas* and the Castilian Prosifications of Escorial Codex T.I.1" in *Studies on the CSM*: Proceedings of the international Symposium on the *Cantigas de Santa María* of Alfonso X, el Sabio (1252-1284) in Commemoration of its 700th Anniversary Year—1981. Madison, Wisconsin: Hispanic Seminary of Medieval Studies, 1987, pp. 253-68.]

Notes

* Reprinted from *Speculum*, 33 (1958), 484-89.

¹ *Primera crónica general*, ed. Ramón Menéndez Pidal, in *Nueva Biblioteca de Autores Españoles*, V (Madrid, 1906); Alfonso el Sabio, *General Estoria, Primera Parte*, ed. A. G. Solalinde (Madrid, 1930).

² *Los libros del saber de astronomia*, ed. M. Rico y Sinobas, 5 vols. (Madrid, 1863-67); *Lapidario del Rey Don Alfonso X*, ed. in facsimile J. Fernández Montaña (Madrid, 1881); *Libro de ajedrez, dados y tablas*, ed. in facsimile J. G. White, *The Spanish Treatise on Chess Play Written by Order of King Alfonso the Sage in the Year 1283*, 2 vols. (London, 1913).

³ *Las Siete Partidas del Rey Don Alfonso el Sabio*, published by the Real Academia de la Historia, 3 vols. (Madrid, 1807).

⁴ *Cantigas de Santa Maria*, ed. Leopoldo Augusto de Cueto, Marqués de Valmar, 2 vols. (Madrid, 1889).

⁵ Alfonso X of Castile, *Patron of Literature and Learning* (Oxford, 1951), pp. 24-46.

⁶ *Miniatura gótica castellana: Siglos XIII y XIV* (Madrid, 1956).

⁷ *Las Cantigas: Estudio arqueológico de sus miniaturas* (Madrid, 1949), p. 14.

The Art of Illumination
in the Books of Alfonso X*

ORTUNATELY FOR ART HISTORY, Alfonso highly esteemed picture books and lavished his patronage upon them. We read in his prologue to his *Primera crónica general* (p. 4), for example, that "mandamos ayuntar cuantos libros pudimos aver de estorias" ("we order collected as many books as we could have of stories"), in which the word *estorias* means "illustrations." Indeed he so prized one series of volumes of a single work, the *Cantigas de Santa María* or *Canticles of Holy Mary*, most probably because these books contained so many illuminations, that in his last will and testament he provided for their archiving in that church in which his body would be interred, which turned out to be the Cathedral of Seville. He even commanded that the *cantigas* be sung there on feast days of the Virgin. There the books remained until Philip II removed them to his new library in the Escorial, where the most important volume is today.[1]

Most of Alfonso's books contain illuminations. But the others— the *Lapidaries*, the *Book of Chess, Dice and Backgammon*, the *Book of Astronomy*, the *Histories*, and the *Seven Divisions of Law*—do not display the many artistic devices and techniques found in the *Cantiga* MSS, which were the king's favorite books. Spanish art historians and critics have therefore devoted more study to the *Cantigas* than to the other Alfonsine manuscripts. Also, the Escorial codex of the *Cantigas*, the richest by far in miniatures, is the only Alfonsine book from which a complete and authentic facsimile has been published. This facsimile makes it possible for scholars to study with confidence all the illuminations, calligraphy, and musical notation of the original, which could not be accomplished by referring to the black-and-white facsimile in the 1949 edition by José Guerrero Lovillo which has served us well insofar as it could.

It is possible that a few people may not be entirely familiar with the *Cantigas de Santa Maria*. Let me briefly offer a few remarks by way of orientation. The complete corpus of *Cantigas* consists of four manuscripts, which *in toto* contain more than four hundred Marian miracles and songs of praise.[2] The *Cantigas* are written in Galician-Portuguese verse rather than in Castilian, and the entire anthology offers the most copious assemblage of poetic meters in the Peninsula, representing all poetic meters known in Spain before the Renaissance, except of course the sonnet (see Clarke, Chisman). Since each poem required a separate melody, the *Cantigas* is Spain's richest anthology of medieval song (Anglés). Encyclopedic also is the *Cantigas'* most varied presentation of sociological patterns, for the illuminations reveal a vast diversity of facets of the panorama of medieval life. All the masses and classes meet the eye from emperors and kings and cardinals to the lowest serf and the most humble cleric. Miracles depict the hunt, travel by land and sea, naval battles and wars on land, Moors, Jews, and native Spaniards, as well as folk from foreign lands. They show rural life and urban, both past and present, for some of the miracles took place in earlier centuries; and in many miniatures one sees the Blessed Virgin and her Son as they and their angels wage eternal war against Satan and his minions.[3] The miniatures in the two manuscripts of the *Cantigas* which visualize events have no equal anywhere as to quantity and quality of narrative art and iconography.[4] In these illuminations students of art can study pigments and the manner of their application, various devices for presenting visually the nine elements of narrative—plot, conflict, setting, characterization, theme, style, effect, point of view, and mood or tone—as well as the richest portrayal of medieval humanity, nature, theology, superstition, ethics, folklore, and daily life to be found in medieval books. Even so, to date the art of the *Cantigas* has hardly been researched, due to various factors such as inaccessibility of manuscripts and the difficulties of medieval Galician-Portuguese, which most scholars do not read with ease. The opportunities for original research are truly virtually untouched.

The sources of the miracles in their written form have not been completely uncovered.[5] Alfonso apparently looked everywhere for miracles and quite naturally turned first to the great collection in Latin dispersed across medieval Europe. Later he included miracles of purely Spanish vintage and thereby preserved some interesting motifs which would almost surely have been lost. He even included miracles he claimed to have witnessed personally and others which had been wrought for members of his family and his servitors.[6] In this way he may be the only collector and renderer of miracles who linked himself so closely to this work.[7]

I shall not concern myself here with motifs and their literary sources, but must cleave to another kind of source—that is, to the manuscripts and other art genres from which the king's illuminators might have drawn inspiration and to the "schools" of illumination which might have influenced them. What do we know of "artistic" influences or what models might Alfonsine artists have emulated? Within the last few years we have learned a considerable amount. Some of this knowledge is admittedly based upon speculation; but some of it too is more factual, coming from comparisons between miniatures in the *Cantigas* with miniatures from abroad. Perhaps art work other than illuminations in books may have inspired Alfonsine miniaturists, since miracles were depicted in stained glass, ivory and wood carvings, sculptures, and frescoes and other paintings. I might point out one miracle in a stained-glass window of the church of Le Mans[8] and refer to what has been said about the influence of French painted-ivory diptychs concerning their influence upon the frames or friezes which encompass the miniatures in the *Cantigas* (Guerrero Lovillo, 20). The burden of such influences may never be weighed with exactitude; but since so many of the miracles found in the *Cantigas* appear in the graphic arts in Spain and abroad, it is not at all unlikely that art forms other than illuminations in books influenced the king's artists. And viewed from the other end of the spectrum, the miniatures of the *Cantigas* might have suggested much to artists practicing other kinds of art. This too is an area barely explored, if at all. Also uninvestigated, but worthy of study, is the possible parallel between illuminations in the *Cantigas* and the little-known medieval dramas of Spain, both in Latin and in the vernacular. Here again virtually nothing has been published.[9]

The fine arts in Spain, especially in churches, palaces, and monastic houses along the Camino de Santiago, flourished and were excellent and sophisticated. Anyone who visits the Collegiate Chapel of the Cathedral of León to view the frescoes, gazes at the visualizations in the stained-glass windows of the cathedral proper, or peruses the illuminated Bibles in the treasury, will be convinced of Spain's artistic excellence. But the frescoes and Bibles represent Romanesque art, and that art form was not considered by Alfonso and his illuminators to be stylish, which led them to prefer the more modish Gothic art.

Alfonso, an innovator in many aspects of his work, turned to the current and more fashionable Gothic style therefore, and managed to develop what may be rightfully termed "Spanish Gothic," a genre colored by various foreign schools. Spanish Gothic as represented in the *Cantigas* was seemingly shaped by transpyrenean illuminations, chiefly French but possibly also German and Italian, and probably too from other European areas and, it now appears quite likely, from illuminations developed in various areas of the Islamic world. Whatever the influences may have been, we can be certain that they were "Hispanified" to a degree, just as were literary works which had their origins abroad, for example the *Auto de los Reyes Magos* (ed. 1900) and the famous *Cavallero Cifar* (ed. 1929).

Obviously in this short article I can only touch upon some of the most likely foreign importations which helped to form Marian miniatures. Those interested in pursuing the matter in depth may consult some of the studies cited in footnotes. Some of the most knowledgeable critics see French influences as the strongest.[10] Even a person like me whose expertise has been primarily limited to the study of medieval literature, if he studies French miniatures and compares them with those in the *Cantigas*, is bound to see certain similarities, as well as elements not similar at all. Perforce he has to admit that much of iconography, imagery, devices, and techniques in the *Cantigas* derive from French models. But what are we to make of the aspects of Alfonsine miniatures which are not present in the miniatures of France? Some scholars see German models, others Italian (e.g., G. Menéndez Pidal). Alfonso's mother was Beatriz of Swabia, granddaughter of Frederick Barbarossa; and it is quite logical to believe that a princess with the pretensions of Beatriz would have brought in her train musicians and illuminators (see Ballesteros-Beretta). And after the royal marriage surely Hispano-Germanic culture and political relationships would have been numerous.

The same may be said for Italian ties, for Alfonso was united by either ties of marriage or blood with royalty in Italy. For that matter, he had similar ties in Portugal, England (his half-sister, Leonor, married Edward I), Rumania, Norway, Constantinople, Sicily, Aragon, and Hungary. From any or from all of these realms might have come models employed by the illuminators of the *Cantigas*.

Thus far I have mentioned European art; but when dealing with medieval Spanish culture one can never overlook the Moorish factor and by extension the Islamic impact from several areas of the world. Some will perhaps contradict me, stating that the Koran forbade idolatry and that all depictions of Allah's creatures, except those of a floral nature and even then in very stylized forms, were regarded as idolatrous. At one time I would have supported such allegations, but now I must take a different view. We now know that liberal-minded erudites in the Umayyad Kingdom of Andalusia, as well as in Egypt, Syria, and especially Persia, did not cleave too strictly to Koranic tenets concerning the fine arts, since they argued that the harsh rulings against art had been required in the "epoch of ignorance," by which they meant the formative and puritanical period of Islam's development (G. Menéndez Pidal, p. 44). Art work was esteemed and collected by those who could afford it, and this was true in much if not all of Islam—art in the form of mosaics, carvings, paintings, sculptures, and illuminated books. It is likely that in Persia the art of illumination never flagged, even in the period of the rise of Islam and while the Prophet still lived. If erudite Muslim rulers in Andalusia were the patrons of Moorish and Jewish poets who added primitive Christian Spanish folk songs, or *jarchas*, to their courtly verse, why would they not have accepted and emulated the best of Christian art?[11] I realize that not much proof exists, since in the course of the long and bitter wars against the Spanish Muslims, culminating in the fall of Granada to Ferdinand and Isabella, the destruction of things Islamic depleted the treasury of eastern art in Spain.

Proof exists elsewhere, however, or partial proof at least, which points to illuminations that seem to belong to the same school of the illuminator's art found so copiously represented in the *Cantigas de Santa Maria*. Some of these Eastern miniatures are so close in design and artistic presentation, and above all in visualization of stories and actual historical events, indeed so very like the miniatures in the *Cantigas*, that one can hardly doubt there was some influence upon them from the East or that the Eastern manuscripts and the Alfonsine manuscripts derive from a common art.

I am not considering those Arabic manuscripts of a scientific nature filled with compasses and astrolabes and the other paraphernalia needed in navigation and astronomy, though these too surely were copied by the king's artists in his scientific works. Nor do I mean the wonderful miniatures in the *Book of Chess, Dice, and Backgammon*, many of whose illuminations depict Moors and Arabs playing these games, even though this book surely contains much in art work which may stem from eastern skills in the making of miniatures. What I have in mind is picture books, like the *Cantigas de Santa Maria*, actually portraying events and incidents which visualize fiction and history.

An Eastern work possibly seen by Alfonso's artists was a novelesque piece which in good part can be traced back to the *Panchatantra*. This particular manuscript is a translation of the Hindu work from Persian into Arabic, in which language it was known as *Kalila wa-Dimna*, or to us *The Fables of Bidpay*. The Arabic version containing, as had the Old Pahlevi, much material not found in the Indian work but added to it from the great storehouse of Middle Eastern fiction, was called by Alfonso *El libro de Calila e Digna*.[12] *Calila e Digna* may have been the first translation of fiction from Arabic into Castilian; but unfortunately the three extant manuscripts do not contain the kind of illustrations found in the manuscript of Baghdad penned and illuminated only a few years before the Alfonsine translation which was made in 1251, one year before Alfonso's coronation.[13] The only illustrated text of *Calila e Digna*, probably of the fourteenth century, contains many interesting miniatures in the form of line drawings without color. It is obviously the work of a Western artist, for all the human characters wear European clothing.[14]

I do not insist that Alfonso's illuminators saw one of the colorfully illuminated books of Eastern vintage; but they might have, because long before Alfonso's time such books had been brought to Spain by Arabs from the Middle East and North Africa. Seville, Cordova, and even Toledo in the Learned King's lifetime were still international centers of culture to which people from across the world gravitated. The ruler of Egypt for example, although he himself did not travel to Spain, nonetheless sent his ambassadors to Alfonso in Seville, ambassadors who in memory of Alfonso's father, Ferdinand III, brought exotic animals. We may see these creatures in a miniature of the *Cantigas*, in what may be the first European depiction of some. One sees clearly a giraffe, a zebra, an elephant, as well as exotic birds like the ostrich and the ibis, all of which humble themselves before the

Blessed Virgin. One may read some mention of these in the *Crónica de los reyes de Castilla*.[15]

Gonzalo Menéndez Pidal points to two additional eastern manuscripts which he sees as possible models used by Alfonsine artists. One was penned and illuminated in the Frankish kingdom of Jerusalem around 1250-1254; the other is dated 1288, too late to have influenced the *Cantigas*, completed a year or so before Alfonso died in 1284. Of these two, the *Universal History* was illuminated in Acre in 1286; the Bible, illuminated in Acre between 1250 and 1254, was finished even as Alfonso was beginning volumes of the *Cantigas*. They divide each illuminated page into six separate panels separated by decorative bands and framed by colorful bands in the same motifs (Menéndez Pidal, 42-43). Gonzalo Menéndez Pidal sees these Franco-Palestinian manuscripts, with their arrangement of action and scene in six panels, as possible models, since these books were made in the Middle East. He may be correct, for perhaps the six-panel plan is of Eastern origin. We know, however, of four-panel arrangements of events in twelfth-century England and have a right to wonder if the plan of grouping into clusters of panels of miniatures might have arisen in England and migrated to the Frankish kingdom of Jerusalem. Of course, migration of this artistic device might have arisen in the East and penetrated to the West.[16] Alfonso's illuminators parallel quite closely the techniques and devices employed in the two manuscripts from Jerusalem, but true influence remains to be more carefully investigated.

In the aforementioned article of Gonzalo Menéndez Pidal another important probable influence is mentioned. He refers to the *Maqamat de Hariri* of the School of Baghdad in 1237, a manuscript apparently made in Catalonia. He compares two miniatures which do indeed contain many similarities with the *Cantigas*, and to prove it he publishes in black and white the miniatures from the *Maqamat* and two from the *Cantigas*.[17] In folio 19 of *Hariri* and in the miniature from *Cantiga* 185 there is much which is similar. In the *Maqamat* a contingent of Muslim horsemen march forth, standards unfurled and trumpets lifted as they are sounded. The same arrangement appears in the *Cantiga*, and in both miniatures one can see the horizon almost filled with huge banners punctuated by raised lances. Very similar, too, in the two miniatures is the manner of indicating the presence of horses, not seen, through the device of revealing only their hooves. Folio 94v and *Cantiga* 165 resemble one another even more. The *Maqamat*, since it was illustrated in Spain, could well have been seen by Alfonso's artists.

The miniatures of the *Maqamat* present another device very well represented in the Marian illuminations. This is the device of placing one or more arches within the various panels so as to divide the action and to impart the impression of a series of events. These and other techniques of parallel nature suggest the strongest possibility of artistic influence upon the *Cantigas*, since so many are common to the Alfonsine manuscript.[18]

Ecclesiastical art was used as a model for the *Cantigas*, of course, as would be expected in miracles of the Virgin, since many of the same miracles had long since been depicted in monastic scriptoria. One finds Christian imagery—the floral images of the Virgin, the cloud floating above the miracle-in-progress to indicate her presence (as when in *Cantiga* 164, after the Virgin has saved her pious devotee from the bull, the cloud seen through an archway indicates her benevolent presence), and the fingers extended in blessing. Quite as would be expected too, one sees the usual votive candles, candelabra on altars, ornamental tiles, columns, and the arches of churches and monastic houses. One should not consider the miniatures of the *Cantigas* as purely pietistic works, however, for the entire concept of the miracles and their depiction leans far toward the secular. Careful consideration reveals that most of the miracles probably are not what we generally regard as pietistic, save of course for the role of the Virgin. Coupled with what is known about the Alfonsine miniaturists, who seem not to have been clerics, this leads me to agree with scholars who regard the miracles as secular books in their conception and in their verbal and visual presentation. This dichotomy is a fine example of the well-known *sic et non* so prevalent in medieval literature; but even *sic et non* cannot explain the intense secularity of the *Cantigas*.[19]

How then did it come about that the *Cantigas* include so many non-pietistic stories to demonstrate the powers of the Virgin? Consider only two *cantigas* whose content may contribute to an answer. Number 135 has not had its source established; but it is surely one of those *romances* (the same genre as the French prose *roman*, not a *romance* in its connotation of a "ballad" later to emerge in Spain) whose length and complexity and detail, insofar as plot is concerned, caused the miniaturists certain problems as they depicted its development. All that makes this rather spicy story a miracle is the insertion of the Virgin, who saves the heroine from rape and brings her and her beloved to an extremely carnal union in their nuptial chamber, all of which is naively and explicitly depicted in the last miniature in the series.[20] One wonders if a clerical artist would have dared so much. Number 42 also stems from the secular world, and indeed had been a secular tale written in twelfth-century Latin by some raconteur in France. The original story has stood the test of time, for it would appear again in *La Vénus d'Ille* of Prosper Mérimée centuries later. In the Latin account the Virgin played no role, nor did she in the earlier Latin account, for it was the goddess Venus who was the nemesis of the young man who betrayed her.[21]

My explanation of the narrative art of the *Cantigas de Santa Maria* can best be presented by referring to one *cantiga* only and by describing the devices used by its artists to visualize the written account. I feel that it is one of the most representative of all the miniatures and that it contains as many narrative devices as any. Its colors are excellent moreover, and it was surely the work of one of the "better artists" of the codex. No summary of a *cantiga* can be as effective as a complete translation; and since *cantigas* are often very brief, number 42 will be presented here.[22] In passing, let me state that I believe this to be one of the most "literary" of all the *Cantigas* in its careful attention to structure and presentation. This is probably due to the fact that the story was already old when Alfonso and his poets used it as the background for this miracle. The old story of Venus and her devotee had had time to be polished and improved; when it reached the Learned King there was little to do to embellish it, save to substitute the Blessed Virgin for the pagan goddess and to change the savage dénouement of the original into the miracle's ending in a more humane and Christian fashion.

This is how the postulant placed the ring on the finger of the statue of Holy Mary and the statue curved its finger around it.

The most glorious Virgin,
Spiritual Queen, is solicitous
of those she loves, for she
does not want them to do wrong.

Concerning this, I shall tell you a beautiful
miracle, agreeable to hear, which the Virgin
Mother of Our Lord performed to save from
great error a fickle admirer who often changed
his fancies.

It happened in the land of Germany that some
people wished to renovate their church.
Therefore, they removed the statue of Holy
Mary, which was on the altar, and put it
at the entrance to the town square under
the portico.

In that square there was a lush green park
where the local folk went to take their
ease and there they played ball, which is
the favorite game of all young men.

There chanced to come there once a great
troop of young men to play ball, and among
them was a youth who was in love. He wore
a ring which his beloved, a native of that
town, had given him.

This youth, for fear that he would twist
the ring when he hit the ball, looked for
a place to put it. He saw the beautiful
statue and went to place the ring on its
finger saying: "From this day forth
that lady whom I loved means nothing to me,
for I swear to God that these eyes of mine
have never seen anything so beautiful. Hence
from now on I shall be one of your servants
and give you this beautiful ring as pledge."

Kneeling before the statue in reverence and
saying "Ave Maria," he promised Her then and
there that from that moment on he would
never love another woman and would be
faithful to Her.

When he had made his promise, the youth
arose and the statue closed its finger
around the ring. The young man, when he
saw this, was taken with such great fright
that he began to shout: "Oh, Holy Mary,
protect me!"

The people, when they heard this, came
running up to where the youth was shouting
and he told them what we have just recounted
to you. They advised him to enter the order
of the monks of Claraval at once.

They all believed that he had done so, but
on the advice of the devil he did otherwise,
for what he had promised to the Virgin of

great worth melted from his thoughts as
water melts salt.
He never more gave thought to the Glorious
Virgin, but fell in love again with his
first lady love. To please his relatives,
he married her soon after and left the joys
of the other world for earthly pleasures.
After the nuptials were over and day was
done, the bridegroom lay down and went
quickly to sleep. While sleeping, he saw
Holy Mary in his dreams and She called to
him angrily: "Oh, my faithless liar!
Why did you forsake me and take a wife?
You forgot the ring you gave me. Therefore,
you must leave your wife and go with me
wherever I so will. Otherwise, from now
on, you will suffer mortal anguish."
The bridegroom awoke, but he did not wish
to depart. The Glorious Virgin made him
go to sleep again and he saw Her lying between his bride and himself to separate
them. She called to him angrily: "Wicked,
false, unfaithful one,
do you understand? Why did you leave me
and have no shame of it? If you wish my
love, you will arise from here and come at
once with me before daybreak. Get up in
a hurry and leave this house! Go!"
Then the bridegroom awakened and was so
frightened by this that he got up and
went on his way without calling even two
or three men to go with him. He wandered
through the wilderness for more than a
month and took up lodging in a hermitage
beside a pine grove.
Thenceforth, as I found written, he served
Holy Mary, Mother of the King Most High,
who then took him with Her, as I believe
and know to be true, from this world to
Paradise, the heavenly realm.

Color plays a truly important role in the illuminations of the
Cantigas, for color symbolism is very important. But color also makes
clear and understandable what black and white fails to do. Indeed, a

black and white reproduction often actually conceals important elements. Sometimes the original's pale pinks and beiges, for example, when outlined by the original's white, may run together, obscuring outlines. The expression of a face may change from its representation in full color when it is reduced to black-and-white. It would have been prohibitively expensive to offer a color plate, so we must make do for the present with the pale reproduction [offered here]. It can at least lay out the general design or presentation, depict the actual events as they take place in each of the panels, provide some impression of background with its details, and indicate (but only fairly well) how medieval artists could visualize all or most of the nine elements of the classic design of verbal narrative.[23]

Ideally one should view the original in the Escorial Museum or else the published facsimile in color. Here the reader should turn, as he reads, to the page illustrated in black and white in order to follow what I attempt to describe. Perhaps he will be able, since I describe in some detail the colors found in the panels—of flowers, garments, rooftops, columns, and so on—to visualize how the miniatures looked in their pristine form. The viewer's eye should move from left to right, just as it does when reading a comic book today. Above each of the six panels is a caption in either scarlet or azure calligraphy which explains what appears below it. The lions rampant and the three-towered castles, each of which appears in a corner of every panel, symbolize Alfonso's kingdoms of León and Castile. The six miniatures, which I shall term "panels," are framed together by a colorful band of ornate design, and this motif is repeated in a perpendicular band running down the middle of the page, separating the three panels to the left from the three to the right. Similar bands separate the three pairs of horizontal panels. Every page of illumination in the codex is so arranged, although the designs in the panels' borders and in the bands sometimes vary.

Above panel 1 we read: "Como lavravan huna eglesia et poseron a omage de Santa Maria no portal" (How they were working on a church and placed the image of Holy Mary under the portal). From the very first the viewer sees elements of daily life portrayed. Masons at the right hand of the panel work: one mixes mortar with a spade; another fills a bucket, which a man above lifts by means of a pulley; a fourth lays blocks of stone. All are secular workers. Three wear leather hats to protect their heads, and one wears a white kerchief to contain his

hair. The statue of the Virgin with the Christ Child on her lap appears at the left of the panel under an arch, which focuses attention upon her role in the story.

Panel 2 offers an example of something characteristic of *cantiga* illumination, that is, the amplification of a very minor element. The artists in this panel simply took the opportunity to illustrate something they found attractive, something from the daily life around them which they felt would surely interest the viewer. Even the caption, "Como iogavan a pelota os mancebos en un prado" (How young men played ball in a meadow), is spun out visually into one of the codex's finest miniatures. The batter at the left, in a pastel puce tunic, holds a bat which tapers as do ours today. He stands with one knee bent, his arms in the perfect position for batting the ball which is about to leave the hand of the pitcher in an underhand pitch. The pitcher in deep blue stands far too close to the batter; but medieval people understood the need to conserve parchment and were familiar with the lack of proportion and attention to space. Had the players been painted to scale, the artists could not have included such details as the open-work shoes with colorful hose showing through and the many flowers of the meadow. Three men in the outfield stand, joined palms upraised and open, exactly as players would stand waiting to catch a ball. The artists displayed great taste in the distribution of color in the clothing of the ball players—pale puce on the batter, blue for the pitcher, pale puce for the man just behind the pitcher, pale lavender for one outfielder, and blue for the player barely seen. All wear the characteristic white kerchief men of all classes and occupations wore to contain their nape-length locks. The men are all blond, as indeed is the case with a majority of people of both sexes in nearly all the illuminations, except of course for Moors and Jews.

Another device needs explanation. Two balls can be clearly seen in the miniature—one in the pitcher's hand, the other high in the air above the expectant outfielders. This is the device I designate as "double action," and it is employed often in the illuminations of other cultural areas as well as in Spain. Sometimes in the *Cantigas* one sees examples of "triple action." The technique of depicting two or three different moments of action in a single illustration enabled the artists to expand the theatre of events and to impart in one miniature what might be expected to appear in more than one. The first action in the panel in which the ball game is in progress reveals the ball in one game;

it has been batted and is seen high in the air as it moves above the outfielders, or perhaps at the very moment it descends toward their outstretched hands. A sequel to this action is found in the stance of the batter and the pitcher as another ball is about to be launched. Probably we are seeing two separate ball games or, at the very least, two separate sequences in one.

Panel 3, "Como o omage de Santa Maria encolleu o dedo con a anel q'lle deu o donzel en sinal damor" (How the statue of Holy Mary closed its finger around the ring which the youth gave her in token of love), encapsulates a single dramatic instant in time. The youth in deep blue, his long blond curls hanging unconfined, the better to frame his countenance, stands in terror before the image of Our Lady whose upraised stone hand reveals the ring, as well as the familiar orb. The "hand language" of the young man expresses eloquently his fear as he sees the stone finger closing around the ring.

Most of the color in this panel is concentrated in the scene in or before the arch under which the Virgin's image appears. The young man wears a deep blue tunic, the Virgin a puce gown, over which her blue robe falls in realistic folds. More color is provided by the gold in her surplice, her throne, her crown encircled by a deep blue nimbus set with crimson floral designs, and by the golden columns which hold up the arch. Color also flashes from the blue gown of the Christ Child whose golden collar, and bright halo in scarlet and gold, contribute to the jewel-like quality of the scene. The entire right-hand side of this miniature, which contains no human figures and no action at all, is of gray stone, with only the barest touch of brown lining the three windows seen in the wall. One might at first regard this stark half of the panel as an example of poor balance against the colorful other half, but actually the very starkness is deliberate, since it contrasts with and focuses upon the scene and the action beneath the arch.

Panel 4, "Como o donzel casou con outra moller e leyxou Santa Maria" (How the youth wed another woman and deserted Holy Mary), depicts the wedding feast. The robes of the diners are blue, as are those of all the servants save one, who wears pink. Brilliant blue roof tiles and a series of pale pink turrets, running the full width of the panel, contrast with the panel's frame design in blue, red, green, white and gold. The groom, to the far left, now wears the white kerchief as do one of the guests and two of the servants who have entered the banquet hall with covered dishes of gold. The bride, flanked by the groom and a lady wearing a white wimple, blazes in a golden wedding gown and crown. The table and its setting provide interesting depictions of what a medieval dinner was, for one sees hexagonal rolls, bowls and goblets, and knives on a white tablecloth; the tablecloth descends halfway to the floor, enabling the viewer to see the hems of the robes of the diners and their feet.

In this panel the device of using golden arches plays an important role and is illustrative of their part in many other pages of illumination. The largest, to the left, frames four people, among them the bride and groom; the second or middle arch has only two; the third encompasses the standing or advancing servants. The eye moves from left to right and catches at least three moments of time. Here then, as in many ecclesiastical illuminations, arches focus upon the flow of action, offering a means of spatial transition from one separate point of time to another. The concept of a picture within a picture—that is, an arch within the square frame of the panel—serves to refine and intensify both the main action of the entire panel and the encapsulated action under the arch. Here most definitely the artists have made the dramatic arch a very integral part of their visualizations. And perhaps, too, they believed that this subtle bow to sacred significance might somehow excuse or diminish the amorous elements of the miracle. The arches in the *Cantigas* may be an attempt to cast a pietistic patina, then, over stories of rapine, murder, carnal lust, incest, and devil worship. Since arches frequently served as the backdrop of contemporary dramas, separating different stages of dramatic plot, viewers of these Marian miniatures might well have associated arches with drama, and might thereby have experienced something akin to what they felt when they watched a play. The simple focusing device of the arch allows the viewer to see and interpret these separate actions in panel 4 and can even be regarded as a technique of "visualization."

Panel 5, "Como Santa Maria fez levantar o novio de cabo da novia et xo levou" (How Holy Mary made the groom arise from beside the bride and took him away), is the most colorful of all the panels in *Cantiga* 42. It represents pictorially also the climax of the miracle. In the larger of the two arches appear the two protagonists—the Blessed Virgin and the groom—as well as the sleeping bride. The varied and brilliant colors in this panel were laid on harmoniously and tastefully, with considerable attention to contrast, framing of action, and detail. The arch just mentioned has a great deal of meticulous portrayal of scene: the four-poster bed covered by its deep blue counterpane, whose crimson lining shows here and there as the cloth falls in graceful folds to the floor. Above the bed a filmy white canopy with its golden design bifurcates in a kind of arch all its own. The arch itself is cusped, and gold and scarlet are evident in it. The same gold and scarlet are picked up in the halo of the Virgin and in the gold epaulettes of her angelic escort, seen in the left-hand arch. Gold also flashes in Our Lady's robe, from columns, and from the golden four-poster. The lavender and deep blue counterpane is also spangled with golden designs; and the bolster beneath the bride's and groom's heads is a riot of multi-colored designs upon a field of gold. Color is present too in the city's skyline—in the purple-tiled tower at the left and the domes and turrets in puce, blue, and red. And of course the aforementioned framing designs supplement the colorful interior of the panel.

In this remarkable miniature the artists have captured most, if not all, of the nine elements of the classic design—plot, conflict, setting, characterization, style, theme, effect, point of view, and mood or tone. The groom stares up from his bed into the eyes of Our Lady, who grasps him firmly by the wrist, preparatory to dragging him away from his unconsummated marriage. With his free hand he seems to repel her. Both he and the bride appear to be nude, but only the upper parts of their bodies can be seen. Perhaps the Virgin's close proximity governed this modest covering of their nether parts. Reference to the translation will remind the reader that the Virgin entered the bed and lay between the bride and groom to separate them, but the artists seemed not to dare to portray her in such an unbecoming position.

The sixth and last panel is captioned "Como aquel novio se meteu en huna hermida u fez muy santa vida" (How that bridegroom placed himself in a hermitage and made a very pious life). This is a crowded panel and yet it pleases the eye, since the crowding is necessary to the rural quality of the scene. As background, the hermitage in neutral pale-tan tones is roofed with blue-gray tiles. Around it and behind it rise pine trees, and to the right and left one sees flower-spangled hills. Surely consciousness of perspective is evident here, or at least a very good understanding of depth of scene and how to portray it. The vivid red-brown boles and branches, the bright green of the pine needles, and the colorful blossoms, aided by the framing design, lend most of the color to this panel. The hermit wears a grayish-lavender habit and a lavender cap. His skin tones, as well as those of all the people in the six miniatures, are true to life. The man's hoary hair and beard would seem to indicate some passage of time, and certainly more than the month mentioned in the penultimate stanza of the poem. He seems to be much older, so that it may be that the artists have portrayed him as he would have appeared after many years of devoted service to the Virgin.

I believe that the artists have managed to parallel the written word quite well. Setting is almost exclusively the creation of the miniaturists, however, since no details of this narrative element were given in the verbalization. Plot and conflict follow in visualized form most of what the miracle relates. The artists have developed characterization through gestures, facial expressions, stances, and movement as indicated by the flow and fall of garments. The gestures of the groom for instance in panel 3, his hands open and thrown up in an attitude of terror at the sight of the statue's finger closing around the ring, most graphically portray his feelings. The Virgin's purposefulness could hardly have been more manifest than in the way she holds him by the arm as she forces him to leave his bride.

All narratives require theme, and theme is developed in this *cantiga* through the expression of the Virgin's grace in forcing the recalcitrant devotee to keep his promise and save his soul. Indeed, there may be a lesser or perhaps a broader theme. Is not the personal problem of the ball player, whose very way of life is changed, a theme all its own? And surely there is the allegorical theme with peripheral implications that the protagonist's dilemma is also humanity's—that is, the everlasting conflict between this world and heaven. The artists seem to me to have consciously applied themselves to this.

Even style is reflected in the illuminations of this miracle, as well as in most of the others; the omniscient point of view is ever-present; and mood or tone in the hands of the Alfonsine artists has been evoked with greater effect than by the written word. I mentioned above that the presentation of the *Cantigas de Santa Maria* is a three-fold communication. The words, even in translation, provide the reader with proof of the poems' literary quality, and this is especially true of Number 42. The miniatures, as we have seen, relate more effectively than any words the events and background of the story. And music surely intensified the miracle's impact.

Although an explication of the content and presentation of *Cantiga* 42 can delineate many of the most representative artistic techniques of visualized narrative, one cannot treat all of the many utilized by the artists. We have reviewed the use of the dramatic arch, multiple action, perspective, condensation of large fields of scene and action into a small space, and amplification of a minor part of verbalization into a significant visualization. We have also treated gesture, facial expression, stance, and movement created by the fall and flow of garments. Some other aspects should be listed, with the understanding that not all such devices can be included without a very intensive study by art historians and art critics with special qualifications as medievalists.

Associated with double action, but not actually the same device, is that of depicting more than one event in the same panel by separating the two by a wall, a cliff, a line of trees or by some other physical boundary. In *Cantiga* 64, for example, two scenes are divided by a wall. To the left a young man employs an old go-between to help him seduce the wife of a man absent due to a journey. In the same panel and to the right, separated by the wall, we see the mediator talking with the wife. In a single panel, then, two separate scenes appear, either of which might have occupied the entire space. This device is much less confusing than double action in *Cantiga* 42 wherein we see either two separate ball games in one panel or two different sequences of one.

Throughout the *Cantigas* one finds examples of the fusion of realism and impressionism, which at first may seem to the reader to be an anomaly. Even so, Alfonso's illuminators were forced to work with both and to blend the two acceptably. In some pages realistic treatment of the subject was so detailed that no vestige of impressionism needed to be included. In these illustrations a kind of "photographic" quality obtains, in which the artists have painted in great detail and exactitude. The human figure, both clothed and nude, animals rendered with great attention to authenticity, buildings, plants, and seascape might almost have been photographed, so clear and realistic are they. A good example is in *Cantiga* 18, in which are depicted silkworms with every pseudopod and true leg visible. It is true that all the worms are greatly enlarged, indeed to the dimensions of good-sized sausages—so that the viewer can readily realize what they are. Painted to scale in so small a space as a *cantiga* panel, the larvae could not have been recognized, nor could they have been seen weaving or spinning two wimples for images of the Virgin Mary. Examples of enlargement are frequent in the miniatures.

Medieval man loved nature and lived in close association with animals both wild and domestic. The artists therefore portrayed all sorts of beasts so clearly that the viewer could identify them and feel at home with them. The magpies in *Cantiga* 175, not mentioned at all in the verbalization, nonetheless enabled the artists to depict a scene of travel in a remote area much better than they could have without these birds so often seen in the wilderness. The same may be said of the partridges in *Cantiga* 44, or of the farm animals and fowls in *Cantiga* 148 with three white geese, a sow with five piglets, a dovecote with pigeons going in and out, and a rooster scratching for food for a hen.

The finest details emerge in some *cantigas* illuminations: the marks on dice as gamblers play seen so clearly that one can read the score (*Cantigas* 93 and 174); a pilgrim frying fritters (*Cantiga* 157); and in *Cantiga* 63 a fierce battle raging between Christians and Moslem warriors in truly amazing detail, even to the flow of blood from wounds. I know of no medieval illustration more filled with action. Frequently realism blends in a single panel with impressionism. This was often due to the need to conserve paper, especially when space for detail had been used up and some few impressionistic touches alone could be added. An example is the frontal depiction of a horse in which one sees only the head, chest and forelegs and must visualize the hidden parts of the animal (*Cantiga* 63).

The "aquarium" device is another interesting facet of *cantiga* art. This is extremely well developed in *Cantiga* 142 in which a swift river flows toward the viewer who can see the underwater channel, with steep banks rising on both sides, while one of Alfonso's huntsmen struggles beneath the turbulent surface. This technique appears also in *Cantiga* 86, in which a woman can be seen up to her neck in the sea as the Virgin walks across the surface to assist her. Related to this is the device which shows events on the surface of the earth and others beneath the ground or in hell. In *Cantiga* 131 the Emperor of Constantinople has entered a mine which caves in upon him, and the viewer can see him in two parts of his adventure. One of the frequent pictures of hell can be seen in *Cantiga* 192 in which, as though a portion of the earth had been cut away, one can see a Moor in hell fighting with the Devil. Transition is sometimes accomplished by having a person or animal cross the perpendicular framing design and enter another panel, as occurs in *Cantiga* 63 in which one sees the posterior of a horse in panel 3 and the animal's fore parts and the knight riding it emerging into panel 4.

I believe that this paper has touched upon the major narrative devices found in the more than a thousand panels of manuscript T.I.1. Many, many more interesting devices may remain to be discovered and researched. When professional students of medieval Spanish art realize the treasure of these miniatures, the scholarly world will begin to understand their significance to art, literature, and their interdisciplinary ties, and will be able to enter areas of investigation hitherto not even suspected.

Notes

* Reprinted from *Thought*, 60 (1985), 388-406.

1 See Alfonso's testament in the facsimile *Cantigas* (II): "Likewise we order that all the books of the *Canticles of Praise of Holy Mary* be in that church where our body shall be interred, and that they be sung on the feast days of Holy Mary. And if that one who inherits legally and by our will what is ours, wishes to own these books of the *Canticles of Holy Mary*, we order that he therefore make good compensation to the church from where he removes them so that he may have grace without sin." See also Filgueira Valverde (47).

2 The manuscripts are: Biblioteca Nacional, 10069, formerly the Manuscript of Toledo; El Escorial, T.I.1, formerly EI, and B.I.2, formerly E2; Florence, Biblioteca Nazionale, Banco Rari 20, formerly II.1.213. T.I.1 and Banco Rari contain the visualized miracles.

3 A good study of the devil in the *Cantigas* is Nelson (1964).

4 MS T.I.1 contains 194 pages of illumination, and since each page has six panels, save one which has eight, the sum of individual miniatures is 1,172.

5 It seems that Gautier de Coincy's *Miracles de la Sainte Vierge* was known to Alfonso, as well as the *Speculum Historiale* of Vincent of Beauvais, actually mentioned in Alfonso's will, the *Miraculis Beatae Mariae Virginis* of unknown authorship, the *Liber Mariae* of Gil de Zamora, a friend of Alfonso's who seems to have assisted in the preparation of the *Cantigas*, Walter of Cluny's *Miraculis Beatae Virginis Mariae*, the *Scala Coeli* of Johannes Gobius, the *Liber Miraculis Sanctae Mariae Dei Genetrix*, possibly composed by Patho, the *Mariale Magnum*, attributed to Isidore of Seville, and most probably the *Milagros de Nuestra Señora* of Gonzalo de Berceo, also a contemporary of Alfonso. As the volumes of the *Cantigas* increased across the king's life, sources from popular lore and contemporary miracles were included.

6 As Procter (32-33) pointed out, 28 poems in the *Cantigas* refer to the king and members of his family and court, a personal element without parallel in other collections.

7 So avid was Alfonso in the gathering of miracles that he traveled to the sites of several and seems to have taken others from traditions of his family, perhaps learned at his mother's knee. For example, *Cantiga* 235 relates an illness he suffered in Valladolid from which the Virgin saved him; in another, No. 349, Alfonso cures a girl of scrofula; and in No. 375, when the horse of a servitor fell ill, the Virgin cured it.

8 Mâle (264) mentions the miracle of the painter who painted the devil

hideous and the Virgin fair. He had not seen the *Cantigas*.

9 In our edition of *Calila* (1967, 92-93) we suggest some means of identifying parallels between medieval theatre and certain miniatures in the *Cantigas*.

10 Gonzalo Menéndez Pidal (25-51) treats the actual preparation of parchment, lists the names of those who may have been artists of the *Cantigas* miniatures, and gives an account of the various authorities as to their tracing of sources or schools of art emulated by the king's illuminators.

11 The *jarchas*, variously spelled, were discovered or at least identified for what they are in the late 1940s. They were "tail pieces" to poems written by Andalusian Moorish or Jewish poets in Arabic and Hebrew. The *jarchas* themselves, are in Spanish though written in Hebrew or Arabic characters. Because they were in the two Semitic scripts, and were discovered in Cairo, they were overlooked until the middle of this century.

12 Several editions have been made. The most recent is ours (1967).

13 It has been fashionable to deny the patronage of the translation of *Calila* to Alfonso, but in recent years the king's patronage seems to be gaining ground. If Alfonso's brother was the patron of the translation of the *Libro de los engaños* from some text of the *Book of Sinbad* (also known as the *Book of the Seven Wise Masters* or as the *Seven Sages*), if his nephew Don Juan Manuel wrote in his own inimitable style his *Conde Lucanor* with many versions of Arabic tales, especially from *Calila*, and if Alfonso's own son Sancho IV was a patron of such stories in his *Castigos e documentos para bien vivir*, it is reasonable that Alfonso was the patron of *Calila*. After all, he is given credit for *Calila* in the explicits.

14 Solalinde's edition of 1917 (48, 109) published two of the line drawings; we publish the full seventy-odd.

15 *Crónica* (8): "And King Alfonso being in Seville, and all the people with him in this honor which they were doing his father, messengers came from the King of Egypt.... And they brought to this king Don Alfonso gifts of many fine fabrics of many varieties, and many noble and very exotic jewels. And likewise they brought him an elephant and an animal which they call *azorafa* [giraffe], and an ass which was striped, for it had one band of white and the other of black, and they brought creatures and animals of many kinds."

16 For a treatment of panels in miniatures see Pächt.

17 Gonzalo Menéndez Pidal (three pages of *láminas* at end of article).

18 Menéndez Pidal among the *láminas* publishes miniatures in black and white from the *Maqamat de Hariri* and the *Cantigas de Santa Maria*.

19 For additional comments about the secularity of the miniatures in the *Cantigas* see Filgueira Valverde.

20 The young couple can be seen in their nuptial bed, nude but covered to the waist by bedclothing. The groom with one arm hugs the bride close, while with his left hand he fondles her breast. It is unusual for the Virgin in the *Cantigas* to condone or assist lovers, even when married, in amorous acts. Recall how she separated the bride and groom in *Cantiga* 42.

21 See Baum (1919) and my article of 1959.

22 The translation is that of Kathleen Kulp-Hill who has translated all of the 400-odd *cantigas*.

23 My explication of *Cantiga* 42 also relies on the observations of Kinkade.

Works Cited

Alfonso el Sabio. *Cantigas de Santa María*. 2 vols. Madrid: EDILAN, 1979.
——————. *El libro de Calila e Digna: Edición crítica*. Ed. John Keller and Robert W. Linker. Madrid: CSIC, 1967.
——————. *Calila y Dimna: Fabulas*. Ed. A. G. Solalinde. Madrid: Calleja, 1917.
——————. *Primera crónica general*. Ed. Ramón Menéndez Pidal. Madrid, 1906.
Anglés, Higinio. *La música de las "Cántigas de Santa María" del rey Don Alfonso el Sabio*. 3 vols. Barcelona, 1943-1964.
Auto de los Reyes Magos. Ed. R. Menéndez Pidal. *Revista de archivos, bibliotecas y museos*, 4 (1900), 453-62.
Ballesteros-Beretta, Antonio. *Alfonso X el Sabio*. Barcelona: Salvat, 1963.
Baum, Paul F. "The Young Man Bethrothed to a Statue." *PMLA*, 34 (1919).
Chisman, Anna M. G. "Enjambment in *Las Cantigas de Santa Maria* of Alfonso X, el Sabio." Unpublished doctoral dissertation, University of Toronto, 1974.
Clarke, D. C. "Versification in Alfonso el Sabio's *Cantigas*." *HR*, 23 (1955), 83-98.
Crónica de los reyes de Castilla. Ed. Cayetano Rosell. BAE 66. Madrid: Atlas, 1953.
Filgueira Valverde, José. "El texto: Introducción histórico-crítico, transcripción, versión castellana y comentarios." In Alfonso, *Cantigas* (above), II.
Guerrero Lovillo, José. *Las Cántigas: Estudio arqueológico de sus miniaturas*. Madrid: CSIC, 1949.
Keller, John. *Alfonso X, el Sabio*. New York: Twayne, 1967.
——————. "The Motif of the Statue Bride in the *Canticles* of King Alfonso the Learned." *Studies in Philology*, 56 (1959), 453-58.
——————, and R. P. Kinkade. *Iconography in Medieval Spanish Literature*. Lexington: UP of Kentucky, 1984.
El Libro del Cavallero Zifar. Ed. C. P. Wagner, Ann Arbor: Univ. of Michigan Press, 1929.
Mâle, Emile. *The Gothic Image*. New York: Harper and Row, 1972.
Menéndez Pidal, Gonzalo. "Los manuscritos de las *Cántigas*: Cómo se elaboró la miniatura alfonsí." *BRAE*, 150 (1962), 25-51.
Nelson, Charles L. "Literary and Pictorial Treatment of the Devil in the *Cantigas de Santa Maria*," Unpublished M. A. thesis, UNC, 1964.
Pächt, Otto. *The Rise of Pictorial Narrative in Twelfth-Century England*. Oxford: Clarendon Press, 1962.
Procter, Evelyn S. *Alfonso X of Castile, Patron of Literature and Learning*. Oxford: Clarendon Press, 1951.

The Miracle of the
Divinely Motivated Silkworms:
Cantiga 18*

CHOLARS WHO STUDY brief narratives and *exempla* in the Middle Ages in Spain, indeed in any western culture, often fail to take into consideration the very large number of narratives in verse. I have made a beginning, but only insofar as pietistic verse narratives are concerned,[1] and have barely opened the way to those who are confronted by the vast repository of verse narratives in the *Cantigas de Santa Maria* of King Alfonso X, el Sabio, that is "the Learned" or "the Wise" (ruled 1252-1284).

Besides the *Cantigas*, one encounters another volume of versified miracles, the *Milagros de Nuestra Señora* by Gonzalo de Berceo who lived at approximately the same time as the Learned King and who might even have known him.[2] Both these devotees of the Blessed Virgin Mary produced collections of her miracles, and some of the same miracles are found in both the *Milagros* and the *Cantigas*. The *Milagros* contain twenty-five miracles, whereas the *Cantigas* embody more than four hundred. A few other incidences of brief narratives in verse in medieval Spain can be found, but it is the *cantigas* which form the most important corpus.

Even scholars whose speciality is medieval Spanish literature tend to overlook the *Cantigas*, and this has delayed for decades a comprehensive study of these poems. The reason is obvious and it has even caused historians of Castilian literature to omit the *Cantigas* entirely or to give very little space to them. The *Cantigas*, instead of being written

174

in Castilian, the official language of King Alfonso's realm, are in Galician-Portuguese, the tongue regarded by Spanish poets as the most apt medium of lyric verse. This preference lasted until well into the fifteenth century. Indeed, from the thirteenth, scarcely five examples of lyrics in Castilian have survived the ages.[3] Literary historians, who for the most part did not read or understand the significance of the *Cantigas*, simply avoided their study, and thereby damaged their own presentation of lyric poetry's development.

Fortunately this has changed to a considerable degree within the past few years. New and better tools of investigation exist. There is a definitive critical edition; we can now study the miniatures of the *manuscrito rico* in a remarkably authentic facsimile edition; an up-to-date and continuing bibliography is in circulation; translations into Castilian and into English exist; there is a motif-index under way, prepared in acordance with the world-standard *Motif-Index* of Stith Thompson; transcriptions exist of the entire corpus of musical notation; a recently established newsletter will inform all *cantigueiros*, a term recently coined to describe *cantigas* scholars, of all research and publication connected with the works sponsored by the Learned King, and, of course, the *Cantigas*, are included.[4] As more scholars study the *Cantigas*, hear their melodies on the many discs and tapes now available, and view the illuminations, an unusual amount of interdisciplinary interest is making itself felt. Scholars in many areas now can turn to the *Cantigas de Santa Maria* for information; historians, art historians, sociologists, folklorists, musicologists, theologians, legists, scientists, and students of literature and linguistics can study them as to thematology, imagery and symbolism, narrative techniques, poetics, etc.

The four volumes of the *Cantigas* should be regarded as a single work, open-ended in that as new *Cantigas* were written and melodized and illuminated these could be added to the original text.[5] Apparently the production of the volumes ran across many years of Alfonso's life. He regarded the *Cantigas de Santa Maria* as his favorite book and even provided for their archiving in his last will and testament.[6]

The present article is one of a series in which the writer is preparing to demonstrate the impact of the *Cantigas* upon the society of Alfonso's time. To treat this impact fully would require a very long book, but one can—and this is the writer's plan—exemplify the narrative techniques in verbal, melodic[7] and visual form and indicate the uniqueness of many of the motifs included in the miracles. Many, perhaps most of the *Cantigas*, were drawn from the great collections of miracles written in Latin in various parts of Europe, but some appear to be of folkloric origin, and this seems to be true in the case of *Cantiga 18*, the subject of this article. [AUTH. The plate that illustrates this *Cantiga* has already been printed on p. 145.] No other miracle in the *Cantigas* reveals so well the king as a gatherer of oral tales. Indeed, in one of the six miniatures he is depicted as he hears the account of number 18 from the mouths of those who were closest to it and who may have witnessed it. This is a most unusual portrayal, both in verbal and visual form, for rarely if ever does one encounter in Western medieval culture a king who moved among his people to the extent that Alfonso did,[8] who placed himself in his works, and who actually traveled to shrines where he had heard that miracles occurred. He may well be the first of Europe's medieval folklorists.[9]

In order to follow the treatment of narrative techniques in their three-fold form—melodic, visual and poetic—the reader should first read the miracle itself. It has been provided in English translation through the generosity of Dr. Kathleen Kulp-Hill who has translated the entire corpus of more than four hundred.[10] With the actual story of the miracle in the mind, the reader can better understand how the *cantigas* were produced, and with the added aid provided in the black and white facsimile of the illuminations of Number 18, arrive at a reasonable understanding in this article.

This is how Holy Mary made the silkworms spin two wimples, because the lady who kept them had promised Her one and had not given it to Her.

1 It pleases Holy Mary to perform Her beautiful miracles each day in order to free us from doubt.
   To prove Her worth to us, She performed a great miracle in Extremadura, in the city of Segovia, where dwelt a lady who
5 produced much silk in her home.
   The lady lost some of her silkworms and had little silk. Therefore she promised to give a length of silk for a wimple to honor the statue of the Peerless Virgin, in whom she fervently believed, which was on the altar.
10 As soon as she made the promise, the silkworms thrived and did not die. But the lady became negligent about her promise and kept forgetting to give the silk for the wimple.

Then it happened that on the great feast in August, she came to pray before the statue at midday. While she knelt in
15 prayer, she remembered the silk cloth she owed. Weeping in repentance, she ran home and saw the silkworms working diligently to make the cloth. Then she began to weep with happiness.
When she stopped weeping, she examined the cloth. Then
20 she called in many people so that they could come to see how the Mother of God could weave with miraculous skill. The people, when they saw it, praised the Mother of God with great joy and went out into the streets shouting: "Come see the great miracle which She who is our guide has
25 performed!"
One by one and two by two they came quickly to the place and saw. Meanwhile, the silkworms made another wimple, so that there might be a pair, and if someone wished to take one of them, there would be another left.
30 Therefore, King Don Alfonso, as I learned, brought the more beautiful of them to his chapel. On holy days, he has it brought out to eradicate heresy in those who foolishly doubt the Virgin.

Anyone who knows even a little about the culture of silk will be interested to see how it was produced in the thirteenth century in Spain. And any one with such knowledge will realize immediately that there are two miracles involved. The first, easily overlooked or overshadowed by the more significant miracle of the actual weaving of the cloth by the divinely motivated silkworms, is the curing of the sick worms. The larvae of the larger moths, silk moths included, are subject to virtually incurable diseases produced by molds or viruses. That the Virgin could heal the woman's sick worms would have greatly impressed those who heard the account of the miracle.

The illuminated page of *Cantiga 18*, like all such pages in this Alfonsine anthology, is divided into six panels or sections, each of which move from left to right, beginning with the topmost two panels and continuing in the same way until all six have been perused, virtually in the exact way in which one looks at a modern comic book. Above each panel appears in either scarlet or azure calligraphy a very brief statement as to what is depicted in it. With this in mind, with the

translation as a reference, and with the reproduction of the illuminated page, the writer believes that he can make the *cantiga* live for the
modern reader.

In Panel I ("How the woman begged Holy Mary to cure the
silkworms and that she would make her a wimple in return") lays the
scene, and lines 5-9 amplify it somewhat.[12] Incidentally, the caption
here is unusual in that it fills the usual space for captions and runs
down into the wall behind the woman as she presents the sick worms
to the Virgin's image. The use of the large cusped arch in this panel, as
well as the appearance of arches in other panels, suggests dramatic
presentation, since medieval plays sometimes used dramatic arches as
frames or stagings for successive incidents.[13]

Under the left-hand arch is the altar of the Blessed Virgin, who sits
on her throne with the Christ Child on her knee. The larger arch
frames the woman, who kneels as she presents a shallow dish of sick
worms to the statue. The dish is tilted on its rim so that the viewer can
see that it is filled with silkworms, all depicted a great deal larger than
they are in life so that they can be seen. Normal-sized worms would
not be visible in detail. In subsequent panels they will appear even
larger, where the viewer can see them in their entirety, with all their
segments, pseudopods and true insect legs. The poem does not treat
this scene until lines 5-9.

Panel 2's caption ("How, being before her altar, she remembered
the wimple she had promised Holy Mary and was troubled because of
it") gives almost as much information as lines 14-16 in the text, which
add only that she was very sorry and hurried home. The statues still
occupy their altar in the lefthand arch. In the righthand arch the
woman walks toward the door of the chapel, and her motion is
visualized by the hem of her robe trailing behind her and the
impression which her knee makes in front as she strides toward the
door of the chapel.

Panel 3 ("How the woman went home and saw the worms were
making a wimple") in its caption parallels lines 16-19 which, however,
gives more information. The miniature reveals under a narrow left-
hand arch the door of her house half open with blue tiles of the roof
plainly visible. The larger arch, cusped and supported by columns with
carven capitals, contains a very unusual scene. The woman kneels in

amazement as she views the tray upon which the worms are kept. Her hands are thrown out in a gesture of astonishment. On the tray, up-ended in the same way in which was the dish of worms in panel 1, are visible fifteen sausage-sized larvae eight on one side and seven on the other of a white wimple which they are weaving. The green mulberry leaves upon which they feed can be seen clearly in the color facsimile and the original, but only barely in the black and white reproduction. In this *Cantiga* may appear the only picture extant which shows how silk was produced. Surely the artists must have used living models.

In Panel 4 ("How she ran into the street to call the people, and the worms commenced to make another wimple") the miniature offers more detail, although the poem itself, in its lines 21-24 barely expands what the caption stated. At the left appears the façade of the woman's house with its tiled roof and door before which the woman stands and speaks to five or six people. Here the artists give two separate scenes of action. Having depicted the woman in the street talking to the citizens, they use the right-hand side of the panel to portray the group which has entered the silkworm shed to kneel in adoration of the Virgin. This latter scene is paralleled by lines 23-26.

Panel 5 ("How the woman gave to the friars the completed wimple") contains three arches. Under the left-hand arch appear the same images. The center arch frames two priests as they stand and receive the wimples from the woman who stands under the right-hand arch, though her hands extend into the middle arch as she places the wimples in the hands of the clerics. Behind her stands another woman who steeples her hands in prayer. Here the three arches lend considerable dramaticity to the panel as they encapsulate the three moments in time which the viewer sees—the images, the priests, and the woman and her companion.

Panel 6 ("How King Alfonso took one to hang in his chapel") is a very unusual miniature. Its three arches seem to depict or catch three moments or incidents. The left-hand arch presents the images of the Virgin and the Child. The center arch portrays Alfonso himself as he faces three clerics who seem to be telling him about the miracle. One supports the wimple on one side, while the king supports it on the other. With his right hand he points or traces figures, some with crowns, which can be seen in the original and the color facsimile, but cannot be seen in black and white. Under the right-hand arch and behind the king stand three gentlemen, their hands steepled in adoration as they hear what the clerics are saying. Since the poem does not actually state that the king went to the chapel, but only suggests it in words (lines 31-34), the artists must have gleaned from other sources the information which allowed them to portray him there. We believe that Alfonso went over the *cantigas*, as he stated he did in the case of other books, and we feel that it is correct to assume that he told his illuminators of his journey, the culmination of which they depict so realistically here.

Cantiga 18's illuminated page is one of some twenty-four which contain in the lower margin, immediately under the frame of the six miniatures, a summary of the poem in Castilian prose, which has been edited.[14]

All the nine elements of the classic design—plot, conflict, scene, characterization, style, theme, effect, point of view, and mood or tone—can be found in the verbalization, although scene, as is often the case in written accounts, is barely presented. In the miniatures, on the other hand, scene is the most prominent element. Plot is well-handled and conflict, too, in the very brief poetic narrative, while in the illuminations the artists have gone far toward making these elements visible. Characterization in both verbal and visual form is clearly manifested. Point of view is either omniscient or is the king's. The theme is that the Virgin's ever present mercy will assist her devotees, even in little ways such as curing worms, and is likely to be manifested in even more striking ways. Effect, style, and mood or tone can be identified in verbalization and visualization, but each viewer in Alfonso's time, as well as in our own, may be affected in his own particular or personal way.

Cantiga 18, then, exemplifies what a *cantiga* was to Alfonso and his helpers, how it was planned and produced in three media--poetry, melody and illumination—and how subject matter need not have stemmed from the great literary collections of Our Lady's miracles, but might have been drawn from oral lore or contemporary events.

Notes

* Reprinted from *Hispanófila*, 82 (1984), 1-9.

1 See my *Pious Brief Narrative in Medieval Spanish and Galician Verse* (Lexington: University Press of Kentucky, 1978).

2 See the edition of Brian Dutton, *Obras Completas, II, Los milagros de Nuestra Señora*: (London: Támesis, 1971) and Alfonso X, *El "Códice Rico" de las Cantigas de Santa María* (Madrid: Edilan, 1980).

3 Frede Jensen, *The Earliest Portuguese Lyrics* (Odense: University Press, 1978).

4 The definitive critical edition is that of Walter Mettmann, Alfonso X, O Sábio, *Cantigas de Santa María* (Coimbra: Acta Universitatis Conimbrigensis, 1959-1972), 4 vols.; the facsimile edition is the *Códice Rico* mentioned in note 2; the bibliography is that of Joseph T. Snow, *The Poetry of Alfonso X, el Sabio*. William R. Davis at Mercer University is preparing the motif-index and will assign numbers to *cantigas* on request; José María Lloréns Cisteró's transcription of musical notation is in the volume which accompanies the facsimile edition; José Filgueira, "Transcripción textual de las *Cantigas* contenidas en el *Códice Rico, Códice T.I.1*," in the volume accompanying the *Códice Rico*; Kathleen Kulp-Hill of Eastern Kentucky University has translated all four hundred odd *cantigas* and has generously offered to allow those who need translations to use them; the newsletter is the *Bulletin of the Cantigueiros"* (Lexington, Ky.).

5 Mettmann, viii-xv.

6 Antonio Ballesteros-Beretta, *Alfonso X, el Sabio* (Barcelona: Salvat, 1963), p. 1053.

7 See Richard P. Kinkade's and my *Iconography in Medieval Spanish Literature* (Lexington: University Press of Kentucky, 1983).

8 Joseph T. Snow, "The Central Role of the Troubadour *persona* of Alfonso X in the *Cantigas de Santa Maria*," *Bulletin of Hispanic Studies* 56 (1979), 305-16.

9 See my "A Medieval Folklorist," *Folklore Studies in Honor of Arthur Palmer Hudson* (Chapel Hill: University of North Carolina Press 1965), 19-25. [AUTH. Included as the second article in this volume.]

10 The translation of *Cantiga 18* and the translation of the calligraphy above the six panels in the illuminated page are by Kathleen Kulp-Hill.

11 Actually one page of illumination contains eight panels, i. e. *Cantiga 1* "*Esta la primeira cantiga de loor de Santa Maria, ementando os sete goyos que ouve de seu' Fillo.*"

12 According to Webster, a wimple is "a woman's head covering of medieval times, consisting of a cloth arranged about the head, cheeks, chin and neck, leaving only the face exposed." The long pieces of cloth woven by the worms reveals the appearance of a wimple before it is wrapped around the head.

13 Otto Pächt, *The Rise of Plectorial Narrative in Twelfth-Century England* (Oxford: Clarendon Press, 1962).

14 For a complete transcription of these see James A. Chatham, "A Paleographic Edition of the Alfonsine Collection of Prose Miracles of the Virgin in *Oelschläger Festschrift. Estudios de Hispanófila* (Chapel Hill, Estudios de Hispanófila, 36, 1962).

An Unknown Castilian
Lyric Poem:
The Alfonsine Translation
of *Cantiga* X*

HE DEARTH OF lyric poems written in Castilian during the Middle Ages has not perplexed scholars, because they have known the reason: a preference for lyrics couched in Galician-Portuguese rather than in the native tongue of the court poets whose works have survived. But this rarity has, nonetheless, given cause for disappointment. The discovery of even one additional poem, then, in Castilian of the thirteenth-century is reason for some surprise and delight. That such a poem could have lain undetected in a book of lyrics as well-known and as much investigated as the *Cantigas de Santa Maria* of Alfonso X, el Sabio, is surprising indeed, since every one of the four hundred-odd poems, edited by the most careful and scholarly of researchers, is unquestionably in Galician.[1] How could this have come about? The answer lies in the presence of what I can only term lacunae in scholarship, particularly in editing, as well as in a failure to see, even when edited, the Castilian poem because it had been set down in what appeared to be the lines of a Castilian prose translation of *Cantiga* X.

Long ago scholars had noted that in the bottom margins of the pages containing miniatures for *Cantigas* II through XXV, there appeared prosifications of the poetic content of the miracles illustrated by these miniatures.[2] Some of these prosifications which are Castilian renditions of the poems are lengthy and therefore are penned in extremely minute characters, which makes reading difficult and even at times impossible without infrared light. It is strange that no one has taken the trouble to edit what is obviously a body of Alfonsine material written to summarize or clarify the content of twenty-four of the famous *Cantigas de Santa Maria*. It is even more strange when one realizes that the indefatigable Menéndez Pidal long ago indicated the need and pointed the way by editing *Cantiga* XVIII, and that as recently as 1965 his transcription of that *cantiga* was published again, this time in the *Crestomatía del español medieval*.[3] It is even more inconceivable that, in my own studies of the *Cantigas*, I failed to detect the Castilian poetic translation of *Cantiga* X, since Robert W. Linker and I had in collaboration edited the entire corpus of the prosifications and I had even read proof of our edition (recently published by the Real Academia Española).[4] My failure to notice that the poem appeared as prose occurred, I believe, because as we transcribed, we did so word by word with our attention focused upon individual letters; also, as I read the transcription for sense and for the purpose of typing it in a reliable and readable form, I again failed to realize that the prose-like lines were in reality verses. Even now the Castilian poem would remain undetected had I not, by merest chance while reading proof, decided to read the transcription of number X aloud. At first nothing poetic emerged as I read, since the first several lines of the Castilian were no more than a lengthy prose expansion of the Galician prose title. But beyond this point the Castilian verses emerged from the prose. There seemed to be four stanzas and this proved to be correct once the lines had been set down in poetic form. After the fourth stanza of the Castilian text, the poetry ended and the translator reverted to prose and ended his treatment of the *cantiga* with several lines of observations and statements in praise of Our Lady which did not appear in the Galician poem.[5]

The most effective way to present the form and content of the *cantiga*, and to show how close a translation it is of the Galician, is to present the two poems together. The Galician version is from the edition of Walter Mettmann. The Spanish transcription appears in our edition of the *cantiga* prosifications as published by the Real Academia. The Galician poem reads:

Esta é de loor de Santa Maria, com'é fremosa e bõa e á gran poder.

Rosa das rosas e Fror das frores,
Dona das donas, e Sennor das sennores.

Rosa de beldad' e de parecer
e Fror d' alegria e de prazer,
Dona en mui piadosa seer,
Sennor en toller coitas e doores.
Rosa das rosas e Fror das frores.

Atal Sennor dev' ome muit' amar,
que de todo mal o pode guardar,
e pod-ll' os peccados perdõar,
que faz no mundo per maos sabores.
Rosa das rosas e Fror das frores.

Devemo-la muit' amar e servir,
ca punna de nos guardar de falir;
des i dos erros nos faz repentir,
que nos fazemos come pecadores.
Rosa das rosas e Fror das frores.

Esta dona que tenno por Sennor
e de que quero seer trobador,
se eu per ren poss' aver seu amor,
dou ao demo os outros amores.
Rosa das rosas e Fror das frores.

The Castilian text reads as follows:

Esta estoria es de como la muy santa, e muy alta, e muy noble,
e mucho onrrada, e mas bienaventurada que otra criatura, Virgen
gloriosa salua Ssanta Maria, rreyna del cielo e de la tierra es
nuestra Señora e nuestra Abogada e medianera entre Dios; e nos
fue, e es, e sienpre sera com...de fermosura, e de beldat, e de
sçiençia, e de piadat, e...ria en todas las otras virtudes e bien aver,
e al...ar, e que es[6]

Rrosa de las rrosas e flor de las flores
e dueña de las dueñas, e Señora de las señoras.
Rrosa de beldat e de parescer
e flor de alegria e de plazer,

e dueña muy piadosa en nos toller
nuestras cuytas e nuestros dolores.
    e que es
Atal Señora que devemos mucho amar,
porque de todo mal nos puede guardar,
e nuestros pecados nos faz perdonar,
que nos fazemos por malos sabores.
    e que
La devemos sienpre [amar e servir],
que p[unga] de nos guarir [de falir],
e de los yerros nos faz rrepentir,
que nos fazemos como pecadores.
    e que
Devemos sienpre trabajar
por todavia su amor ganar,
ca es valiosa e muy celestial,
e non valen nada los otros amores.

E dize en esta estoria que por quanto el buen rrey don Alfonso el
Sabio, seyendo en grades peligros, le saco a su onrra todavia d'ellos
que tornon [sic] perder el su amor e al...r della tanta merçed que
se apartava a la loar en cantigas e en llores por se q...rar...del
diablo e de sus tenptaçion...que en cobdiçia de la costunbre...a
los grandes señores por lo que esta señora le...perdon del su
glorioso fijo e lo llevo a la santa gloria de parayso...seamos dignos
de yr al su serviçio...

The obvious differences between the Galician and Castilian poems
need not be emphasized, but should be pointed out. Apparently, the
translator saw no need to repeat the refrain to match the one in the
original Portuguese; or perhaps, since space was very limited, he
simply could not repeat the refrain five times. More striking is the
difference between the last stanza of the Castilian and the last in
Galician, which the Castilian definitely does not translate, but instead
offers an entirely original stanza containing none of the concepts or
images found in the Galician.

There is a slight divergence in the syllable count of the verses in
the two languages. The first line of the refrain in Castilian contains

twelve syllables, the Galician ten, a difference owed to the higher frequency of elision in the latter. The same is true in the case of the second line of the refrain: the Castilian runs to thirteen syllables, the Galician to twelve. Lines not in the refrain vary somewhat from language to language, usually because of divergences in syllable count for the refrains, but sometimes because the Castilian omitted a word or added words not matched in the Galician.

The similarities are even more evident than the differences: the rhyme is virtually identical throughout the two poems. Only in two lines, before the last Castilian stanza, could there be differences, and, if allowances can be made for the logical insertions I have made—that is, of *servir* as the last word of line 1 in the third stanza, and of *falir* as the last word in line 2 of the same stanza—then there are no differences. Why the scribe omitted these end rhyme words is unknown.

Our discovery, then, is of a poem of four stanzas in thirteenth-century Castilian, three of which are almost literal translations from the Galician and one of which is original to the Spanish. The presence of this hitherto undetected poem adds to the very meager repertory of lyric verse written in medieval Castilian and is a reminder that other poems may likewise lie concealed in what appears to be prose.

Notes

* Reprinted from *Hispanic Review*, 43 (1975), 43-47.

For more information, see Dorothy Clotelle Clarke, "Additional Castilian Verse and Early *Arte Mayor* in the Marginal Passages in Alfonso X's *Cantigas de Santa María*," *Kentucky Romance Quarterly* 23 (1976): 305-17. Our inability to read letters, which are edited and substituted by dots, has been remedied by James R. Chatham in his "A Paleographic Edition of the Alfonsine Collection of Prose Miracles of the Virgin," *Oelschläger Fetschrift* (Estudios de *Hispanófila*, 35, Chapel Hill, 1976), 73-111.

1 *Cantigas de Santa María de Don Alfonso el Sabio*, ed. Leopoldo Cueto, Marqués de Valmar (Madrid: Real Academia Española, 1889); Afonso X, O Sábio. *Cantigas de Santa María*, ed Walter Mettmann (Coimbra: Acta Universitatis Conimbrigensis, I, [1959], II [1961], III [1964], IV [1972]).

2 Mettmann, p. xi, reprints the description as printed by Valmar: "Al pie de las páginas, y a todo el ancho de las dos col. del texto unas veces, dividido también en dos columnas, y otras, en fin, debajo de las miniaturas, se halla la explicación de cada cantiga, en prosa castellana, y letra de la misma época

que la de aquellas. Este comentario, que en algunas hojas casi ha desaparecido por el roce constante, sólo llega a la *Cantiga* XXV."

3 R. Menéndez Pidal, *Crestomatía del español medieval*, ed. R. Lapesa and M. S. de Andrés (Madrid, 1965), I, 252-53; 2nd. ed. (Madrid, 1971), I, 252-53.

4 R. W. Linker and my article, "Las traducciones castellanas de las *Cantigas de Santa Maria*," *BR*, 54 (1974), 221-93.

5 Needless to say I have now read the other prosifications aloud, but so far have found no other poetic renditions.

6 The words *que es, e que es,* and *e que,* printed above the stanzas are simply a part of the translator's commentary.

Cantiga 135:

The Blessed Virgin

As a Matchmaker*

HE ROLE OF the Blessed Virgin in certain of the *Cantigas de Santa Maria* has been studied,[1] but by and large research in the area of her characterization as well as the motifs in which she plays a part is a new and unexplored field for investigation. Most students of the great anthology of her miracles and hymns see her as a stern supporter of heaven's laws, an inexorable and determined warrior in her Son's endless warfare with the forces of hell, a benevolent Queen of Heaven who protects her devotees, punishing their enemies, who even heals and saves dumb animals, not excepting insects such as bees and silkworms. Well known, too, are her tolerance toward sinners who repent, her willingness to guide them away from sinful ways, and her repeated and successful attempts to lead lovers away from carnal desire and into the paths of chastity and devotion to her, even in cases when the lovers are legally married.[2] It is rare, therefore, to find the Virgin actively abetting lovers and bringing them together in a romantic marital passion in defiance of the wishes of their parents. Nevertheless, such is *Cantiga* 135," Como Santa Maria librou de desonrra dous que sse avian jurados por ela quando eran menyos que casassen ambos en uno, e fez-lo ela conprir."[3]

No. 135 has a most attractive motif in addition to its thematic rarity among Marian miracles. To date the few remarks devoted to this miracle appear in the volume which accompanies the recent facsimile edition of Escorial MS T.I.1.[4] This *cantiga* may derive from one of those romances in written form in French and Spanish prose which seem to have been modeled upon the Byzantine romance.[5]

Certainly No. 15 stems from a well-known romance in Spanish, and I believe that subsequent research will reveal similar origins for other *cantigas.*

The possibility of oral sources should not be overlooked, since folklore derivation is evident in many *cantigas.*[6] The fact that the poem, put into the mouth of Alfonso, states that he heard it told

> Desto vos quero dizer,
> per com' oy retraer...
> [2:98, II. 8-9]

may or may not indicate an oral source, but it surely suggests one, as does still another statement, also attributed to the king.

> Pois os dous ben de raiz,
> segund' este conto diz...
> [2:102, II. 144-45].

Unfortunately we may never know.

Cantiga 135 is even close to being an abbreviated sentimental novel, and it very definitely contains the element of true *divertimiento.* Indeed, the poet says as much:

> un miragre, ond' aver
> podedes gran gasallado
> [2:98, II. 10-11]

The original Galician-Portuguese from the Mettmann edition follows; it serves far better than any summary could for acquainting the reader with the events narrated, while the music of the *cantiga* is best studied in the transcription of Higinio Anglés or in his text as reworked by José María Lloréns Cisteró, the latter found in the volume which accompanies the facsimile.[7]

Cantiga CXXXV

[C]omo Santa Maria livrou de desonrra dous que sse avian jurados por ela quando eran *menÿos* que casassen ambos en uno, e fez-lo ela conprir.

> Aquel podedes jurar
> 5 que e' ben de mal guardado
> o que a Virgen fillar
> via por seu acomendado.

1

Desto vos quero di*zer,
per com' oy retraer,
10 un miragre, ond' aver
podedes gran gasallado
des que fordes entender
o que a Virgen fazer
e mostrar foi no condado
15 *Aquel podedes jurar...*

2

De Bretanna a Mẽor
por *dous* que sse gran[d]' amor
avian e gran sabor
de viveren sen pecado;
20 onde foi ajudador
esta Madre do Sennor,
cug' é do Ce' o reynado.
Aquel podedes jurar...

3

Estes de que fal' aqui
25 moç' e moça, com' oy,
foron e, com' aprendi,
cada un deles criado
foi cono outr'; e des i
est' amor poseron y
30 u moravan, e jurado
Aquel podedes jurar...

4

Foi pela Madre de Deus,
assi que ambos por seus
ficaron, amigos meus.
35 E pois esto foi firmado,
seus padres, maos encreus
do que mataron judeus,
partíronos mal seu grado.
Aquel podedes jurar...

5

40 Ca o padre del fez yr
o fill' e dela partir;
e a moça foi pedir
un ric-ome mui[t]' onrrado
por moller. E quen cousir
45 quan changid' o espedir
foi o deles e chorado,
Aquel podedes jurar...

6

Gran doo aver pod' en.
Mas estes dous, que gran ben
50 se querian mais d'al ren,
foi ontr' eles ordiado
que se lles falass' alguen
en casar, per niun sen
sol non lle foss' outorgado.
55 *Aquel podedes jurar...*

7

Mas o padr' enton fillou
ssa filla e a casou
con outr' ome que achou
rico e muit' avondado,
60 a que a moça contou
seu feito como *passou:*
e pois llo ouv' ascuitado,
Aquel podedes jurar...

8

Diss': "Amig', assi farey
65 que cras con vosco m'irei
e atanto buscarey
aquel que foi esposado
vosco, que o acharey,
e logo vo-lle darey
70 por aver a Deus pagado."
Aquel podedes jurar...

9

Log' outro dia sen al
se foron; e en un val
aque o ric-ome sal
75 que cuidara seer casado
con ela, que mui mortal
queri' a seu padre mal.
E fez come om' yrado;
Aquel podedes jurar...

10

80 Ca log'ambo-los prendeu
e el en carcel meteu,
e pois que anoiteceu
con ela seu gasallado
quis aver; mas faleceu
85 y, ca log' adormeceu.
Ben tro eno sol levado
Aquel podedes jurar...

Dormiu e abriu enton
os ollos, e ssa razon
90 la menỹ, [e] en bon son,
disse: "E non é guisado
de me forçardes vos, non,
ca à Virgen dei en don
meu corpo, tenp' á passado.
95 *Aquel podedes jurar...*

12

Poren nunca mi averá
erg'a quen m'ela dará;
e vos, quitade-vos ja
d'irdes contra seu mandado,
100 mais levade-m' acolá
u ést' o que seerá
meu marid' e meu amado."
Aquel podedes jurar...

13

Quand' est' oyu, "a la ffe",
105 diss' el, "eu yrei u é
aquel, e este que ssé
aqui ben enferrollado
farei soltar. E en pe
sse levou e diss': *"Aqué*
110 *m' estou tod' aprestidado*
Aquel podedes jurar...

14

De log' ir" E diss' "ai, fol,"
a un seu ome, "vai tol-
ll' os ferros a est', e prol
115 será minna que livrado
seja; e quant' hũa col
do seu non filles, ca sol
por tanto serás rastrado."
Aquel podedes jurar...

15

120 Outro dia ant' a luz,
en un cavalo de Cuz
que corre mais que estruz,
no camỹo foi entrado,
dizend': "Ai, Deus que en cruz
125 morreste, mui ced' aduz-
nos u aquel ben-fadado
Aquel podedes jurar...

16

É, que aja com' el quer
esta moça por moller."
130 E tan tost' a Monpesler
chegaron e y achado
[o ouveron, e disser-
ron-lle que ll' era mester
de ser log' apparellado
135 *Aquel podedes jurar*...]

17

De casar con Don' Alis,
pois Santa Maria quis.
E fezérono ben fis
que nunca mais destorvado
140 fosse per eles, e gris
e pano vermell' e bis
ouvesse logo conprado.
Aquel podedes jurar...

18

Pois os dous ben de raiz,
145 segund' este conto diz
e dissemos, a Fiiz
ouveron todo contado,
graças à Emperadriz,
ond' eu este cantar fiz,
150 deron muitas e de grado.
Aquel podedes jurar...

19

E logo tost' e vïaz
Fezeron vodas assaz
onrradas e muit' en paz;
155 e pois ouveron jantado,
o novio fez como faz
novio a novia en solaz;
e assi foi acabado.
Aquel podedes jurar...

Before continuing, some comment must be made here in passing
about the importance of the two pages of illumination devoted to this
cantiga. All *cantigas* whose last number ends in 5 are illuminated by two
full pages of miniatures, and 135 is no exception. To grasp the full
impact of the miracle a very close scrutiny of the accompanying
illumination can be quite profitable. Visualization, taken together
with verbalization, often brings out matters which might not emerge

from mere perusal of written content. Sometimes the visualized story diverges amazingly from the written account, as has been pointed out recently.[8] Such verbal-visual variations may uncover sources of the *Cantigas de Santa Maria*, elucidate narrative devices and techniques, and prove conflict of interest between writer and illuminator, to name but a few possibilities. With the truly fabulous facsimile mentioned above we now have a reliable medium for such investigation, for without full color no serious study of this remarkable art can be undertaken.

The length of No. 135 and the fact that it was deemed worthy of the two-folio presentation of its miniatures, which depict the story in twelve separate panels rather than the six devoted to most *cantigas*, indicate the lengthiness of the romance from which it was derived. This is also true in the case of *Cantiga* 15, mentioned in note 5, which is even longer. And surely knowledge of the source of 15 lends credence to the origin of 135 in some presently not-identifiable romance.

Frequent reference on the reader's part to the color facsimile will make the approach to the study of this miracle's development more meaningful, but even the accompanying black-and-white reproduction is helpful. In all the miniatures of the *Cantigas* the eye is intended to move from left to right and top to bottom until all three bands of the two panels have been viewed. Thus panel 1 is in the upper left and panel 2 in the upper right, panel 3 mid-left, etc.

The artists in panel 1 begin their illumination with stanza 3, since the first four lines of the poem are mere introduction and are to be repeated after each narrative stanza in the form of a refrain, and since the second stanza does no more than state the author's (Alfonso's?) purpose, i.e., to recount an enjoyable miracle. The caption of panel 1 ("Como un menino e huna menina iuraron par Sancta Maria que-s casassen ambos") reveals the subject matter of the panel or what is taking place in it. In this case the artists certainly follow the caption. We see a lad and a damsel who appear, from their height, to be in their early teens or even of more tender years. They stand facing one another under a vaulted ceiling supported by four golden pillars with carved capitals. The youth holds his sweetheart's hand in his left hand, while with his right he seems to confirm his vow. Hand language and facial expression to a lesser extent reveal the mood of the young people.

Panel 2 ("Como estos meninnos criavan de sso uno e os padres os partiron mal seu grado") matches stanza 4. Dramatic arches are employed in the illuminations of *Cantiga* 135 as they are in many of the illuminations of the *Cantigas*.[9] Here the action unfolds under three triangular cusped arches supported by golden columns. Separate elements of plot can be encapsulated under a single arch, allowing the artists to achieve something which often approaches the dramatic movement successfully captured by modern cinema. Even transition can be cleverly developed under a series of arches. Aided by the depiction of characters in motion, indicated by their stances and the flow of their garments, the artists did much to create a sense of action and movement from place to place.

Under the left-hand arch the damsel—her name will be seen to be Alis toward the end of the poem—is seen as her father, holding her hand, pulls her from under the middle arch.[10] The flow of her robe shows that she is moving toward her father, while the extension of her hand into the left-hand arch shows transition. Under the middle arch, too, we see the youth drawn by his father away from Alis and toward the right-hand arch. The idea of forcible separation is certainly well-depicted, and the viewer feels as though he actually sees the motion involved in this scene of action.

It is in panel 3 that the artists depict beautifully the request of the rich man who asks for Alis' hand and is refused by her father, as described in stanza 5. The caption reads "Como un ricome onrado pidiu por moller e o padre non quis." Arches again divide the panel into three parts or incidents: in the left-hand arch we see the suitor's retainers; the center arch reveals the suitor pointing to the damsel as the father pushes his daughter toward the right-hand arch into which her hand already projects as her mother grasps it and pulls her away from the suitor, clearly refuting his suit. One hardly needs the caption to understand what is taking place.

Panel 4 ("Como casaron a meninna con outr'ome rrico e muyt' avondado") illustrates stanza 6. Again we see the action divided by the three arches. Under the left-hand arch stand wedding guests and family. The scene depicts the ceremony itself with two priests officiating, one with his hand extended in the symbol of benediction, while the bride and groom kneel under the center arch to take their vows. The right-hand arch focuses attention on the altar with its colored tiles, the candle atop it, and the host in its paten covered by its white corporal. A tall and ornate cross on the altar lends balance to the scene.

Cantiga 135, Escorial MS. T.I.1, folio 190ᵛ

Cantiga 135, Escorial MS. T.I.1, folio 191ʳ

This panel and its verbalization might lead the reader to wonder how Alis can ever marry her sweetheart, in view of the ceremony underway. But recall that early in the poem and depicted in panel 1 is the matter of the couple's vow of eternal fidelity to one another. This kind of personal and private betrothal without benefit of clergy is sometimes known as "the marriage made in heaven," and is an age-old motif present in many cultures. Prominent in Hindu writings such as the *Panchatantra* and the *Mahabarata*, in Byzantine romances and in some Islamic tales, as well as in the medieval literature of Christendom, this motif will enable the young people to rise above Alis' marriage to the man we see her wed. It is a concept vital to this story, just as it was to the account of Cardenio and Lucinda in *Don Quixote* when such a pledge foiled the designs of Don Ferdinand.

Panel 5's caption ("Como a meninna dis a o novio com' era iurada con outro e ele disse cras yrey buscalo e dárvolo ey") summarizes more or less what is narrated in stanza 7. To be noted is the fact that this caption is so lengthy that the calligrapher had to run it into the space under the arch and just above the figure of the groom seated on the bed. This serves to link even closer verbalization and visualization and may be an incipient attempt to produce in art what modern cartoonists do in their comic strips as they allow the reader to realize what each character is saying. In the visualization we see determination clearly depicted in Alis' face as she explains to her groom why she cannot be his wife. Her gestures certainly confirm this. Under the left-hand arch, in what is to us a dramatic scene, she is seen speaking to her husband, while in the arch to the right the groom sits crosslegged on the same bed, his actions separated from hers by the arches. The meaning of his gesture language—one hand is open and extended as though he feels astonishment or perhaps wishes to stop the flow of Alis' speech—is clear, and the perplexed expression on his face confirms it. We can almost hear him stating his plan to reunite Alis with her true love.

The counterpane in colorful designs in scarlet and azure stripes ornamented with golden x's has not even been turned back, allowing the reader to realize that the marriage has not been consummated. Thus panel 5 with its gestures, its facial expressions, and the way the events are encapsulated beneath the arches, enables the artists to suggest audible conversation.

Panel 6 ("Como encontraron en un val o ricome que cuydou casar con a meninna e os pres amos") illustrates the content of stanza 9.

Here arches are abandoned and all the action, in one moment of time and no more, occupies the entire panel in a truly exceptional scene. The artists have produced here one of the most uncluttered settings in the *Cantigas* and one of the most beautiful of all the miniatures. We see the entire action unfolding between two craggy cliffs, one at each side of the panel, and each crowned by a bright green leafy tree. In the foliage of this tree to the left perches a tiny white owl, and beneath the same tree sits a rabbit, one of the many which grace rural scenes in various *cantigas*. Neither animal has anything to do with the story, in my opinion, and both were probably added, as was the profusion of brilliant blossoms spangling the grass, to indicate the rurality of the setting and because in the thirteenth century, as Mâle has so graphically pointed out, artists loved to embellish their work with the beauties of nature.[11] Perhaps the owl symbolizes wisdom (the wisdom of the trip to find the sweetheart?) and perhaps the rabbit signifies love, but I doubt that any symbolism is intended. After all rabbits appear in too many *cantigas* to list, and most appear in scenes of the chase, in journeys by knights, in short, in any sort of rural scene in which love has no part at all. No one to my knowledge has investigated the appearance of so many rabbits in the miniatures of the *Cantigas*, and I am inclined to agree with Mâle as to their presence and the presence of many other small animals, birds, and plants.

The groom has been forced to dismount, his hands are bound in front of him, and one of the wicked rich man's retainers holds a long dagger to his chest. Alis, still mounted, although her horse is hidden by the standing figures of men, steeples her hands in prayer as she looks in concern at her captor. Two lances rising immediately to her right lend an attractive balance to the scene. Color here is especially brilliant—in the green of the trees, the scarlet hose and equine accouterments, and in the multi-colored flowers.

Moving to the next folio and its six panels, we find even greater action and color. Panel 1 ("Como o ricome se deytou con a meninna e dormeceu logo tras eno sol rayado") depicts the action recounted in stanzas 9 and 10. We see at the far left the good rich man, that is, the groom, in a cell, his hands folded in prayer, and the arch created by the ceiling of the cell encapsulates him and presents his part of the story. To his right under two golden arches we see Alis and the wicked rich man in bed together. He has tried to have his way with her, according to stanza 10, but "he fell asleep," according to the narration. We see revealed a good deal more than was described in the caption. Two arches dramatize what occurs. Under the left-hand arch above the colorfully tiled rooftops is a blue sky with a ring of feathery white clouds in the center of which glows a golden sunburst, and from it, piercing the roof and penetrating the left-hand arch falls a bolt, touching the legs of Alis' sleeping captor. Bed covers conceal him from the chest down. His shoulders reveal that he is wearing a nightgown. The bride is sitting up in bed, her hands joined in supplication, as she calls upon Our Lady to save her from her tormentor. Stanzas 11, 12, and 13 relate the conversation between Alis and her captor after he awakens from his trance. This is not illustrated in the panel.

Panel 2 ("Como o ricome mandou sacar da carcer o esposo da meninna que presera") illustrates stanza 14. Actually, four moments of time are seen. The first occurs as the groom is being pulled from his cell, which encapsulates a part of this action, for we can see the groom half in the cell and the cruel rich man's retainer in the act of pulling him into the left-hand arch. In the center arch we see the rich man himself as he gives peremptory orders, employing an imperative gesture. The right-hand arch contains only the figure of Alis, her hands, as usual, steepled in prayer.

Panel 3 ("Como o rricome e o esposo da meninna foron buscar o meninno con que fora iurado"), which illustrates stanza 15, is an artistic jewel with exceptional colors and arrangement of characters in a beautiful rural setting. One is led to agree with Mâle in his statement that medieval artists often were motivated to illustrate nature by the sheer joy of depicting the world about them. The three leafy trees make an attractive skyline. The horses and the bride's dappled palfrey move sedately from border to border of the panel. Alis, wearing a stylish pink gown and seated sidesaddle, holds in her lap a small dog, which some scholars might regard as a symbol of devotion, but which I see, after some thirty years of studying the miniatures in the *Cantigas*, as no more than another of the artists' characteristic embellishments. From the animal's ears I judge it to be a spaniel. Alis' headgear is a lovely conical creation of green leaves which sweep down from a golden pompom to a brim formed by what appear to be rose or carnation buds. If roses, they could, of course, symbolize the Virgin. The rich accouterment of her palfrey is in brilliant blue spangled with golden x's. The wicked rich man, now reformed, turns in his saddle to speak to Alis, one hand holding the reins, the other, his right, possibly encouraging her to follow. Behind her rides the groom, his sombrero strapped flat against his shoulders, his hair contained by the characteristic white kerchief. The trees, the blue and scarlet accouterments of the horses, the profusion of color in the flowers literally sprinkling the ground, make this an unusually rich miniature.

Panel 4 ("Como acharon o donzel e disseronlli que s'aparellas de casar con dona Lis"), frames no less than five golden arches under which the action unfolds. The first arch to the left reveals only an open door; the second contains two men, probably the reformed rich man's retainers; arch number three encapsulates the good rich man as he, with hands in a gesture one might use to explain, faces three men in the fourth arch, one of whom must be either the reformed rich man, who is seen gesturing, or possibly Alis' sweetheart; the fifth arch at the far right shelters Alis, her hand holding a glove, probably to give a characteristic feminine touch rather than to provide any sort of symbolism.

Panel 5 ("Como os casaron amos por prazer da Virgen Sancta Maria por en seia loada amen") in three arches reveals the ceremony as Alis and her young man are legally wed. The left-hand arch contains only an altar with colorful tiles, a golden monstrance, a candlestick holding a tall lighted candle, and, of course, the sacramental paten containing the Host, covered with its corporal. The center arch rises above Alis and her young man on their knees with two priests officiating, one of whom blesses the union with an upraised hand. The right-hand arch is filled with men and women witnessing the ceremony. Stanzas 16-17 parallel the depiction.

The last panel is one of the most unusual among all the miniatures in the *Cantigas de Santa Maria*. The caption helps to explain this peculiarity: "Como os deytaron amos e fezeron como fez novio a novia en solaz." A scene of carnal love is presented with extreme simplicity, naïveté, and explicit frankness. The bed is covered with rich bedclothing in blue, scarlet, and gold. Above it a canopy embroidered with designs of gold and blue towers over the couple. Lighted sconces affixed to walls and a column illuminate the scene. The panel is divided into the usual three arches, but to the left of the arches is a section of the panel separated from the rest by a band or column of interspersed castles and lions, symbols of royal power in Spain and almost always found in the corners of each panel throughout the volume. This is one of the two cases where these royal symbols invade and divide the interior of a panel. The other miniature appears in the illuminations of *Cantiga* 138, which has nothing to do with royalty.

The first arch, the one to the far right, is larger than either of the other two, and beneath it the artists have set the most important aspect of the action. In the larger four-poster, and sheltered under the high canopy of lacy white with its designs in blue and gold, we see Alis and her true spouse lying nude and side by side with the covers pulled up to their waists. Her left arm is around his body and is hidden by it. Her right arm extends across his body and her fingers, curved and intended to indicate movement and probably purpose, seem ready to draw back the sheet from his midriff.

The action of the groom is much more explicit. His left hand encircles his bride's neck and his fingers seem to squeeze her shoulder. His right hand unabashedly fondles her breast crowned by a papilla. This posture is, of course, a traditional representation of carnal love, but to see it in the *Cantigas*, a work in which the Virgin repeatedly prevents such love, is startling. Even so the caption tells us that the groom "did as does a groom to a bride in *solaz*" (2:102, ll. 156-57).

Perhaps it is this carnal motif intensified by the explicit miniature that led the artists, probably at Alfonso's suggestion, to omit the portrayal of the Blessed Virgin in the illuminations, although certainly in the caption of panel 5 of the second folio, in the first four lines of the *cantiga*, and in the first stanza the Queen of Heaven is mentioned. Nor can we forget that in panel 1 of the second folio her symbolic cloud appears as she prevents the wicked rich man from having his way with Alis. But her actual depiction, usually included in the miniature of other *cantigas*, is conspicuous by its absence in *Cantiga* 135. The only visual hint of her presence, aside from the aforementioned cloud, lies in the representations of the altar in the first folio, panel 4, and in the second folio, panel 5, since both altars, seen in the backgrounds of Alis' two weddings, resemble the Virgin's altars so often depicted in other miniatures.

One last point should be developed—Alis' coronet in most of the miniatures.[12] I see no likelihood that she can be considered to be a member of any but a fictive royal family or of some royal family which had become the subject of fiction, as was the case in the *cantiga* which stemmed from the romance about the empress of Rome mentioned earlier. Therefore I believe that, since she wears her coronet in eleven of the twelve panels devoted to her story, we must consider her as royalty. No symbolism seems to lie behind her coronet or crown. This would strengthen my opinion that Alis' story derives from a romance, since the heroines of romances generally were of royal stock.

Cantiga 135, unusual in many ways—in its artistic presentation, its subject matter, its permissiveness on the part of Our Lady and her romantic regard for the young couple under her protection—can lead to hitherto unexplored facets of her character in Alfonso's great Marian anthology.[13]

Notes

* Reprinted from Florilegium Hispanicum. Medieval and Golden Age Studies Presented to Dorothy Clotelle Clarke, ed. John S. Geary, et al., (Madison: Hispanic Seminary of Medieval Studies, 1983), pp. 103-18

1 Albert I. Bagby, Jr. ("The Jews in the Cantigas of Alfonso X, el Sabio," Speculum 46 [1971]: 670-88, and "The Moslem in the Cantigas of Alfonso X, el Sabio," Kentucky Romance Quarterly 20 [1973]: 173-207), in treating the two religions of necessity treats also the Virgin's character. Sara Sturm, "The Presentation of the Virgin in the Cantigas de Santa Maria," Philological Quarterly 49 (1970): 1-7, is directly concerned with the Virgin's character.

2 Number 42 is the most convincing. See my "The Motif of the Statue Bride in the Cantigas of Alfonso the Learned," Studies in Philology 56 (1959): 453-58, where I also indicate the strength of the Virgin's character and her aversion to carnal love. Other Cantigas in which the Virgin does not help lovers in their love affairs are number 16, 68, 104, and 105.

3 All quotations or references from the Cantigas come from the edition of Walter Mettmann, Cantigas de Santa Maria, 4 vols. (Coimbra: Acta Universitatis Conimbrigensis, 1959-72). The title of Cantiga 135 appears at 2:98.

4 Alfonso X el Sabio, Cantigas de Santa Maria, Edición facsimil del Códice T.I.1. de la Biblioteca de San Lorenzo el Real de El Escorial, Siglo XIII (Madrid: Editora Internacional de Libros Antiguos, 1979).

5 Many French and Spanish romances are very long, so lengthy, in fact, that most have not been edited and published. A. D. Deyermond, in his The Literary History of Spain: The Middle Ages. (New York: Barnes and Noble, 1971), pp. 155-56, discusses Spanish romances and their French originals, as well as some which do not seem to be translations from the French or to stem from French sources, for example, El libro del Cavallero Cifar. Anita Benaim Lasry, "Noble cuento de Carlos Maynes de Roma e de la buena emperatriz Seuilla su mujer," and "Fermoso cuento de una santa emperatriz que ovo en Roma e de su castidat" (Ph.D. diss., Columbia University, 1979, [now published in the Juan de la Cuesta series as Two Romances]), provides excellent treatment of the two romances she edits in her introductions. The latter was used in the writing of Cantiga 15. The debt of the Cantigas to the romance may be greater than we know.

6 Evelyn S. Procter, Alfonso X of Castile Patron of Literature and Learning (Oxford: Clarendon Press, 1951), pp. 25-32, discusses local and folk miracles, and my

"Folklore in the *Canticles* of Alfonso X," *Southern Folklore Quarterly*, 23, no. 3 (1959): 23-25 reveals considerable proof of the extent of popular sources.

7 The music of the *Cantigas* can best be studied in the transcription of Higinio Anglés, *La música de las "Cantigas de Santa Maria" del Rey Alfonso el Sabio: Facsímil, transcripción y estudio crítico*, vol. 2 (Barcelona: Diputación Provincial de Barcelona, 1943), 126 pp. of text, 462 pp. of transcription.

8 See my *Pious Brief Narrative in Medieval Castilian and Galician Verse* (Lexington: University Press of Kentucky, 1978), pp. 111-12.

9 For an excellent study of "dramatic arches" see Otto Pächt, *The Rise of Pictorial Narrative Art in Twelfth-Century England* (Oxford: Clarendon Press, 1962), pp. 31 ff.

10 Alis' name does not appear in *Cantiga* 135 until the 17th stanza. It is written Lis, but this was understood as "Alis." The name of her sweetheart and finally husband never does appear, although in the Spanish translation found in the volume accompanying the facsimile of the *Cantigas*, the word Fiiz is rendered "Felix," and connected with Alis' young husband. Kathleen Kulp-Hill, who has translated the *Cantigas*, believes that this is incorrect, and I agree with her. She states that Fiiz is no more than some person who is in authority. The mention of Fiiz is not integral to the story and would seem to be an afterthought to sustain the rhyme in *-iz*. And certainly in stanza 18, where Fiiz appears, he is not the young man, because the line reads that the two, that is Alis and the young man, told everything to Fiiz; he would not have been telling it to himself. Dorothy Clotelle Clarke may have a better idea: she thinks that in the poem's stanza 18 *fiz* in 1.146 means "end," which would be the logical balance to *raiz* in 1. 144. In other words, the story is told "from beginning to end." Mettmann's glossary, vol. 4, lists two others whose name is Fiiz, one a bishop in *Cantiga* 125, 1. 124, and the other an abbot, in *Cantiga* 353, 1. 81.

11 Emile Mâle, *The Gothic Image*, trans. by Dora Mussey (New York: Harper and Row, 1972), p. 51.

12 In the miniatures of the *Cantigas* royalty is usually identifiable by the crowns worn. Alfonso usually appears in a crown, even when he lies ill in bed. In *Cantiga* 10, usually known as *Rosa das rosas* from its first line, we see the Queen of Heaven in her crown. In the first panel she is "Rose of the Roses" and she sits in a bed of these favorite flowers; in panel 2 she sits crowned among flowers and is "Flower of Flowers." In panel 3 she is "Lady among Ladies," and of the many ladies near her not one wears a crown. In panel 4 she is "Queen among Queens," and here she sits crowned and surrounded by many queens all with royal crowns to identify them as queens. It seems unlikely that Alis would be depicted as crowned unless she were indeed of royal blood.

13 I believe that I have for the first time in print attempted to coordinate verbalization and visualization in a *cantiga*, indicating how picture and written word complement one another and how, at times, they are at variance. It can be hoped that this interpretation of the verbal and the visual may lead others to further study of this important matter.

Monserrat in the
*Cantigas de Santa Maria**

 CROSS MOST OF the years of his reign (1252-1284) Alfonso X caused miracles and songs of praise (*loores*) to be gathered, written in verse, set to music, and in some two hundred and more cases, to be illuminated by a multitude of miniatures.[1] This is the richest of all collections of Our Lady's miracles, either in Spain or beyond her borders, containing the most copious outpouring of verse forms (all those used in Spain before the Renaissance, except the sonnet), the most comprehensive anthology of musical notation (more than 400 melodies), and the most lavishly illuminated corpus of medieval miniatures illustrating a vernacular work.[2] The three-fold impact created by the team of workers employed by the Learned King—poetic (the narratives), melodic (the musical notation), and visual (the miniatures and possibly dramatic productions[3]), makes the *Cantigas de Santa Maria* a very unusual and extremely valuable work. Scholars from many fields can gain much from the study of these Alfonsine anthologies: art historians, literary historians, musicologists, thematologists, geographers, political and social scientists, folklorists, medical doctors, botanists, zoologists, geologists, and many others, since the miniatures are a world within themselves.

Alfonso was interested in any and all miracles of the Blessed Virgin. Therefore he caused the great corpuses of miracles in Latin to be researched, as well as those miracles which abounded apparently in legend and tradition to be collected, many of these from obscure Spanish and Portuguese shrines, and even from informants among the folk.[4]

205

In recent years, ever-increasing study of the *Cantigas* has developed, so that presently a number of excellent tools for research have been created: bibliographies, translations, studies in daily life, in folklore, and in the areas listed above.[5]

This essay will treat for the first time those six miracles which are associated with Our Lady of Montserrat, one of Christendom's greatest shrines, dating from very early times and to this day the focal point of pilgrimages from many parts of the world. Moreover, shrines of Montserrat exist in many Spanish-speaking countries. It is not strange, then, that Alfonso, noting the power and attraction of Montserrat as a magnet of pilgrimages from much of the western world, should devote six miracles to that great shrine.[6] The Learned King must surely have had access to Montserrat miracles written in Catalan, for such collections existed. Moreover Alfonso had reason to show interest in the Virgin's miracles in the Kingdom of Aragón, since King James I was his uncle and since his wife Violante was an Aragonese princess.[7] Therefore he set some seventeen miracles in Our Lady's shrine at Salas.[8] But, strange to say, the *Cantigas* contains no miracles concerning Nuestra Señora del Pilar in Saragossa, an intriguing mystery, fertile in possibilities for speculations and research.

The six miracles about Montserrat have a simple and ingenuous charm, not only in their motifs and verbal and melodic presentation, but also in their visualization which so well illustrate the terrain of the region. Actually only four of the six—numbers 48, 52, 57 and 113—are illustrated and found in the manuscript T.I.1, known as the *manuscrito rico*, archived in the Escorial.[9] The others, 302 and 311, appear in unilluminated manuscripts.

All four of the illustrated miracles of Montserrat contain suggestions of the terrain at or near the shrine and monastery, but numbers 52 and 113 are noteworthy in the depiction of landscape there. It is these two miracles and their illustrations which will be treated fully, with emphasis placed upon the locale of Montserrat. Special attention will be given also to the techniques and devices of verbalization and visualization employed by the artists. To date no one has treated the setting of Montserrat in the *Cantigas*, although other areas in Spain which were the sites of miracles have been studied—Seville, Murcia, Toledo and Segovia, for example.[10] Nor has any one interpreted the narrative techniques used in these two *cantigas*. This approach, original to the author of this article, is straightforward, but not simplistic. It is used because the miniatures and their captions can pose problems and can be misunderstood. Persons not expert in or familiar with thirteenth-century Alfonsine miniatures can be led astray by such devices as "double" or even "triple" action taking place in a single panel of miniatures; imagery and symbolism may be strange to others who view the illuminations; details important to plot and characterization ("hand language" and gesture) might confuse others; moreover, even the captions which explain the content of the divisions of the illuminated pages, since they are in Galician-Portuguese rather than Castilian,[11] can produce still more misunderstanding by the appearance in the captions of peculiar medieval abbreviations. When all is said and done, even though thirteenth-century Spaniards could understand Galician-Portuguese well enough, modern readers not carefully trained in that language can easily mistake one word for another or may not be able to supply some diacritical accent mark omitted inadvertently by the scribes. To this day even specialists sometimes differ as to what a given word means in the *Cantigas de Santa Maria* or exactly what a miniature contains.

Before reading the commentary on *Cantiga* 52 and later 113, it will be well if the reader understands their content through the translations provided.[12]

Cantiga 52

This is how Holy Mary made the mountain goats come to Montserrat and they allowed the monks to milk them every day.

It is only right that the beasts obey Holy Mary, of whom God was born.

Concerning this, with God's aid, I shall tell you now of a great and beautiful miracle which the Glorious One performed. Listen to me, if you would hear an agreeable tale.

In Montserrat, as I told you before, there is a church, or so I hear, built in the name of the Mother of the King Most High Who died on the cross for us.

That place lies at the foot of a mountain on which many mountain goats roam. A singular miracle occurred, for all the goats came down to the church, which stands in a valley, and lined up in front of the door, standing very quietly until the monks came out to milk them.

How Holy Mary made the mountain goats come to Montserrat
and they allowed the monks to milk them.

This went on for four years, as I heard, and the monks had plenty of milk for themselves, because each night the goats came to give it to them, until a foolish novice stole a kid from the flock and ate it. After this happened to the goats, the monks could never catch them again.

In this way, the Mother of God provided for those monks of Hers and because of this, great processions of pilgrims came to learn about the miracle.

This delightful *cantiga* presents one of many miracles in which dumb animals play a role, which motifs are in themselves unusual and in need of investigation.

In panel 1, ("Como as cabras monteses descendian da montaña que as mongessen os monges"), the landscape of the Montserrat region is unquestionably depicted. Even today one sees the monastery literally built into the cliff which rises above it. In the miniature the rough escarpment of stones surrounds the cream-colored walls, the domed belfry, and the red and blue tile of the roofs. The building occupies the left-hand side of the panel, and an open door is visible in which stands a monk watching the file of mountain goats as it descends the rockstrewn slope toward level ground. Trees, shrubs, flowers, and grasses sprinkle the stones, indicating that then, as now, an abundance of flora was present. Botanists today estimate that one half of the three thousand plants native to Catalonia grow in that barren land.[13] Quite lush vegetation can be seen in panels 1, 2, 5, and 6. In panel 1 a bird in flight appears and one sees it again after it has lighted in panel 2.

Panel 2 ("Como as cabras se paravan todas en az e as mongian os monges"), is a delightful scene with the line of horned does standing placidly while one monk milks and another hands a pail of milk to a third brother just inside the monastery door. A partridge occupies the top of another peak, while lower down the stony slope sits a ptarmigan, and to its right a pair of rabbits. Rabbits, are, by the way, depicted in numerous illustrations of the *Cantigas* when sylvan scenes appear. They may represent something symbolic and significant and much more than the presence of the local fauna.

Kids stand at their dams' feet. Detail here is notable and realistic: one sees also the curved and the pointed horns of the goats with the ridges clearly visible in them. Detailed, too, are the expressions of gratification on the faces of the monks and the details of the monastery, for example, the tiled room and the great bell hanging inside the belfry and seen through an arch. The colors of the blossoms—scarlet and white and blue—and the red and the blue tiles of the roof, in contrast to the white robes of the monks, the pale beige of the goats, and the creamy walls of the building, produce both color and contrast to color.

Both panels 3 and 4 reveal what takes place inside the monastery. Panel 3, ("Como os monges comian leite d'aquelas cabras quanta lles era mester"), reveals six monks under three golden arches. In passing, it should be mentioned that arches, most often of gold, but sometimes of stone, serve to separate facets of scene and can even encompass a series of events in the same panel.[14] They may serve, then as "dramatic arches" employed in medieval drama in the same way, that is, to focus under each arch some incident in a sequence of action. Here it would seem that the arches are utilized primarily to illustrate action in the refectory, but even so the monks are in various poses, some talking, some eating, one pouring milk into bowls from a pitcher, and at the far right one with a second pitcher. Since the eyes move from left to right and from arch to arch, the viewers may have seen a different event under each arch.

Panel 4 ("Como os monges loavan Santa Maria per aquela mercee que lles fazia"), is divided into three golden arches, with monks kneeling in prayer under the left-hand and central arches, while the right-hand arch is filled with the altar of Our Lady, replete with brilliant tiles. Atop the altar sits her statue with its golden crown outlined against her azure halo, while the Christ Child's image, seated on her knee, has blond curls, vivid against His scarlet nimbus. Golden lamps of intricate detail hang in the left and central arches. The Virgin's image holds the stem of what appears to be a lily whose small red blossoms are numerous.

Panel 5, ("Como un crerizon furtou un cabrito d'aquelas cabras e o comeu"), is alive with action. The thieving monk, holding the kid with both hands, slinks through the postern door looking guiltily over his shoulder. Behind him a brother milks a doe, while the others wait to be milked. Kids stand in front of their dams. The backdrop of rocks and crags runs across the full width of the panel. Trees, a host of flowers, and two rabbits, one caught in stasis as it hops along toward the other, which crouches and seems to be waiting, decorate the scene.

Panel 6, ("Como as cabras fugieron e nunca mais y vĕeron por aquel cabrito que tomaron"), reveals at the right the herd of does and kids fleeing up the steep slope toward the crest surmounted by trees. Only one rabbit is visible. At the left a monk stands in the doorway, his hands open in a gesture of sign language, which clearly indicates alarm and surprise, as he watches the disappearing herd. Of course, the goats never return, even though for four years they had allowed the monk to milk them.

Cantiga 113 will be explicated inmediately after the translation of it. Again, as in the case of *Cantiga 52*, we shall delineate narrative devices and techniques, and stress the depiction of the setting at Montserrat.

Cantiga 113

How Holy Mary of Montserrat protected the monastery so that the stone which fell from the cliff would not strike it.

I think it right and proper that stones obey the Mother of the King, because when He died for us, I know that they were split asunder.

Concerning this, I shall tell a great miracle which I heard told which the Virgin performed in Montserrat, as can be seen there today. A great stone shifted and broke loose.

It fell in such a way, if God had let it strike, that it could have destroyed all the church in a moment. However, God, in order to protect the church of His Glorious Mother, Spiritual Queen, would not let it happen.

Therefore, he deflected the stone in such a way that it did him no harm. He made it descend so gently that it could roll no further.

The monks, who were singing the mass of the mother of God, when they heard the loud noise, said: "Dear Lord, we are yours, do not let us perish nor die a bad death."

Saying this, they went out of the church and saw the boulder which had fallen and which God had diverted. They began to bless God and the Virgin and Their great power.

This great miracle which God performed for the One of Good Will, His Glorious Mother, can be seen by all who go to Montserrat. It gives them great joy and they make offerings there.

In panel 1, which has no caption even though there is the usual space provided for one,[15] we see a depiction of the towering massif, described today as a conglomerate of pebbles, principally limestone,

How Holy Mary of Monserrat protected the monastery so that the stone
which fell from the cliff would not strike it.

but with fragments of quartz, slate, and porphyry, all bound together by a natural cement. This produces an extremely characteristic stone, with colorings that have a very striking effect when it is polished. Some, due to atmospheric agents—wind, snow, heat, cold, and mist— have molded the cliff into peculiar shapes. While it is not feasible to identify the perpendicular formation seen in the panels of 113, one can liken them to certain rock formation named by the folk the "sentinel" or "the finger", or the "spellbound giant."[16] In this panel appears a portrayal of King Alfonso himself, one of the peculiarities of this codex of the *Cantigas de Santa Maria*, in which he appears many times, always as a rather handsome man in his late twenties or early thirties. He is crowned, clothed in royal robes of many colors, and he stands and preaches or explains to kneeling gentlemen what appears in panel 2. The king's left hand seems to grant the honor of hearing him, or perhaps it signifies that he is demanding their attention. With his right hand he points into panel 2.

Panel 2, ("Como as pedras se foron fender quando morreu Ihesu Christo e dar os mortos que tïian"), attempts to depict what is described in Matthew 27:52-53, that is, how the earth opened and the saints' bodies emerged. The image of Jesus does not depict one of those grim and emaciated Christs, so characteristic of later centuries than the thirteenth. Instead, His body is that of an everyday man, well-made and comely. Above His head is the plaque on which the Roman soldiers inscribed the mocking words describing Him as the King of the Jews, but no lettering can be seen. At the foot of the cross slabs of stones are being pushed up to reveal two coffins in which are seated two of the saints, while other bodies are seen as they are resurrected. One coffin is blue, one red.

Panel 3 ("Como estava huna grand pena sobelo mõesteiro de Santa Maria de Monsarraz"), brings the viewer to Montserrat. At the left rises the sheer escarpment of creamy stone sparkling with red and blue blossoms. At the top of the cliff one sees a great boulder or outcropping of the cliff as it projects over the building far below. The right-hand side of the panel reveals the interior of Our Lady's shrine, with only the roof and turrets depicted to show its exterior.

Much artistic effort went into the portrayal of the shrine inside the church. At the left and under a pointed arch one sees four monks as they kneel and gaze in adoration into the scene under the large arch which is Gothic and cusped. There they see the typical altar with

brilliant tiles and the seated image of Our Lady with the Christ Child
on her knee as she seems to turn her head to look directly at them as
they pray. As usual, the tiles match the frieze which frames the entire
illumination. The crown of the Blessed Virgin is of gold and is set with
rubies and her halo is deep blue. The Christ Child's head, crowned
only with His golden curls, is outlined by His scarlet nimbus.

Panel 4 ("Como aquela pena se moveo e farira no mõesteiro se
non por Sancta Maria"), almost repeats the details of panel 3. However, a definite change is visible in the hanging boulder which now
appears to be surrounded by a clearly outlined crack in the stone. The
viewer realizes immediately that it is about to topple.

In panel 5, ("Como Santa Maria fez desinar a pena que non feriss
no seu mõesteiro"), can be seen a scene of "double action." The poem
reveals that the Virgin and God did not permit the falling boulder to
strike the church. The miniature shows how the boulder was turned
aside: at the left, which depicts the cliff and the falling stone, we see
two angels, one holding the falling stone from above as he reaches
down from a cloud, while another angel stands on a ledge of the cliff
and with both hands supports the weight of the stone. Also in the
sky, at the right we see Our Lady standing on a fleecy cloud and
accompanied by a female figure, as she points with her right hand to
the action, as though directing the angelic work in progress.

In her left hand she holds a crimson missal. Her robe is scarlet and
gold rather than the customary azure. The second element of "double
action" reveals the boulder after it has rolled to the foot of the cliff.

Panel 6, ("Como os monges loaron muito Santa Maria por que os
assi livrar de mal"), is divided into three cusped golden arches. Under
the one at the left monks in black robes stand and pray before a
lectern on which is an open book. The central arch frames three
clerics, seemingly deacons, with hands steepled in prayer, while on
the steps of the altar a third, hands also in the attitude of prayer,
seems to address the image.

The remaining two illuminated *cantigas* which deal with Montserrat also depict the Catalonian mountain, but not as strikingly. *Cantiga*
48, "Esta es como Santa Maria tolleu a agua da fonte ao cavaleiro en
cuja erdade estava, e a deu a aos frades de Monssarrad a que a el
queria vender", is the title which goes far toward summarizing the
event contained therein. It can be seen in the black-and-white repro-

How Holy Mary took the water from the knight's spring on whose land it was and gave it to the monks of Montserrat to whom he wanted to sell it.

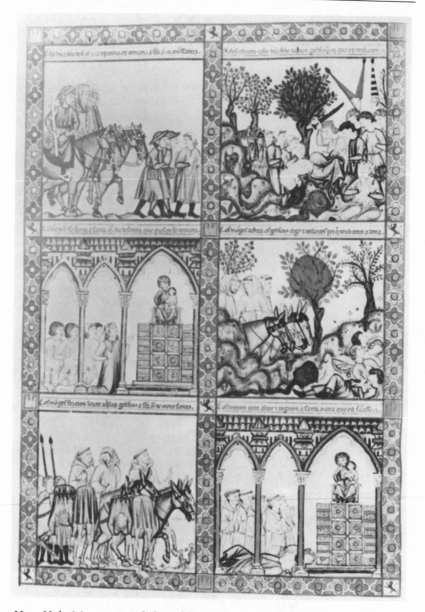

How Holy Mary assisted the robbers who were paralyzed because they had robbed a lady and her company who were going on a pilgrimage to Montserrat

ductions. Its action is fairly obvious and its captions tell its story sufficiently well to suffice here. Panel 1's caption reads: "Como un cavaleiro gardava hũa sa fonte que non collessen agua os monges;" panel 2, "Como o cavaleiro penorava a os monges per que collian agua na sa fonte;" panel 3, "Como os monges rogaron Sancta Maria que llis desse consello por que ouvessen agua;" panel 4, "Como a fonte do cavaleiro se secou e naceu na herdade dos monges"; panel 5; "Como o cavaleiro deu a os monges a herdade u estava a fonte;" panel 6, "Como o cavaleiro deu a os monges a rarta do herdamento con seu seelo."

Cantiga 57, i.e., "Esta e como Santa Maria fez guarecer os ladrões que foran tolleitos porque roubaran ũa donna e ssa cunpanna que yan en romaria a Monssarrad," whose title is also quite explicit as to its content, (see reproduction) is action-filled and depicts events which took place on a pilgrimage to Montserrat. The captions read: 1, "Como ya hũa bona donna con sa companna en romaria a Sancta Maria de Monssarraz;" 2, "Como eles estando cabo d' ũa fonte vēeron golfinnos que os roubaron;" 3, "Como a bõa donna sse quixou a Santa Maria da desonrra que pres en so romaria;" 4, "Como os monges echaron os golfinos cegos e tolleidos por que roubaran a dona;" 5, "Como os monges fezeron levar aquelos golfinos a Santa Maria de Montsarraz;" 6, "Como os deitaron ant'o altar e rogaron a Santa Maria que os sãase." The action in some of the panels is worthy of mention as is the depiction by the artist. In panel 2 one sees the lady as she is stripped of her robe which is being pulled over her head. In panel 4 the monks, who have ridden to the site of the robbery, find the robbers stretched out blind and paralyzed on the ground, and in panel 5, which is extremely well rendered, we see how the clerics placed the robbers across the backs of asses, two to each ass, and how their heads and legs dangle over the sides of the animals.

Notes

* Reprinted from *Josep Maria Solà Solé: Homage, Homenaje, Homenatge*. Barcelona: Puvill, 1984, pp. 67-77.
1 The manuscripts of the *Cantigas de Santa Maria* are four in number: Madrid, Biblioteca Nacional MS 10069, which, since it originally belonged to the Cathedral of Toledo, is usually referred to as the manuscript of Toledo (Tol); the two Escorial manuscripts, T.I.1. (EI) and B.1.2. (E2);

Florence, Biblioteca Nazionale, MS. Banco Rari 20 (formerly II.1.213 (F). The content of all these differs, as do the number of *cantigas* each contains, and they may represent at least two, if not three different editions. The most lavishly illuminated volume is T.I.1.

² The best discussion of the prosody of the *Cantigas* is that of Dorothy Clotelle Clarke. "Versification in Alfonso el Sabio's *Cantigas*," *Hispanic Review* 23 (1955), 83-98. Though still of great value in connection with the musical notation of the *Cantigas* is Higinio Anglés' *La música de las "Cantigas de Santa Maria" del rey Alfonso el Sabio: Facsímil, transcripción y estudio crítico.* (Barcelona: Diputación Provincial de Barcelona, Central, 1943), the more recent text and study of José María Loréns Cisteró, *"Cantigas de Santa Maria* del rey Alfonso el Sabio. La música, datos, transcripción y notas, con un apéndice descriptivo de la grabación discográfica que acompaña este volumen," which appears in the volume which accompanies the facsimile of Edilán, is of greater value today. Anglés discovered the meaning of the thirteenth-century notation: Lloréns Cisteró perfected it.

³ In *Iconography in Medieval Spanish Literature.* (Lexington: University Press of Kentucky, 1983) Richard P. Kinkade and I study the three-fold impact of the *Cantigas,* and I speculate about the dramatic productions in my *Alfonso X, el Sabio,* (New York: Twayne World Authors Series 1967), pp. 92-3.

⁴ I discuss Alfonso's interest in legend and tradition connected with the *Cantigas* in my "A Medieval Folklorist," *Folklore Studies in Honor of Arthur Palmer Hudson* (Chapel Hill: University of North Carolina Press, 1965), pp. 19-24. [AUTH. Included ih this volume as the second article.]

⁵ Among the most valuable contribution to the study of the *Cantigas de Santa Maria* are these: José Guerrero Lovillo, *Las Cántigas, Estudio arqueológico de sus miniaturas* (Madrid: CSIC, 1949): Kathleen Kulp-Hill's translation into English, not yet published, but available through Dr. Kulp-Hill's courtesy to scholars who need it; Antonio Ballesteros Beretta's *Alfonso X el Sabio.* (Barcelona: Salvat Editores and Murcia: CSIC, Academia "Alfonso X el Sabio," 1963); Roger D. Tinnell's *An Annotated Discography of Music in Spain before 1650.* (Madison, Wisconsin: Hispanic Seminary of Medieval Studies, 1980); Israel J. Katz's "The Traditional Folk Music of Spain: Explorations and Perspectives," *YIMFC* 6 (1974), 64-85: Gonzalo Menéndez Pidal's "Los manuscritos de las *Cantigas:* cómo se elaboró la miniatura alfonsí." *Boletín de la Real Academia de la Historia,* 150, (1962), 25-51; Connie L. Scarborough's "Verbalization and Visualization in Codex T.I.1 of the *Cantigas de Santa Maria.* Diss. Univ. of Kentucky, 1983; Joseph T. Snow's *The Poetry of Alfonso X. el Sabio. Research bibliographies and Checklists,* 19 (London: Grant and Cutler Ltd., 1977): Walter Mettmann's definitive edition, *Afonso o Sabio, Cantigas de Santa María* (Coimbra: Acta Universitatis Conimbrigensis, 1959-1973, 4 vols.); Anthony J. Cárdenas' editing of *Noticiero Alfonsí* (Wichita: Fairmont College of Wichita State University, 1982). The first volume of this ongoing newsletter-bibliography, appeared in November of 1982. It is to be published twice a vear. At present volumes II (1983), III (1984), IV (1985) and V (1986) have appeared.

⁶ King Alfonso took a great interest in pilgrimages within the peninsula. Indeed, so interested was he in the shrines of the Blessed Virgin which

attracted pilgrims from Spain, as well as abroad, that he included in his *Cantigas* miracles which revealed how the shrines of Our Lady could cure ailing pilgrims who had with no help from the saint, visited the great international shrine of St. James at Santiago de Compostela. In two articles I discuss this: "The Virgin Mary as Rival of Saint James in the *Canticles* of King Alfonso the Learned," *Middle Ages-Reformation Volksunde Festschrift for John G. Kunstman.* (Chapel Hill: University of North Carolina Press, 1958), pp. 75-82 and "More on the Rivalry between Santa Maria and Santiago de Compostela," *Crítica Hispánica* I, (1979), 37-43. [AUTH. Both of these articles are in this volume]

⁷ Diplomatic ties with the Kingdom of Aragon were always important to Castile, James I was the brother of King Fernando III, Alfonso's father; Alfonso's wife, Violante, James' daughter, brought much prestige to the Castilian realm, and even though she later left it to take her grandchildren back to Aragon to save them from possible destruction by her son Sancho IV, el Bravo, Aragon never ceased to influence the Learned King. The miracles in Catalan can be studied in Cebrià Barnaut.

⁸ The *Cantigas* which treat miracles of Our Lady of Salas in Aragon are numbers: 43, 44, 109, 114, 118, 129, 161, 164, 166, 167, 168, 171, 172, 173, 189 and 247.

⁹ Alfonso X el Sabio, *Cantigas de Santa María. Edición Facsímil del Códice T. I. 1 de la Biblioteca de San Lorenzo de el Escorial, siglo XIII* (Madrid: Editora Internacional de Libros Antiguos, 1979), is a remarkably authentic and significant reproduction of the miniatures of the *códice rico.*

¹⁰ Guerrero Lovillo, op. cit.

¹¹ For a discussion of Galician-Portuguese as the vehicle of lyric poems see Frede Jensen, *The Earliest Portuguese Lyrics.* (Odense, Denmark: University of Odense Press, 1978) and Gerald Brenan. *The Literature of the Spanish People.* (New York: Meridian Books, 1957).

¹² The translation of *Cantigas* 52 and 113 are those of Kathleen Comaes Kulp-Hill.

¹³ The descriptions of the terrain of Montserrat come from a guidebook to Montserrat: *A Mountain Sanctuary / a Monastery / a Spiritual Community /* issued without date by the authorities of the monastery at Montserrat, 7 and 11.

¹⁴ For a fine discussion of dramatic arches see Otto Pächt, *The Rise of Pictorical Narrative in Twelfth-Century England* (Oxford: Oxford University Press, 1951).

¹⁵ Only a few panels in Codex T.I.1 lack captions, but in the Florentine Ms. many lack them, and indeed, in that codex many other omissions are made. For a description of the Florentine manuscript see A. G. Solalinde. "El códice florentino de las *Cantigas* y su relación con los demás manuscritos," *Revista de Filología Española* 5 (1918), 143-70.

¹⁶ *The Mountain Sanctuary...* p. 11.

Iconography and Literature:
Alfonso Himself in *Cantiga* 209*

N OUR STUDIES of iconography and narrative art, supported by a generous grant from the National Endowment for the Humanities, we have photographed and researched various art genres which tell stories. We believe that the importance of this sphere of study is increasingly being recognized and that it can contribute enormously to our knowledge of medieval man's perception of literature and the fine arts. Most interesting parallels and contrasts between the written word and its visualization occur, for frequently miniatures may supply details lacking in the text. It should be noted that in the miniatures of *Cantiga* 209, iconography and text closely parallel each other and that contrast is hardly present except for the fact that scene, not specifically developed in the poem, is detailed in visualized form. The present article took its inspiration in the first of several books which we hope to publish about the interdisciplinary ties between literature and the fine arts.[1]

Among some 400-odd *Cantigas de Santa Maria* of King Alfonso X, el Sabio, some twenty-eight are concerned with the king himself or with members of his family who were benefited by Our Lady's miraculous intervention in their lives. This is a remarkable phenomenon, for no other patron of literature and art in medieval times, insofar as we have been able to discover, included himself to so great a degree and so personally in a work sponsored by him. The noted British historian, the late Evelyn Procter, was singularly attracted by the personal touch accorded the *Cantigas* by the Learned King, and today Joseph Snow and Philip Vandrey have brought to light even more of the king's personal touch.[2] But neither Procter nor Snow approached the matter through the visualization of miracles in which Alfonso appears depicted by his artists as they characterized him visually, and in the process, developed facets of the monarch omitted in the verbalization.

Frequent reference to the color plate that accompanies this article [ED. In *Hispania* it *was* reproduced in color, but here it is only in black and white] will help the reader to follow our treatment of Alfonsine illumination because it enables one to see the royal character in pictorial form. The page of miniatures comes from the Florentine manuscript, and this illuminated page is lacking in the most lavishly illuminated of all the manuscripts of the *Cantigas de Santa Maria,* that is, Ms. Escorial T. I. 1.[3]

The personal quality of this *cantiga* is intense and unique in "biographical art." Both the artist and the poet, who may well have been the poetically gifted Alfonso himself, have produced a remarkably sensitive work of literary and graphic art; and if, indeed, King Alfonso composed the poem, as we believe he did, then *Cantiga* 209 might be called an example of "autobiographical writing." As one reads *Cantiga* 209 today and studies its miniatures he feels that he is actually experiencing much of the king's own suffering as he fights for his life. It is interesting to discover, due to the efforts of Procter, that Alfonso was flat on his back in Vitoria suffering from a mortal illness, a fact which explains why there is no entry of his whereabouts and activities in that time in the chronicle.[4]

It is probable that in Alfonso's time few were privileged to peruse the illuminated manuscripts of the *Cantigas,* but those who were so fortunate could receive the impact of miracles presented to them in three media—the written word, musical notation, and truly fabulous miniatures. To read these poems, to follow their content in the illuminations, and to hear them sung to musical accompaniment, must have been a very moving experience. And today, in the recently published complete and authentic facsimile of the Escorial manuscript,[5] one is now able to read, view, and hear (on the discs which accompany the volume), some of the songs edited by modern musicologists. The Florentine manuscript contains no musical notation, but Higinio Anglés' definitive musical transcription of the most complete of the manuscripts of the *Cantigas* does contain the music of *Cantiga* 209.[6]

This particular *cantiga,* then, is an unusual piece: not only is it a fine short poem and a moving melody, which we think harmonizes with the miracle's subject matter,[7] but it also contains one of the most brilliant of illuminations to be found in either of the narrative codices of the *Cantigas.*

Since Number 209 is brief, we offer it in the original Galician-
Portuguese from the edition of Walter Mettmann and in the translation by Kathleen Kulp-Hill.[8]

[C]omo el Rey Don Affonso de *Castela* adoeçeu en Bitoria e ouv' hũa
door tan grande, que coidaron que morresse ende, e *poseron-lle* de
suso o livro das Cantigas de Santa Maria, e foi guarido.

5   *Muito faz grand' erro, e en torto jaz,*
    a Deus quen lle nega o ben que lle faz

    Mas en este torto per ren non jarei
    que non cont' o ben que del recebud' ei
    per ssa Madre Virgen, a que sempr' amei.
10 e de a loar mais d'outra ren me praz.
    Muito faz grand' erro, en en torto jaz...

    E, como non devo aver gran sabor
    en loar os feitos daquesta Sennor
    que me val nas coitas e tolle door
15 e faz-m' outras mercees muitas assaz?
    Muito faz grand' erro, e en torto jaz...

    Poren vos direi o que passou per mi,
    jazend' en Bitoira enfermo assi
    que todos cuidavan que morress' ali
20 e non atendian de mi bon solaz.
    Muito faz grand' erro, e en torto jaz...

    Ca hũa door me fillou [y] atal
    que en ben cuidaa que era mortal,
    e braadava: "Santa Maria, val,
25 e por ta vertud' aqueste mal desfaz."
    Muito faz grand' erro, e en torto jaz...

    E os fisicos mandavan-me põer
    panos caentes, mas nono quix fazer,
    mas mandei o Livro dela aduzer;
30 e poseron-mio, e logo jouv' en paz,
    Muito faz grand' erro, e en torto jaz...

    Que non braadei nen senti nulla ren
    da door, mas senti-me logo mui ben;
    e dei ende graças a ela poren,
35 ca tenno ben que de meu mal lle despraz.
    Muito faz grand' erro, e en torto jaz...

    Quand' esto foi, muitos eran no logar
    que mostravan que avian gran pesar

de mia door e fillavan-s' a chorar,
40 estand' ante mi todos come en az.
Muito faz grand' erro, e en torto jaz...
E pois viron a mercee que me fez
esta Virgen santa, Sennor de gran prez,
loárona muito todos dessa vez,
45 cada ũu põendo en terra sa faz.
Mu[i]to faz grand' erro, e en torto jaz...

How King Alfonso of Castile Fell Ill in Vitoria and Had Such Severe Pain
That They Thought He Would Die of It. They Laid the *Book of the Canticles* of
Holy Mary upon Him and He Was Cured.

He who denies God and His blessings commits a great error and is
grievously in the wrong.

However, I shall never fall into this error by failing to tell of the benefit I
have received from Him through His Virgin Mother, whom I have
always loved and whom it pleases me more than any other thing to
praise.

And how should I not take great delight in praising the works of this
Lady who assists me in trouble and takes away sorrow and grants me
many other blessings?

Therefore, I shall tell you what happened to me while I lay in Vitoria, so
ill that all believed I should die there and did not expect me to recover.

For such a pain afflicted me that I believed it to be mortal and cried out:
"Holy Mary, help me, and with your power dispel this malady!"

The doctors ordered hot cloths placed on me, but I did not wish it and
ordered Her Book to be brought. They placed it on me and at once I lay
in peace.

I neither cried out nor felt anything of the pain, but at once felt very
well. I gave thanks to Her for it, for I know full well She was dismayed at
my affliction.

When this happened, many were in the place who expressed great
sorrow at my suffering, and began to weep, standing before me in a line.

When they saw the mercy which this Holy Virgin, Lady of Great Worth,
showed me, they all praised Her, each one pressing his face to the earth.

Because the story revolved entirely around the monarch himself,
the artists seem to have lavished more color and gold upon their
production than upon any other folio of miniatures in any of the

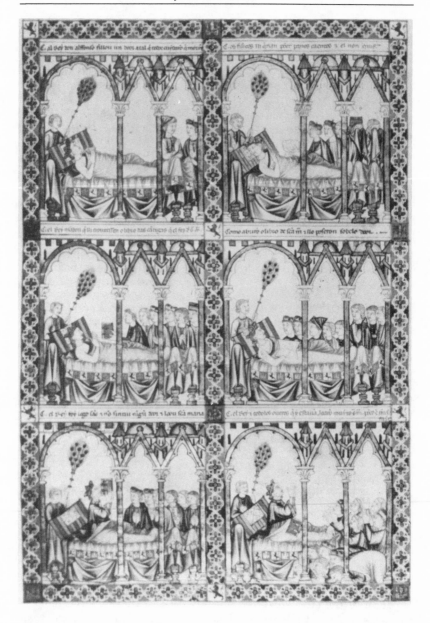

volumes of the *Cantigas*. The page literally blazes with the precious metal—in arches, columns, the king's crown, the great four-poster bed, and in the motif of the castle and the lion which forms the border of his counterpane. Even the frame or frieze glows with exceptionally rich hues and intricacy of design. This is truly a royal illumination, sparing nothing in its conspicuous attempt to be unique among the *cantigas* miniatures.

Since we present it in translation *in toto*, there is no need to discusss the details of a plot whose essential scheme and content are summarized by its somewhat lengthy title. The truly interesting aspects of this miraculous event lie in the iconography and the revelation of the monarch's most intimate feelings as he expresses them in the first person in verse and pictorially. Nowhere have we encountered a similar account of a king's description of how he felt in the midst of the misery of an illness or how he prayed in the depths of his despair. He calls the Virgin *his* Divine Mother, and relates: "I cried out, 'Holy Mother, help *me*, and with your power dispel this malady!'" The caption of the appropriate panel reads, "How King Alfonso suffered a pain so great that all thought he would die."

In panel 1 the visualization parallels and greatly strengthens Alfonso's actions at the height of his illness. He lies supine in his royal four-poster with its pink counterpane drawn up around his body, leaving one arm limply exposed. His head is propped up on a pillow striped in gold and blue, and since he is the king, he wears his golden crown even in bed, for he must be easily recognized by the viewer. The gleaming golden arches, one large romanesque at the left, the center and far right Gothic, frame the action. The first and larger arch focuses attention upon the monarch. At his right physicians consult. Alfonso's face reveals pain, insofar as the artists were able to capture and depict it.

Alfonso in panel 2 has grown worse. The caption reads, "How the physicians ordered hot cloths placed on him but he refused." In the miniature he turns his face away from them as they proffer the cloths and regally waves them back with his hand. Behind the doctors stand two courtiers or members of the royal family, who cover their heads and weep in gestures often seen in medieval paintings and sculptures depicting funerary scenes. At the king's left, and just behind the head of the bed, stands a servant wielding a peacock plumed fan. This personage is, of course, part of the panoply of kingship, but at the same time provides an aesthetic touch of balance to the panel. The poem reveals that Alfonso thought it was better to suffer, making clear his critical opinion of medical science as compared with the power of Our Lady. The poem relates that "I ordered Her Book brought to me."

Indeed, in panel 3, "How the king ordered the *Canticles of Holy Mary* brought," Alfonso is still lying in bed, apparently waiting for the treasured volume, bound in scarlet and silver, which a tonsured priest presents ceremoniously. Doctors and courtiers stand behind the cleric, and the servant with the fan has not deserted his post.

Panel 4 shows Alfonso still supine, but seemingly relaxed with the book's open face resting over his heart. "They put it on me," he wrote in the poem, "and immediately I lay at peace." His body certainly seems at rest. Several people in expectation of the miraculous, or out of respect to the Virgin and Her wondrous Book, have gone to their knees, while others stand and stare in pious awe. The king's palm now lies flat across the pages.

In Panel 5, "How the King was instantly cured, felt no pain, and praised Holy Mary," he sits up in bed, wearing a bright blue bedrobe over his samite gown. He raises the volume in both hands and kisses it devoutly, while all kneel except the fan-bearer. "And," wrote Alfonso, "I didn't scream nor did I feel pain at all, but felt instantly quite well." His face has an expression of devotion. The striped pillow, now that his head is no longer on it, reveals a square doily where it had rested, calling attention once more to artistic insistence upon the inclusion of the smallest detail.

Panel 6 depicts the king still sitting up in bed, the volume now face down upon his lap. All kneel, save the fan-bearer, as Alfonso raises his hands in prayerful devotion. The caption reads, "How the king and the others who were there praised Holy Mary." Indeed, the kneeling, weeping men lower their faces all the way to the floor and press against it, just as the verses recall.

Gesture and facial expression play a strong role in this *Cantiga's* illumination: the king's hand in panel 1, listless on his chest, his face strained; the royal head turned peevishly from the physicians in panel 2, as his hand rejects their cloths; the intense faces of the king and courtiers in panel 3 as the volume is presented; in panel 4, the king's face at last calm, his body relaxed, his hand seeming to caress the open pages, while the faces of the others relax at last; the king's face ecstatic in panel 5 as he holds the book on high and presses his lips to it; and in panel 6 his countenance in complete repose, as he gazes piously upward, his hands steepled in prayer.

In this *cantiga*, perhaps more expressively than in any other, can be found the nine components of narrative in briefest form as well as in detailed and lavish pictorial representation—*plot, setting, conflict, characterization, theme, style, effect, point of view*, and *mood* or *tone.*

The simple, unadulterated *plot* and its conflict never falter and are constantly manifest; *scene* certainly is gorgeous, explicit in detail, laid on effectively against the oyster-white walls of the royal bed-chamber; *characterization* is primarily Alfonso's, for the others are mere minor supporting parts of the scene. The king's definite character emerges: his disdain for worldly cures; his confidence in the divine; his belief in Our Lady's power and willingness to heal him; and his pious respect for the wondrous book which he had caused to be written, set to music, and illuminated in Her honor; even his deep love for his Patroness is apparent as his hands lift the volume so that he can kiss it.

Iconography in these miniatures, as well as *style* in the poem, is so direct, clear and unencumbered, even in the case of the lavish details of the scene, that without captions the viewer can unravel most of the action with little effort. *Theme* is obviously faith and devotion and their rewards; *effect* is powerful and perhaps more complex than meets the eye at first. Viewers might well have been so thrilled at the series of scenes in the intimacy of the royal bed-chamber amid so much luxury and pomp that other effects might have been diffused. *Point of view* is most unusually personal and like no other found either in verbal or visual form in the *Cantigas.* King Alfonso allows the reader to hear him speak and, through the visualization and their captions, lets the viewer see that he is speaking. The king has actually versified a vignette straight from his own personal life and experience and from the depths of his suffering. *Mood* or *tone* is one of deep religiosity. Of all the *cantigas* in which Alfonso appears none is more deeply intimate.

At least five other authors of note in Medieval Spanish letters are remarkable for the revelation of their personal feelings and opinions. Contemporary with Alfonso X was Gonzalo de Berceo, who frequently presented interesting statements of how he felt and what he thought, but without visual representation. The fourteenth century produced three authors, two of the highest literary quality: Juan Ruiz frequently and often daringly exposed his most intimate feelings; Don

Juan Manuel, nephew of Alfonso X, though far less direct, nonetheless expressed his thoughts, especially in his masterpiece, *El Conde Lucanor*; and toward the end of that century one finds strong personal admissions in Pero López de Ayala, especially in *Rimado de palacio*. A century later one can read very personal confessions in the *Sacramental* of Clemente Sánchez de Vercial, Archdeacon of Valderas, although some claim his confessions to be contrived, with which we disagree. But no author equaled the very precise, emotional, and intimately personal disclosures found in those *Cantigas de Santa Maria* in which King Alfonso plays a role in both verbalization and visualization.

Notes

* This article was written with Richard P. Kinkade (University of Arizona) and is reprinted from *Hispania*, 66 (1983), 348-52.

1 *Iconography in Medieval Spanish Literature* (Lexington: University Press of Kentucky, 1984) is the title of the first book resulting from the grant from the National Endowment for the Humanities; the second book will treat iconography and narrative in tapestries; the third in frescoes and other paintings; and the fourth will concern itself with various kinds of carvings and sculpture.

2 Evelyn S. Procter, *Alfonso X of Castile, Patron of Literature and Learning* (Oxford: Clarendon Press, 1951), pp. 32 ff; Joseph Snow, "A Chapter in Alfonso's Personal Narrative: The Puerto de Santa María Poems in the *Cantigas de Santa Maria*," *La Corónica* 8 (1979), 10-21 and "Self-Conscious Reference and the Organic Narrative Pattern of the *Cantigas de Santa María* of Alfonso X," *Medieval Renaissance and Folklore Studies in Honor of John Esten Keller* (Newark, Delaware: Juan de la Cuesta, 1980), 53-66; and Philip L. Vandrey, "A Stylistic Approach to the Authorship Problem of the *CSM* of Alfonso el Sabio," unpubl. diss. Northwestern Univ., 1972, 113 pp, of which an abstract appears in *DAI*, xxxiii (1972-73), 5753A.

3 This manuscript of the *Cantigas* is richly illuminated, but it is incomplete, since not only have ten pages probably been removed at the beginning, but also many pages of miniatures have vacant panels, lack titles, or are otherwise defective. The best description of it is that of Antonio García Solalinde, "El códice florentino de las *Cantigas* y su relación con los demás manuscritos," *Revista de Filología Española*, 5 (1918), 143-79. This codex is known as Biblioteca Nazionale, MS Banco Rari 20, formerly II.1.2.3.

4 Procter, p. 40.

5 Alfonso X el Sabio, *Cantigas de Santa Maria: Edición facsímil del Codice T.I.1 de la Biblioteca de San Lorenzo de El Escorial, Siglo XIII* (Madrid: Editora Internacional de Libros Antiguos, 1979), 2 vols. See my review in *Hispania*, 63 (1980), 605 and that of Kathleen Kulp-Hill, *Kentucky Romance Quarterly*, 28, (1981), 213-15.

6 Higinio Anglés, *La música de las Cantigas de Santa Maria del Rey Alfonso el*

Sabio: Facsímil, transcripción y estudio crítico (Barcelona: Diputación Provincial de Barcelona, Biblioteca Central, 1943) and the edition, based upon that of Anglés, but reworked by José María Lloréns Cisteró in the volume of text, transcription, etc. which accompanies the facsimile volume, pp. 341-90.

[7] Not all scholars believe that the melodies and the stories of the miracles are in any way connected. In our opinions sad miracles are set to sad melodies, warlike subjects to lively melodies, etc. The opinions of both schools of thought are purely subjective, we believe. More research is needed in this area.

[8] Walter Mettmann, *Alfonso X, o Sábio. Cantigas de Santa Maria* (Coimbra: Universidade de Coimbra, 1959-1972) 4 vols. *Cantiga* 209 appears on pages 274-75 of Vol. II.